THE PSYCHOANALYST AND THE CHILD

The Psychoanalyst and the Child explores the unique nature of psycho-analytic work with children. This book is based on more than 30 years of practice and reflection within the framework of the Alfred Binet Centre in Paris, France. The very great diversity of situations encountered at the Centre brings the issue of therapeutic indications to the forefront.

Michel Ody focuses on the diversification of fifteen clinical situations and their theorization, ranging from basic consultation to psychoanalytic treatment. With this framework as his starting-point, he looks at the common features between the therapeutic consultation – a consultation that becomes therapeutic – and the analytic treatment, as well as what differentiates them. This implies examining, at the technical level, the different forms of interventions and interpretations presented as well as their metapsychological articulation. Ody draws on decades of clinical expertise to set out not just the basic considerations and problems typically encountered in work with this patient group, but clear guidelines for methodology and technique.

Psychoanalysis can be an intellectual process, dependent on the ability of the patient to express themselves verbally, which can make working clinically with children challenging. *The Psychoanalyst and the Child* seeks to help psychoanalysts through the most challenging of clinical treatments with this patient group.

Michel Ody is a psychiatrist, psychoanalyst, and honorary training member of the Société Psychanalytique de Paris. He was a member of the Management Committee of the SPP Training Institute for twelve years and Chair of the SPP Scientific and Technical Committee for five years. Since 1975 he has gradually taken responsibility for a multidisciplinary team at the Alfred Binet Centre. He is the author of two books and more than 100 psychoanalytic articles in French and was awarded the Maurice Bouvet Prize in 1988.

PSYCHOANALYTIC IDEAS AND APPLICATIONS SERIES

Recent titles in the Series include

THE PSYCHOANALYST AND THE CHILD

From the Consultation to Psychoanalytic Treatment

Michel Ody

R Routledge
Taylor & Francis Group

LONDON AND NEW YORK

First published 2019
by Routledge
2 Park Square, Milton Park, Abingdon, Oxon OX14 4RN

and by Routledge
52 Vanderbilt Avenue, New York, NY 10017

Routledge is an imprint of the Taylor & Francis Group, an informa business

This book is a translation of a work previously published in French by Éditions In Press as *Le psychanalyste et l'enfant: De la consultation à la cure psychanalytique* (2013).

Translated by Andrew Weller.

British Library Cataloguing-in-Publication Data
A catalogue record for this book is available from the British Library

Library of Congress Cataloging-in-Publication Data
Names: Ody, Michel, author.
Title: The psychoanalyst and the child : from the consultation to psychoanalytic treatment / Michel Ody.
Other titles: Psychanalyste et l'enfant. English
Description: Abingdon, Oxon ; New York : Routledge, 2019. | Series: International Psychoanalytical Association ideas and applications book series | Includes bibliographical references and index.
Identifiers: LCCN 2018032460 (print) | LCCN 2018034952 (ebook) | ISBN 9780429424038 (Master) | ISBN 9780429753794 (Web PDF) | ISBN 9780429753787 (ePub) | ISBN 9780429753770 (Mobipocket/Kindle) | ISBN 9781138389250 (hbk : alk. paper) | ISBN 9781138389267 (pbk. : alk. paper) | ISBN 9780429424038 (ebk)
Subjects: | MESH: Psychoanalytic Therapy–methods | Child | Child Psychiatry–methods | Psychotherapeutic Processes
Classification: LCC RJ504.2 (ebook) | LCC RJ504.2 (print) | NLM WS 350.5 | DDC 618.92/8917—dc23
LC record available at https://lccn.loc.gov/2018032460

ISBN: 978-1-138-38925-0 (hbk)
ISBN: 978-1-138-38926-7 (pbk)
ISBN: 978-0-429-42403-8 (ebk)

Typeset in Palatino
by Apex CoVantage, LLC

CONTENTS

For Maïté

ACKNOWLEDGEMENTS

I would like to express my thanks to Elsa Schmid-Kitsikis and Rémy Puyuelo for the support, help and advice they gave me as I was writing this book, and to all those with whom I have worked at the Alfred Binet Centre for the last thirty years or so.

SERIES EDITOR'S FOREWORD

The Publications Committee of the International Psychoanalytic Association continues, with this volume, the series "Psychoanalytic Ideas and Applications".

The aim of this series is to focus on the scientific production of significant authors, whose works are outstanding contributions to the development of the psychoanalytic field and to set out relevant ideas and themes, generated during the history of psychoanalysis, that deserve to be known and discussed by present psychoanalysts.

The relationship between psychoanalytic ideas and their applications has to be put forward from the perspective of theory, clinical practice, and research, so as to maintain their validity for contemporary psychoanalysis.

The Publication's Committee's objective is to share these ideas with the psychoanalytic community and with professionals in other related disciplines, in order to expand their knowledge and generate a productive interchange between the text and the reader. This goal has been achieved here in of the English translation of Dr Ody's volume, first printed in French entitled: *Le psychanalyste et l'enfant. De la consultation à la cure psychanalytique.*

In this volume Dr Ody describes in great detail the process that takes place from the first consultation to the analysis of a child. He does this by drawing upon work that he has published over a period of twenty-five years. Throughout the five chapters of this book, the reader will witness Dr Ody's remarkable and rich experience as a psychiatric consultant and leader of a multidisciplinary team in the Alfred Binet Centre in Paris, and as a psychoanalyst.

Throughout this book, Dr Ody highlights the crucial importance for psychoanalysts of centering our reflections on the distinctiveness of the psychoanalytic method in face of the changes in psychoanalytic practice that have arisen in the last decades. The author considers that, in order to safeguard the uniqueness of psychoanalysis, psychoanalysts should ". . . re-examine its fundamentals, to put the texts both of Freud and those of post-Freudians to the test in order to give fresh stimulus to the analysis of complexity, coherence, and its limits"

Dr Ody has effectively organised the book in two parts that reflect his main interests. The first addresses the relationship between the psychoanalytic therapeutic consultation and psychoanalytic work proper. The second addresses methodological and technical questions and puts forward metapsychological considerations. The book offers a synthesis of important theoretical and clinical insights. It is filled with a variety of rich and detailed clinical illustrations. I have no doubt that it will be of great interest to all practitioners working with children and parents as well as professionals who work in an institutional setting.

Gabriela Legorreta
Series Editor
Chair, IPA Publications Committee

General Introduction

T his book is mainly concerned with the place of the child within the corpus of general psychoanalysis, as well as the necessity of focusing our considerations on the uniqueness of the psycho-analytic method in face of the extensions to psychoanalytic practice that have been occurring for over a century now.

Such considerations are particularly useful in an era where thera-pies of all kinds are on offer. In this context, the cognitive-behavioural therapies are currently at the forefront. It is worth noting in passing that they employ notions such as cognition and behaviour, which are also present in psychoanalysis, since cognitive and behavioural moments are also part of the process of analytic work.

However, it would be a mistake to think that psychoanalysts, in their national and international exchanges, adopt a sort of ecumeni-cal position in favour of the uniqueness of the method. There is much talk of the risk of a babelisation of the psychoanalytic language, even though the gaps between analysts can be reduced and clarified each time they meet together to discuss a clinical situation. This is part of the redefinition, in a work group, of what each one understands by this or that concept – concepts that are sometimes internationally rec-ognised. This takes place either due to oscillations between different understandings or opinions concerning one and the same concept, or due to a community of thought expressed in different forms, which thereby acquires a truly metaphorical function.

General practice, which includes children and adults and grapples with an extreme variety of situations in public or private practice, requires a high degree of methodological rigour if dispersion is to be avoided. This rigour has the advantage of giving coherence to practice as a whole and to the process of reflection that is part of it. Otherwise, each subset, children, adolescents, adults, and its possible subdivisions, including those in psychopathology, risk becoming a specialised zone with its own language, thereby creating a territory that would be located outside general psychoanalysis and its metapsychology.

Consequently, maintaining the coherence of the method requires a constant return to Freud, whose work constitutes the basis of psychoanalysis. It is not just a matter of having read Freud; in some quarters it is considered that, as he belongs to history, it is no longer very useful to read him, and that other authors have gone "much further" than he did. What is at issue here is something quite different. Reading Freud allows one to confront a process of thought and creation with its contradictions, its advances, its backtrackings, and even its regrets. What results from this is a forward march, not as a system, but as *coherence*, even if it has its place within complexity. The most eminent post-Freudians situate themselves, then, within the context of this complexity, thereby opening the way to new discoveries. It is not a matter of being more or less Kleinian, Winnicottian, Bionian, Lacanian, or more or less close to our contemporaries. We can be any of these at any particular moment in one and the same session. What matters is to appreciate, even if retrospectively, if this or that reference to a post-Freudian belongs to the coherence of the ensemble or not. This coherence does not imply the presence of a closed system but rather of a system – notwithstanding the term – that is open to new discoveries. This is reminiscent of the debates between structure and history.

To take one example, among others, the notion of attachment resulted in the disappearance of the drive and its dialectical implications. Reading Bion, or any other author, also means returning to Freud, to some of his writings, including those that one has already read. Such to-ing and fro-ing enriches our understanding of his work. I often point out that this was how it was for the psychosomaticians of the Paris School in their return to the texts of Freud of the 1890s, in particular with regard to the concept of actual neurosis and trauma. I have personally had a similar experience concerning the Freudian concept of "boundary idea" (Ody, 1999a, pp. 1633–1636), a concept that is very aptly-named if one considers, among others, the contemporary notion of "borderline state".

As regards the method, everything begins with the famous model of standard or classical analysis, which is a purely theoretical model, for it cannot be found in practice. This model is a basic reference for any form of practice or "clinical thinking", to use André Green's expression. It is necessary for thinking about the gap between that which corresponds to it and that which evokes all the other situations of psychoanalytic work. What corresponds to the model constitutes the situation of the "analytic pair", to use another of Green's expressions, where free associations, expressions of the unconscious, of the infantile situation, of history, etc., are expressed in sufficiently harmonic terms, in transferential resonances, including conflicts, too, so that the process of analysis can find its rhythm with a beginning, a middle, and an end. If the model is taken to its extremes, it might be supposed that, once the analyst has ensured his presence and his listening, the analysand can do his or her work alone, including that of interpretation.

This was how Winnicott, in the light of his experience, came to consider that it was more profitable for the patient to discover the pertinence of his or her own interpretations at this or that moment of the analytic work. It remains true, however, that thinking about the gap between theory and practice, of which Donnet speaks, a gap that is structural for analysis, helps to guarantee the possibility of remaining an analyst at work in any situation that deviates more or less from the model of reference. At the extreme pole, one only needs to evoke the contributions of Balier (2005) in connection with the psychic functioning of serious criminals to see that such work is clearly psychoanalytic. Balier, with his methodological rigour, beginning with that which he applies to the setting, and even to the "context of the setting" ("*cadre du cadre*") on the basis of his work in prisons, gives us a demonstration of how a psychoanalytic process is established.

These considerations lead me to refer to certain current situations, where the considerable extension in the application of the psychoanalytic method, due to the age of the patients and the broadened scope of psychopathology, can lead us to conclude that each situation requires its own technical and theoretical apparatus. Hence there is a certain risk in affirming the idea that each person should follow his own orientation, his own "school", or worse, his own "chapel". On the contrary, this extension in the history of psychoanalysis should oblige us to re-examine its fundamentals, to put the texts both of Freud and those of post-Freudians to the test in order to give fresh stimulus to the analysis of complexity, coherence, and its limits.

The renewed debates on the subject of psychoanalysis/psychoanalytic psychotherapy are part of this dynamic. During an international debate, a few years ago now, Marilia Aisenstein engaged in an exemplary exercise. Being deliberately provocative, she put forward the idea that psychoanalytic psychotherapy does not exist. Drawing on an illustration, underlining the provocative aspect of her intervention, of a very difficult case conducted face-to-face, she showed how demanding it can be to carry out what is clearly psychoanalytic work, in the form of a *psychoanalysis in the face-to-face situation*. In other words, the difficulty of the situation had not tilted the technique towards supportive psychotherapy, or focal psychotherapy. Quite to the contrary, she showed that the term psychotherapy, which reduced psychoanalysis to a qualificative, watered down the psychoanalytic specificity of the method practised.

Let us now take the further example of analytic work with a child. It is well known that analysts do not see eye to eye on this issue. One of the parameters of this opposition is the number of sessions. It could be said that such a parameter, by having an "over-parametrising" effect in some countries, risks fetishisation. It is true that a genuine analytic process is not determined by the number of weekly sessions, even if the importance of the frequency of the sessions may facilitate the process. It is worth recalling the well-known example of Carine, in *La psychanalyse précoce* (Diatkine and Simon, 1972). The psychoanalytic work took place on a once-a-week basis, not because this choice was an indication in itself, but because of the conditions of feasibility, geographical distance in particular. This did not prevent a real analytic process from taking place. It is obvious, though, that when we are dealing with a clear indication for psychoanalytic work, and the practical conditions are in place, the choice of three or four sessions per week is preferable for the patient and the analyst alike. But, as we all know, such conditions can only be obtained in a minority of situations, where a child or adolescent is concerned, whether in public or private practice. This is a further reason for not watering down the method, as is suggested by the old and now well-known term of "psychoanalytically-inspired psychotherapy".

But the divergences between analysts do not only concern the number of sessions. Thus, for some, the work done with children and adolescents cannot be recognised as psychoanalysis, which, in effect, amounts to saying that child psychoanalysis "does not exist". Cahn's (2002) approach in his very interesting book *La fin du divan?* is a case in point. He proposes the following formulation: "The psychoanalysis of children, or rather the psychoanalytic psychotherapy of children" (p. 208), a formulation that contrasts with that of certain analysts who prefer not to speak of child psychoanalysis, but go much further by asserting that those who are "only" adult psychoanalysts do not have sufficient analytic experience . . .

At the point we are at, it seems that as far as the uniqeness of the method is concerned, this may be said to include, ultimately, *any form of psychoanalytic work*; at the same time, this would exclude all methods that do not refer to psychoanalysis, in other words, several hundred of them. But in the context of the work with a psychoanalyst, it is also important to add that whether we qualify the work done with a child or an adult on at least a once-a-week basis as psychoanalysis or psychoanalytic psychotherapy is not the central problem. The priority is to know if the work involved is psychoanalytic in its method. If that is the case, an analytic process, irrespective of the age of the subject, can take place on a once-a-week basis, even if it is clear that several sessions favour the expression of the process.

But such prerogatives raise the problem of the indication and its feasibility. When there is a process, it possesses qualities linked to the period of life in which the work is being carried out, but it also has its limits, such as those, in the child, concerning the elaboration of masochism or the limitation of insight. This also concerns the quality of the psychopathological dimension, that is, for a psychoanalyst, the quality of the functioning of the "psychical apparatus". This functioning is related to the clinical aspects of the relationship to the analyst, whereas what is psychoanalytic is only definable retrospectively (*après-coup*), implying, therefore, the issue of two phases (*temps*). The same is true during the therapeutic consultation, in particular with a child and his/her parents. It is the second consultation that enables us to appreciate, from a metapsychological point of view as well, whether the first had an effect or not, whether it was really therapeutic or not.

To return to the basic referent, the further we deviate from the model, the more the analyst is its *guardian* (analogically to the dream as a guardian of sleep), for he or she has, as it were, to tackle the problem of the degree of deviation from the model. If the work is to remain analytic, it is important that the analyst speaks second and that interpretation is based on the patient's material and as closely as possible to the words expressed or that are potentially present. By the patient's material I mean that his/her functioning is at the very least constituted by two *elements* (Bion), from the proto-representational to the most represented, such as fantasy or historical elements, the ensemble being animated by the movement of the transference/countertransference. These two elements are separated in time, whether this time period is that of immediate concatenation in the case of micro-processes or that of several years. The linking up of these elements by the analyst may be a rapprochement of an analogical type or a rapprochement through opposition. This linking leads, when the patient's negativity does not permeate the entire transference (which is another form, so to speak, of "indexation" – i.e. the way the subject responds to the analyst's words – as a consequence of the analyst's intervention), to an associative movement of the patient, the *third term* completing a triangular process, a sort of triangular *cell*, which means that associativity can follow its course.

All of the above can, after a certain time *x*, *constitute* an element that participates in turn in a new triangular and processual movement. Generative triangulation, let it be noted, is implied in the very movement of the analyst's intervention or interpretation, since it is the constituent of a third term that links the two intial elements. There are perhaps echoes here with the notion of "tertiary processes" defined by André Green (2002a, p. 82) as processes linking primary processes and secondary processes, even if elements of "primitive logics" (Neyraut, 1997, p. 208) may be involved. These expressions of triangulation also coincide with the "ternary strategy of interpretation" described by Michel de M'Uzan (1994, pp. 106–107). It is clear, then, that in such situations, it is not a question of interpretations of content but interpretations of process, or, more precisely, of interpretation of the *relation between content and process*.

The result of this is that such an ensemble is applicable in any situation of analytic work, from the consultation to the analytic session approximating most closely to the model of the standard treatment, irrespective of the subject's age. What will differentiate the consultation from the analytic session is that in the session the levels of regression (topographical, formal and temporal) are reached thanks to the couch/armchair situation (for the adult) and the frequency of the sessions. This standard (or classical) setting also allows for the interpretation of unconscious phantasies, beginning with the so-called primal phantasies of seduction, castration, and the primal scene.

What I have just described as a *basic model of interpretive work* implies conditions of a metapsychological order. Speaking in second place preserves the analyst from introducing ideas, which, from the point of view of the transference, would inevitably have the function of a purposive idea, in the Freudian sense of the term, so that the only alternative left to the patient would be to submit to it or oppose it. Certain classical figures come to mind in such a context: the Lacanian "desire of the desire of the other", or the Ferenczian "confusion of tongues", both of which are expressions of the problem of seduction. There is then an even greater risk that the patient will not associate much, which, apart from periodic moments in the couch/armchair analytic situation, can manifest itself already in the first consultation with both the child and the adult. We then find that we are falling short of constituting a triangular cell.

In the individual case, it is not necessarily a question of so-called *free* associations, but of an *associativity* in the general sense (Ody, 2012), which is related to any form of concatenation, however minimal the differential qualities of the two successive elements (verbal element, representable or not, motor or somatic element, affect) may be. As long as the triangular cell has not been constituted, the analyst is waiting for possibilities to elaborate it. This waiting is not one of a leaden silence (we know that there is silence and silence in analytic work), which, put in other terms, means that the words of the analyst are not interpretive; rather, they are in the nature of what could be called an *accompaniment for associativity*. Concerning this accompaniment for associativity, we may think, among other things, of the analyst's function as a protective shield, as well as that of the tutelary superego. It is a question of leading the patient to imagine what it is that prevents him/her from continuing, and which might eventually concern the person of the analyst, while differentiating between the latter and him/herself as the support of an imago projection. These circumstances could lead, among other things, to an enactment of the situation, in analogy to a psychodramatic scenario, which would help to get the process going again. If this is still not the case, one has to wait again, sometimes in silence, until a new attempt is made. It is quite exceptional for an impasse to prove itself to be absolute; this would signify the presence of a negativity just as exceptional. But as the impasse can exist, it becomes a fundamental issue of concern by becoming centred on the negative narcissistic aim of *destroying the function of the analyst*. We can understand, then, that the evolution of the definition of the fundamentals of the method led to certain clarifications at the same time as psychoanalysis was evolving towards complexity. This is what gives rise to a paradox, said to be *organising* by certain contemporary epistemologists.

Over the course of time, complexity was enriched thanks to the consideration that was given to the role of the object, with its external valency,[1] that of its functioning and that of the countertransference of the analyst, as an "external object". Now this is taken into consideration in the very first meeting, regardless of its evolution as far as the indication is concerned. It is for this reason that the two fundamental referents – "speaking in second place" and referring to the patient's material as a support for the intervention and/or the interpretation – are already at work in the first meeting. The result is that the clinical appreciation regarding the indication is certainly less dependent on psychopathology alone, regardless of the important role that it plays, unless one can speak of it as a dynamic psychopathology. As psychoanalysts, we are not the observers of the Newtonian model, but rather those, more recent, of the quantum model. In the context of this model, the observer, who participates in the observation, is not independent of the object. This position gives the need to take the countertransference into account all its pertinence, notwithstanding the risk of only seeing in it intersubjective and intrapsychic factors to the exclusion of drive impulses. This, indeed, was the reproach addressed to the American psychoanalyst Owen Renik. Hence the importance of maintaining a balance by taking into account the dialectic between the intrapsychic and the interpsychic.

The methodological questions that we have just been considering can only be sustained on certain conditions which are related to two basic referents, the *preconscious and triangulation*. As far as the preconscious is concerned, as an intermediate space (*Mittelglieder*) in the relationship between words and things, contemporary psychoanalysis has come to consider that the first topography (unconscious, preconscious, conscious) is no longer relevant to difficult clinical situations. It is said, therefore, which proves to be exact, that Freud had good reason to introduce the death drive, and then the second topography. And yet, in *The Ego and the Id*, Freud (1923b) did not abandon the place of the first topography, and he was still wondering about the preconscious in the *Outline* (1940a [1938]).[2]

We find ourselves once again, therefore, faced with a problem of articulation or dialectics. From an interpsychic point of view, even if the patient's preconscious functioning is deficient and dysharmonious, the analyst's is supposed to function. If this is not the case, he/she will be led to examine more closely the dynamics of the transference/countertransference. It was in this context that César and Sára Botella (2001) emphasised the importance of the analyst's retrogressive (*régrédient*) functioning during the session, thereby permitting access to what they have called "figurability" and the representation of movements that are barely representable or unrepresentable, as well as to the process of putting them into words.

An analyst and his/her patient pass through the hazards of language, its arbitrary nature, and its constricting logics, even if a lot of experience prior to language is expressed in the session. All this "prior experience", of which affect is naturally a part, will permeate language and speech, but it will also permeate, as I have just said, the object and the transference/countertransference. It follows that certain signifiers, in the sense of drive representatives that have finally come to light in difficult situations, will be part of the chain attesting to the relationship between code and body. All these elements will constitute the *triangulular cell* to which I have already referred.

But we could ask ourselves what can be said about the preconscious when we are not in an analytic situation such as that with an adult or an adolescent. Leaving aside affects, adults and adolescents express motricity by means of language. The child, on the other hand, gives priority, when he can, to play and/or drawings, which he/she does not necessarily put into words, even when asked to do so. But this does not prevent us from taking into account the dynamics of the relationship between the child and the analyst, which is the basis of clinical evaluation. The graphic emergence, for example, may be more or less figurative but nonetheless identifiable thanks to the associative concatenation. Here it will be necessary to take into account the topographical changes (which may be rapid) that are particular to the child, at the verbal, behavioural, graphic and play levels. If this graphic emergence is not accompanied verbally by the child, which is frequently the case, it will require the words of the analyst. Lacan has been attributed with the idea that the word is the murder of the thing. For his part, Michel Fain, referring to Freud, has pointed out that the strength of the cathexis of the visual representations (*figurations*) (of the colours in a dream for example) is attenuated as soon as they are put into words through the telling of the dream. An analogy may thus be drawn between this *infantile* material mobilised by the dream in the adult and a child's drawings or play activities which are privileged and hypercathected as modes of expression. Thus the analyst finds himself, according to Marty, in the position of lending his preconscious to the child, providing him with the words that are closest to what is represented, including the most elementary forms. When such work can take place, a "triangular cell" can be formed by linking up the elements that are represented, proto-represented and capable of being named, to which the analyst's interventions and the symbolic/symbolising interpretations belong.

All of the above can be found, more or less, in any psychoanalytic work with a child, from the first consultation to analysis itself. These are the issues that I will be discussing throughout this book, which brings together a series of contributions published over a period of twenty-five years. These texts have not been modified fundamentally, but only in their form, in particular to avoid certain redundancies. They are based on my practice as a psychiatric consultant and psychoanalyst, and my experience of leading a pluridisciplinary team in child and adolescent psychiatry for thirty or so years at the Alfred Binet Centre (ASM 13, Paris).[3] This framework of infant and child psychiatry, situated in a specific geographical sector, aims to respond to any situation that presents itself, and although psychoanalysis remains its central reference, regular exchanges take place with the representatives of other disciplines (speech therapists, psychomotricians, etc.) In this sense the indications for psychoanalytic therapies, on a once-a-week basis, at least, concern less than a quarter of those who come for consultations. It follows that the role of the consultation for the type of indication proposed is of crucial importance.

This book cannot take account of all the types of situations encountered, from the most individual to the most institutional, including "re-educational work", work with schools, and so on. It focuses primarily on the relations between the psychoanalytic therapeutic consultation and psychoanalytic work proper, on at least a twice-weekly or three-times-weekly basis. Secondarily, it deals with methodological and technical questions and, *in fine*, it puts forward metapsychological considerations.

Notes

1 Since it is necessary to differentiate external/internal object, whole/part object, and object/narcissistic object.
2 This question of exploring the preconscious further will be discussed in the conclusion to this book.
3 Mental Health Association in the 13th district of Paris.

PART I
THE THERAPEUTIC CONSULTATION

CHAPTER ONE

Psychoanalytic work with the child: basic reflections

Starting from the therapeutic consultation

A s with the initial conditions for "the evolution of open dynamic systems", the conditions of the unfolding of the first meeting with a child and his/her family will have a bearing on the form of the indication at the end of the meeting. This is true even when the indication is limited to the offer of a second meeting. These conditions are based, first of all, on the child's forms of associativity and their stumbling-blocks in the relationship between the child and the consultant. Next, and linked up with this first phase, it will be necessary to evaluate what can or cannot be shared, and at what level, with the parent(s). Let me add that by associativity (to indicate its difference from the model of free association, which is its reference), I mean, irrespective of the child's age, any concatenation, any sequencing of elements, even the most minimal, playful, graphic, verbal, behavioural, and changes of register with their negative aspects, that is to say, when the latter has the significance of rupture.

Here is an example of a relatively common situation. Eliane, a little four-and-a-half-year-old African girl was brought to the consultation by her parents for timidity and "problems of language" observed in pre-school. The first interview conducted with the parents by an experienced colleague, enabled me as a consultant, to gain access not to a purposive idea, but rather to an anticipatory idea (Freud, 1910d, p. 142) concerning the situation as a whole. To emphasise the essential points, there was a difficult context of immigration combined with the fact that three elder adolescent sons had stayed in Africa. The parents were waiting to enjoy better financial circumstances before bringing them to France. Eliane, who was born in France roughly a year after her mother had arrived, was six years younger than the brother who had preceded her. A second daughter was born two years after her. During my first meeting with Eliane, I felt gradually reassured about her linguistic capacities, because she was able to express herself in short, well-constructed sentences within a process involving essentially graphic associative movements.

I had to stimulate this process regularly, though her inhibition did not go beyond this level. It did not infiltrate the ego in a massive way. After a somewhat repetitive graphic departure (drawing balloons), rendered in a way that was a little beneath her age, even though she was a child of normal intelligence, Eliane gradually managed to depict a parental couple. She confirmed that they were playing with a ball. This symbolic intervention would sexualise the situation in a particular symbolised mode. The child portrayed the rain in yellow, at the bottom of the drawing, and added: "There's no more sun." For a brief moment I felt rather perplexed, but then said, "In the background, they are both playing with a ball, it's warming up! . . . Then, there's rain." This was quite a simple mode of interpretation which came to my mind associatively, while at the same time I felt that the situation was more complex than that because it was overdetermined.

This symbolic mode of interpretation had two consequences. First, Eliane wanted to change the sheet of paper she was drawing on, as if she wanted to change the subject. Then, she drew "the baby", as she said, and her associations seemed to confirm my interpretation. Eliane then moved towards a less directly sexual register, saying that the child would grow up, which, beyond the "culturally correct expression" of phallic narcissism, was a good way of introducing temporality. The rest of the consultation with the parents confirmed that Eliane had been making progress since they had intervened on her behalf. It was not possible on that day to go much further. We separated with the next consultation in view. I should point out that the method of working adopted up to then had remained at the level of "spaced" therapeutic consultations. These consultations, separated by several months, continued for two years. They were suspended on the initiative of the child, who was still evolving on the personal level as well as at school, as her teachers confirmed. Eliane now began to have a more outward approach towards others, and also no longer needed her mother's presence when going to sleep; up till then she had needed to have her by her side. I will limit my remarks to the first three consultations.

Though I was reassured at the end of the first meeting about this little four-and-a-half-year-old girl's capacities to organise an infantile neurosis, due to her access to the primal scene phantasy (Freud, 1918b[1914] p. 96), the sense of perplexity that I experienced entered at the same time into resonance with a latent thought questioning the impact of the absence of the three elder sons. It was possible to discuss this question with the father during the following consultation, even though nothing from a dynamic point of view made it possible to intervene at this level during this first contact. This confirms that this way of working cannot be used anamnestically, as is the case in a medical consultation. My meeting with Eliane confirmed for me the singularity of her functioning. In her drawing I found again the portrayal of the signifiers sun and rain of the first meeting. She confirmed that the rain was falling on the man. Not only did he not have an umbrella, she told me, but "he had nothing at all". I associated to her words, "There's no more sun" from the last consultation. She seemed surprised by the strength of her negation. She was perhaps all the more surprised owing to the transferential connotation that this reaction can contain, not to mention the overdetermination of the content of the verbal expression. Indeed, Eliane was about to introduce a yellow sun right at the top of the drawing, and in the house.

Then the child drew a second sun, green like the man, and this time almost at the man's feet. As with my perplexity in the first consultation, I came up with quite an ordinary formulation, probably nourished by the latent thought that I referred to above: "Is he happy that the sun has come to see him?" This had two consequences. As in the first consultation, Eliane wanted first to change the sheet of paper. Then she threw herself into a series of drawings of little squares – I was going to say "distributed" at the top of the drawing among the clouds – to which she clearly had no intention of associating. The child reacted briefly with surprise when I made a link between these squares and the form of the paper. I then changed register by offering her the box of games. It was not very surprising, given this child's inhibition as well as her recourse to a strange, and even abstract, counter-cathecting symbolism, that Eliane systematically left in the box any animal that was aggressive, let alone one that was ferocious. She was now ready to close the box again (just as she was ready to change the sheet of paper, as we have seen). She then told me that otherwise the wild animals would eat the others, and she was also able to tell me about a nightmare for the first time.

What was especially interesting was the process that led her to tell me about it, for the content of the nightmare confirmed the oral theme that had already been raised. Indeed, after telling me that she did not dream, but that she had . . . nightmares, Eliane could not tell me about any of them. I pulled back a bit and then asked her what happened to her when she had a nightmare. This time she gave me an interesting response: "I think in my head." She had thought about the nightmare and was able to tell me about it. It was about wolves eating children. She confirmed by nodding her head which indicated that she was ready to close the box so that there would be no risk of anything happening in her play like in the nightmare (through regression to an animistic mode of thinking, Freud would say). Her father had come alone that day. Apart from the progress that he noticed in his daughter, he was able to show, with finesse and emotion, that he thought that he and his wife had overprotected their daughter, which perhaps explained Eliane's difficulties in going to sleep. But, what's more, he was able to make a link between this overprotection and, as he put it, the hole, the void that the absence of his sons had caused. Eliane was attentive to what her father was saying.

From the third consultation, I can recall a key moment in the process of drawing. The child began by drawing a sun (this time at the top of the sheet of paper) and a flower at the same level, drawn very delicately for the first time, which was a sign of how her drawing skills were developing, and also the transference with regard to the continuity of the symbolic themes. Then she drew clouds. This symbolic situation developed in such a way that the rain coming from the clouds fell onto a little house that she had drawn in the meantime. But above all, independently of these themes that were repeated in a sort of developing spiral, she went on to draw a boy. "What's happening?" I asked her. "It's raining," Eliane replied. She could not say anything more, except by drawing clouds above the line of rain. This time, from one stage to another, the necessary conditions were finally in place. I then asked the child if she was happy for me to tell her about an idea I had about her drawing. "Yes," she said. So I gave her the possible version of a boy who was crying because he was sad, just as she might imagine her brothers were sad to still be in Africa while she and her sister were with their parents.

Eliane looked at me and nodded her head affirmatively, but above all added: "That's right!" I learnt from her father in the second part of the consultation, that he had been to see his sons in Africa since the last consultation. He also told me that his father had embarked on an "exodus" when he himself was eight or nine years old, and that he had only returned for good on the birth of his first son. He also told me, in connection with his plan to bring his sons back to France, that if they stayed too long in Africa, they might be led to repeat the same thing with their own children. While increased awareness does not necessary modify a person's destiny (particularly when that person is unemployed), it is still true that I have not often come across such psychic qualities in this kind of consultation, especially when one is dealing with cultural differences and such a degree of social vulnerability. For the purposes of my presentation, I will limit myself to these first three consultations concerning which, it may be said, retrospectively, that they were therapeutic consultations.

This example serves as an illustration on two counts: strategically, in connection with the question of the indication of the analytic work proposed; and technically, in connection with the type of intervention and/or interpretation used. As far as the strategic aspect is concerned, it is important to evaluate the degree of fluidity in the child's associativity as well as to gauge how far what the consultant is trying to communicate to the parents about the child he has seen has resonance for them. In the best of cases the effect of resonance will be translated by the equivalent of: "What you are saying makes me think of . . .". It may involve the confirmation or concretisation of a form of psychic functioning. For example, one can communicate to the parents in everyday language that a transition from one register to another has occurred too quickly during the consultation. While both parents assert that their child can play by him/herself, one of them makes the remark that although the child plays, it does not last long. But it may equally concern the mention by one of the parents of a recollection concerning the child's past, either their own or the child that they once were, etc. The more one goes in such directions, the more the parents will have the tendency to adopt a position suggesting the existence of the unconscious and infantile sexuality. One can also find oneself in a radically opposite situation.

By way of example, a child with a more or less "as if" personality gradually allowed instinctual drive impulses with representational value to emerge in front of the consultant, but would close up again in the presence of his parents. One of them, who only took interest in the child in a primarily narcissistic way, did not allow the child (the future "subject") to express any form of difference, beginning at the instinctual, and thus personal, level. It is this kind of situation which, at least for a certain time, can transform the initial indication of a child analysis into a counterindication. Otherwise the parents will take it upon themselves to interrupt the treatment prematurely. We have seen that Eliane's parents tended so much towards saying, "that makes me think" that they were filled with a sense of guilt; even though they were able to speak about it (especially the father, while his wife remained in a complementary position). At the same time, this evolution in the parents was essential to the evolution of the child, both when she found herself alone with me and when she was with her parents.

Generally speaking, it is not useful to begin psychoanalytic work on a regular basis until one has made sufficient progress with the parents and their own history, and that includes acquiring a sense of their limits. By "history", I mean both the manifest history, with its eventual traumas and situations of mourning, and the details of the oedipal history of each of the parents. Whatever indication is proposed afterwards, it is a matter of evaluating as far possible the difference between what is a burden for the child up to the so-called transgenerational level, and what is of a more structural and personal nature from the point of view of his/her psychic functioning. As for gauging the degree of the child's associative fluidity, it clearly depends on the way in which he/she positions him/herself in the space of the analytic work (between the extremes of the autistic "fortress" and violent and repetitive acting out.) Eliane found herself in a situation of inhibition, which it was possible to mobilise on the condition of offering her fresh incentives and interventions with a potentially interpretive value. Another consultant might have chosen to do a psychotherapy with several sessions per week. Why not? We know, moreover, that above a certain threshold, discussions on indications are less a question of indicating this or that form of analytic work than a question of indication in relation to the analyst's person.

For example, beyond the fact that the analyst is ready to undertake this work, he/she will have to position him/herself between two stumbling-blocks in the countertransference: an unnecessarily prolonged silence or too much activity. In any case, I am not sure that a therapy involving frequent sessions would have been more useful at a time when questions of evaluation concerning therapeutic approaches and health spending were being debated actively. But, at the risk of being somewhat harsh, I would say that I do not really see the usefulness of beginning a treatment involving frequent sessions as long as the child's development is moving forward again and continues to do so with the help of therapeutic consultations at irregular intervals. On the basis of such a principle, there will always be time to embark on this type of treatment if it proves necessary, which will then take place under better conditions and with less risk of the treatment being broken off. But it sometimes happens, albeit exceptionally, depending on the dynamics of the psychopathology in question, that an indication of analysis can be decided on at the end of the first consultation.

Conversely, an initial indication of regular treatment may change owing to the positive evolution of the spaced consultations. The spectrum is thus very wide, as each situation is special and unique, a truism that is perhaps worth recalling in a context where statistics and the quantitative have a major influence. It should be pointed out that from the moment a consultant is not in the role of a "recording chamber", of a supposedly neutral observer in the consultation, but in a role where his/her interventions form part of the "observation", a dynamic opens up with its share of the unknown as far as predictability is concerned, an evolving dynamic which can only be verified during the next meeting. This is a good moment to point out – when the child does not emerge from the first consultation as he/she was upon arriving – that if one is often struck by the connections between a child's productions from one session to another, even though they may be separated by several months, it is not only due to the existence of the unconscious. It is also due to the particular context of the type of encounter that is profoundly unusual for the child. This context necessarily mobilises the primal phantasy of seduction of the child by the adult, with the particularity that the child has never before experienced the type of listening and intervention offered by this adult. All this creates an effect, as far as seduction is concerned, which is reminiscent of the case of Emma reported by Freud (1950[1895d]) in the *Project*, the second phase reactivating the first retroactively, thereby creating a continuity between the two, like the "guiding thread" that unfolded throughout Eliane's three consultations.

The analytic process

Now that all these points have been made, let us return to the question of associative fluidity, which must be sufficient in order to undertake regular and frequent analytic work. What we need to understand is whether this associativity involves repetitions of functioning which have the value of stumbling-blocks in the face of varied psychic events, with a common denominator. It is also necessary to understand whether these mental stumbling-blocks are linked to the existential and symptomatic reasons for which the child and his parents sought a consultation. But, above all, we need to evaluate whether, in spite of the consultation work that has been done, and any positive effects it may have had, the child's evolution remains minimal and resistance persistent. Analysis, or psychotherapy, then becomes necessary. This is the moment to say a few words about the issue of whether a distinction should be made between psychoanalytic psychotherapy and child psychoanalysis. This subject regularly returns to the forefront, especially in international circumstances, whether, moreover, it is the child or the adult that is in question. As it will have been noticed, I often employ the term psychoanalytic work, which for me – and others – is the cornerstone that separates what is psychoanalytic from what is not. This work on the method defines the different states to which I have already referred. If the meeting is favourable between the productive capacities of the child's psychic functioning and those of the analyst, and three to five sessions a week are put in place as an added bonus, we are thereby creating the optimal conditions for child analysis.

The problem is that this only concerns a minority of children. Moreover, we know that the criterion of the number of sessions does not suffice to define the psychoanalytic process. Conversely, a genuine analytic process can take place with two sessions a week, and sometimes even one. As I have said, Diatkine and Simon (1972) demonstrated this with the publication of their book, *La psychanalyse précoce*, concerning a little girl who could only come once a week. Thus, what counts, first and foremost, is to create the conditions for doing psychoanalytic work, which means that one must have as many metapsychological require-ments as technical ones (theory of technique included), whatever the state of this work. It is not a matter of differentiating what is psy-choanalysis from what goes under the name of "psychoanalytically-inspired psychotherapy", or "supportive psychotherapy", or some other title, as was the case in France at a certain time. Rather, one must ask oneself what, within the psychoanalytic work, bears witness or not to a psychoanalytic process. To be somewhat harsh once again, I would say the following: the psychoanalytic process begins – and can con-tinue for a long time – with the work of the preconscious, which Freud also called the dynamic unconscious; it can then follow with the uncon-scious, which Freud called the unconscious proper.

It can be said that it is here that the process of psychoanalytic psy-chotherapy becomes psychoanalysis (which does not mean this is achieved once and for all). This statement calls for a few clarifications. Let us begin at the beginning. With Eliane, we reached an analytic pro-cess during the consultation. The quality of the interpretations was of a symbolic order aimed at the child's preconscious, in other words the links between thing-presentations and word-presentations, with the child's preconscious entering at moments into resonance with that of the analyst. What was new for Eliane were the new symbolic links that I suggested to her between representations.[1] Symbolic interpretations are based on, or constitute, symbols. They do not interpret symbols, that is, their contents. I will come back to this. This is what led Eliane to say, three times during the process, "that's right!". If I had touched on the content too quickly, I might very well have met with a defensive reaction, which confirms the general idea that an interpretation of con-tent is only worth the process of which it is part.

This kind of work can be extended to sessions of psychotherapy and child analysis. It is essential and not necessarily acquired in advance. It suffices to recall whole sessions during which a child remains silent while "reading" a comic strip that he/she brought with him/her, which, depending on the case, is not necessarily negative, if the playful aspect of this reading remains present. But, one thing leading to another, the work can go on like this, and even come to an end, without even touch-ing on the unconscious "proper", except in cases of untimely interpre-tations which, at best have no effect, and at worst reinforce resistances and defences. Moreover, certain "deep" interpretations can have effects, less as a result of their content as such than due to the symbolic value that underlies them. As Freud (1915e, p. 188) said, the preconscious influences the unconscious, which can render obsolete the project of an interpretation that is foreseen for a future opportune moment.

But, even when this dynamic is taken into account, more generally, the analytic process, involving several sessions a week, requires the utilisation of interpretive contents that belong to the unconscious. They are favoured by the frequency of sessions, which has a catalysing effect on regressive processes: topographical, formal, and temporal. These are contents that have never been thought about consciously, and that are related in one way or another to the fundamental phantasies of seduction, castration, and the primal scene, described as primal phantasies by Freud. Establishing these elements alone makes it possible to give coherence to the process that is unfolding, in connection with which the work already done no longer suffices to resolve the compulsion to repeat. The latter is driven by an activation of the contradictions between oedipal pregenitality and genitality or, if one prefers, between the psychotic aspect of psychic functioning (in the Kleinian and post-Kleinian sense of the term) and the neurotic aspect. This means that, whatever the psychopathological states may be – at least within the "limits of what is analysable" – oedipal triangulation, including all its stumbling-blocks, remains the frame of reference. This is also a way to avoid interpreting all the material in terms of the Oedipus complex, which primarily has the function of organising the infantile neurosis (Ody, 2003a), which in turn transforms "early", "pregenital", and psychotic" material, etc. Triangulation, thirdness (Green, 2002b) and the Oedipus remain, moreover, the frame of reference, their links with primal phantasies included, and are located at the very basis of interpretation, beginning with those aspects of it that are related to the analyst's countertransference. It is in "difficult cases", where the dynamic exerts itself in duality, as in a binary system, that the analyst is threatened by a collapse of the countertransference, making him/her lose any kind of third point of reference as well as the so-called ternary strategy of interpretation (M'Uzan, 1994, pp. 106–107).

This is already present, moreover, in the context of symbolic interpretations. An element A that is similar – or opposed – to an element B belonging to the representative (or protorepresentative) movement of the child will, if the link is made in a timely manner, lead to the emergence of an element C, as a third term, and so on. In difficult cases, the analyst "lends" his/her preconscious to the child, which helps him/her "find/create" *représentance* (Green),[2] that is to say, a movement or activity of representation that also includes the affect representative.

An extract from a child analysis

In order to illustrate the above considerations, I will take as an example the analysis of a boy aged a little more than seven years. This analysis lasted roughly four years, on a three-session-a-week basis but was reduced to two sessions a week after two years owing to a change of residence. A work of therapeutic consultations conducted by an experienced consultant had prepared this indication. To limit myself to the essential points, in spite of a certain degree of improvement, anxieties and nightmares persisted which were of a pre-neurotic register. The sessions with Jean-Éric, an intelligent boy, were marked by a state of excitability whose underlying anxiety (Ody, 1997) made it difficult to master discharge by means of a figurative activity (of which formal regression was a part) involving play or drawing.

Verbal activity and motility therefore played a predominant role, the function of the first being mainly to accompany, prepare and comment on the second. Thus, venturing one day to do some drawing, Jean-Éric depicted a lion confined with a witch in a coffin, defecating and urinating. Given the transference connotations implied by the coffin/office, it is not very surprising that "a certain amount of time" was needed to decondense this fantasy and to bring the child back to the drawing. In the meantime, I was able to accompany his motility in a psychodramatic mode by gradually introducing his acting out into a fabric comparable to fairy tales or myths. The child quickly invested himself in the heroic and symbolic journeys thus implied, the developments taking place from one session to another.

Three years later, after the fantasy of the witch and the lion had been decondensed, in a context where the dynamics of identification and conflictuality in connection with paternal images had finally found their place, there was a reactivation of omnipotent maternal images. The link with the preconscious and its latent thoughts had thus become more accessible. Indeed, with reference to the primal scene and its dialectic, the witch in question gave birth with a caesarean delivery, which the child understood as the creation of a link with his mother, since he had understood that she had always given birth in this way. The dynamic of paternal identification involved, of course, the transference, which, given the family history, needed time to elaborate. This work did not take place independently of the work on castration anxiety in particular, given the relationship between symbolic exhibition, sublimation and sexual co-excitation. It could be said that, thanks to this work of elaboration, Jean-Éric became gradually more assured concerning the possession of his penis. So he no longer needed to be a lion, a lion moreover that could only defecate and urinate in front of the witch. He was able to play with pictorial images of symbolic phallic value and let himself draw forms spontaneously without knowing what the outcome would be. The process of putting things into words became a source of polysemy. Three years after the beginning of this analysis, we had moved a long way from the scene that had put an end to any form of graphic expression. There followed an account of a peculiar dream: he was being followed by a self-adhesive label . . . But there was someone in the dream: the President of Iran.

At the same time, the child made a paper plane which, as if by chance, hit me (dream reversal). I said, "There you are. I am the President of Iran", and not the contrary. Jean-Éric laughed, and I added: "Are you going to take his place as a psychoanalyst?" To which he replied, full of humour, "No . . . of course not, I don't have your experience." The plane hit me again. "Well, really!" he said. I added, "Like a son who wants to take the place of . . . his father?" In a sort of flash of brilliance that one sometimes comes across in a child analysis, he said, "That's only possible when there is an heir!" The week after the child deployed the movement that had been initiated. This time it was Peter Pan against Captain Hook. Then, as Jean-Éric's graphic associations were moving in the direction of the unknown, the forms could only be defined retrospectively. The words that came to him were "zombie", "vampire". "Does that remind you of anything?", he asked me, alluding to the period of his nightmares whose content had remained inexpressible and unrepresentable. I linked this formal and temporal regression to the sequence of the President of Iran whose place had been taken by his son and "heir". "Er, no, not at all!" Then I linked this movement to the transference involved in the reversal – for, at that moment, the child was imitating a vampire in front of me – by telling him that this time the roles were reversed. "It's me who's having a nightmare," I said to him.

The boy had another flash of brilliance. "No, you are the psychoanalyst to whom the vampire is speaking about the fear it had when it looked at itself in the mirror." At this stage, Jean-Éric was approaching ten years of age. He was to continue this analysis for one more year.

Therapeutic consultation and the problem of change[3]

The notion of change

Freud did not conceptualise or theorise, strictly speaking, the problem of change. At the same time, as Widlöcher (1970) noted in his book *Freud et le problème du changement*, Freud's whole approach can be understood as a study of change and resistance to change, from the essential observation that remembering leads to the suppression of the symptom up to the ultimate meditation on resistances and the notion of the death drive. It might be thought at first sight that the psychoanalytic treatment has the ambition of taking change beyond the level of modification alone, insofar as it aims at transformation. But first we have to agree on what we mean by transformation. Transformation cannot turn a subject into another subject, for that would raise the question of identity. In this sense, as Widlöcher himself points out in his book, the notions of identity and change are inseparable. He adds that identity should not be conceived in terms of what individualises the person, but rather as what maintains this differentiation and means that this person remains the same.

This is a way of saying that the limit of identity is related to the problem of change; identity is maintained in effect by the dialectic that is particular to each of us between narcissism and eroticism, with the death drive intensifying this dialectic through narcissism. A difficulty linked to narcissism further complicates the question. Because this difficulty involves the mutual cathexes between the parents and the child, it favours alienating and restrictive identifications – almost "imprinted", to use the ethological metaphor – which encumber more or less significantly the advent of an individual (the child "subject-of-his-drives"). In short, however they are described, these identifications restrict identity and oblige us to resort to a so-called transgenerational reading if we want to create a space for vertical thought, to paraphrase Pasche. The opposite is the reduction of determinism to the trauma of birth and to its *varia*. A more sophisticated variant was presented by Laplanche with his central theory of primal seduction. But totalising the latter, even if by employing the Einsteinian metaphor, by passing from the theory of restricted seduction to a general theory of seduction, runs the risk, in the case of the verticality that is attached to thought, as in the case of the Oedipus, of making it pass through the trapdoor of the primal. This was not the case in the article on primal phantasies (Laplanche and Pontalis, 1964), whereas in *New Foundations for Psychoanalysis*, Laplanche (1987) writes: "The sacrosanct universality of the Oedipus can be seen as one of the many solutions to a problem created by the situation in which adults and children relate to one another (and that is universal)" (p. 91).

What appears here to be a sort of polemical game is at the same time perfectly serious. Indeed, if we only consider the technical consequences of the theoretical positions involved, a critique of the aim of repairing traumas may be outmoded. Widlöcher (1980) demonstrated this in his report "Genèse et changement", by introducing the question of the promotion of seduction, while taking into account its risks in the transference/countertransference dynamics. Seduction reverberates just as it "creates" the above-mentioned primal dimension and contributes to the registration of *new* memory traces, and therefore promotes the life drive of the subject, thereby stimulating the dialectic between narcissism and eroticism. This finalistic point of view is not reduced, as far as change is concerned, to repairing narcissistic failures. It should be added that its necessary preconditions are: verticality in the spatialisation of the psychic agencies, as well as the possibility of thinking about the transgenerational, and thus about Oedipus as an attractor. The latter, through the transference/countertransference, opens up the path to the drive movements of the subject which, by being elaborated, will participate, if not in "repairing" traumas, at least in reinforcing narcissism.

The above theoretical considerations will come as no surprise to the psychoanalyst, especially one who cares for children and their parents in a centre where one is often faced with absolutely any kind of initial situation. Consequently, the analyst's experience as a consultant, particularly if he/she adopts a longitudinal development with this or that family in what are generally called therapeutic consultations – in conjunction or not with work carried out at the centre or at school – obliges him/her to reflect on the problem of change, while trying to define and describe both its movements and their limits. The analyst can also relate this experience to the development of the child's analytic treatment, while taking its differences into account, with the same perspective of change in mind. The dynamic of therapeutic consultations relates not only to the work with the child, but more specifically to the relations between the parents, the child and the consultant. We have seen that whatever the state of the child's mental functioning, even when it allows us to envisage an analysis, something on the parental side of the equation is opposed to such an indication. This makes a period of work necessary that is based on the therapeutic consultation, work, moreover, that may go on for several years, call into question an initial therapeutic indication, or even terminate there. It is also worth noting that the time spent working with the participation of the parents, in the presence of the child, may perfectly well prove justified once the analysis has begun, and when it poses a serious problem in the way it is unfolding, on the condition that it is not introduced in an untimely fashion in relation to what is taking place between the child and his/her analyst who, as we know, may already have seen the parents. Finally, it is worth recalling that this type of consultation has every opportunity of success with regard both to the indications of treatment through mediation and to the time needed to evaluate them. I am thinking here of various forms of re-education, pedagogical support at the centre, or at school, etc., and especially when these therapeutic activities have reached their limit. This state of affairs can be due to a conflictual situation – one that is often masked moreover – involving several protagonists.

The whole situation can be mobilised by this form of consultation. The scenarios encountered are infinitely varied. When one wishes to illustrate a point of view with reference to psychoanalysis and its methodology, the monograph is essential due to the multiplicity of examples it offers (the number of which makes a summary necessary), while presenting a risk of reductionism and reification. While trying to avoid jumping out of the frying pan into the fire, the quantitative forming a "mass", I will present three situations: a process of anti-change and a process of change, both of these occurring within the context of a longitudinal therapeutic consultation; and thirdly a process of change in the setting of child analysis. As a conclusion to this progression I will take up at a theoretical level the distinction between therapeutic consultation and analysis.

Magda, or the violent risk of change

Magda was almost six when she was referred to me for secondary encopresis. She is the second of four children. Her father, who is Oriental, is the fourth child, the only boy, and the youngest of his own sibling group. Magda's mother is Latin-American and, due to her family life, gave up a profession that meant she had to travel a lot. Her parents met each other in Paris. Magda was a pretty and clean girl, and her encopresis seemed to be connected both with entering kindergarten at the age of three and a half years and with staying for the first time with a Swiss family during the summer holidays before beginning kindergarten. Her parents suggested this connection themselves, while at the same time not wanting to recognise it. When I met Magda at the age of six-and-a-half years, I was struck by a significant sequence.

After being asked about her dreams, she told me that her father had dreamed about her grandmother who is now dead. As she was drawing a second female character, she took a black felt pen with which she filled in the outline of the dress of this character. I interpreted this situation for her symbolically saying that this girl had a black dress just at the moment Magda was speaking to me about her father's dream. The effect of this allusion to triangulation was spectacular; Magda now took a red felt pen and evoked a friend who had "cut her arm at school" and had to go to the hospital. I will not dwell here on the transference connotation, through castration, that this movement implies. The child then added brown fingers to the character she had drawn. This made her think of nothing else but crayons, especially as this figurative image clearly referred to the "faecal stick". This manifestation of anality in this encopretic girl was completed by what she said about her dreams: "It's not good . . . we mustn't talk about them", as if their content was fecalised in this movement of anal regression. This particular pressure of the primal process was clearly worrying. Her mother, whom I saw next – unaccompanied by her husband – told me that since the previous summer, when her daughter had once again been to a neighbouring country in the same conditions as two years earlier, the encopresis had almost stopped; and furthermore, that Magda had begun to speak spontaneously.

The situation concerning the symptomatic changes is as follows. Although pleasant, the woman cannot avoid controlling her daughter by saying things such as "stand up straight". Her previous profession

evoked fantasies of prostitution in those around her, which is not unrelated to the dirtiness and anality that I have referred to in connection
with Magda. Given the fact that the symptom had almost disappeared
as well as my concern about the child's mental functioning, I suggested
we should meet again two months later. By then she had totally overcome her encopresis and, at the same time, Magda was almost mentally
"sphincterised". For example, she hardly spoke at all and her drawing
was absolutely stuffed full of colours: it was of a house that disappeared
under this mass of grey and mauve colours (the colours of her father's
tracksuit). Her play was also very restrained, even in a dramatisation
that I gradually encouraged her to play out. In it she was paralysed in
front of a group of soldiers, who looked as if they were going to shoot
at a woman. Her parents were satisfied with how things were evolving.
The only intervention of their daughter concerned her drawing, which
she did not take with her – an intervention that turned out to be significant. She said something that was related, but this only became evident
much later on, to her father's profession, which I had no knowledge of
at that moment because he had changed his line of work. In any event,
I was unable to make them sensitive to their daughter's "block". They
accepted the principle of coming regularly for consultations. In fact, I did
not see them again until one year later, when their daughter was seven-
and-a-half. Several appointments had been postponed in the meantime.
The father came alone and continued to come alone to each consultation,
whatever I said about about it. Magda was now speaking again with a
certain degree of spontaneity. She had the tendency to describe building games to me with very few images. Later on, she talked to me about
the last child of her sibling group, a sister three years younger than her,
as if she was her baby. She even went as far as to say that in the future
she she wouldn't need to have a child because she already had one! Her
drawing, which continued to be characterised by control, gradually portrayed a series of birds between a house and a girl outside. When I drew
her attention to the fact that the birds were between the house and the
girl, Magda symbolised the process excessively by decorating the house
with a multitude of multi-coloured points. For the father everything was
always fine. He remained mistrustful, yet polite. He "agreed" with the
principle of continuing the consultations provided that he was the one
who made the appointment each time.

I heard about Magda six months later at her school. She was now
eight years of age. She was in a special needs class with a good teacher

whom I knew well. The child was described to me as "almost delusional". During a visit to a park she had "seen" knives in the trees and assassins. She would talk repeatedly about making gifts to her teacher, speak to adults whom she didn't know, and kiss several mothers as she was leaving the school. In class, she was only productive for short moments, even though she was considered to be an intelligent child. She was a "real pain" and the "scatterbrain" among the other children who, as a result, marginalised her.

Her parents had an appointment with the teacher who told me that the father had reacted in an authoritarian manner and was not ready to listen to anything except one thing with which he agreed, namely, that his daughter was from time to time "elsewhere". The teacher insisted on continuing with the consultations in spite of the father's voiced opinion that speaking and drawing were a waste of time. Another six months went by. I saw no one. I learnt at a school meeting that since our last encounter there had been a clear change, in the sense that Magda was no longer in a state of "crisis" and had apparently resumed her usual mode of functioning. Then I had no more news for almost four years. In September, Mrs A. came to the Centre to inform the secretary that they had not come the previous year because of the birth of a baby. I saw them two months later, that is to say, only the father and daughter together. Magda, who was now twelve, was in the 5th year of primary school (in France, *cours moyen*, CM2). To explain the mother's absence, Mr A. turned towards his daughter and said to her in an apparently detached and final way: "I think your mother's at work this morning." He then told me that things were going better. Mr A. meant that Magda's eagerness to be helpful to others to the point of disconcerting them had diminished. Magda responded by saying that she only did this when she knew the person.

Once again, a modification occurred when a consultation was in sight. Mr A. exposed himself more this time, and involuntarily, by associating his daughter's conduct with the fact that she was very affectionate, particularly with him. I then learnt – because I was completely unaware of this – that Magda's eldest sister, the first child, was in fact a half-sister, born of the mother's first marriage (which backed up what I was saying about the mother's profession). And Mr A. defended himself by saying that it wasn't a secret since I had never asked him anything. He agreed, however, that his daughter was highly sensitive. He was able to make a link – but for him this was a perfectly egosyntonic explanation – between the love he had for Magda (and, of course, for his other children, he added immediately) and the love that he had received both from his parents and from his sisters (he was the only boy and the youngest), thereby denying any ambivalence. Magda, whom I saw alone afterwards – and with whom I eventually raised the subject of the meeting at school four years earlier – told me, in a sort of reconstitution, that at that time she had felt a bit lost in the new class (the special needs class) where she knew no one. Now, she added, she "introduced herself" instead of addressing others directly. She apparently could not remember the content of the past consultations, but when I suggested that she might like to see her drawings again, she reacted immediately by saying: "I don't want to." In fact, she said she was afraid she might have nightmares. I suggested that perhaps she would like to see her drawings later and asked her when we would see each other again. Immediately she exclaimed, and this is typical of the mental functioning of this child, "The sooner the better!" The father, whom I then saw in the presence of his child, was perplexed by the summary I gave him, with Magda's agreement.

Our consultations resumed, but they did not come to the next one. At a school meeting in March I learnt that Magda was falling behind in arithmetic. The consultation took place one month later. Magda talked to me about her difficulties with fractions. I did a few with her and realised that, when she had understood, she inevitably began making errors again shortly after. She had a clear tendency, in the activities she talked to me about, to give priority to what had an appearance of veneer. This resembled her earlier need for decoration and control. This defensive mode is characteristic of her structure. For example, in class she had built a trader's letter box decorated with sweet papers wrapped around stones. If I drew her attention to the playful function of this activity, Magda replied that she didn't do it to have fun but to learn things. This is an example of alienating identification.

Nevertheless, the instinctual drive made its return and, as before, a sudden shift occurred which was linked to this consultation. After talking about her reading of Mickey Mouse, she told me, contradicting what she had said the time before, that she "really liked being afraid" and watching "horror films". Moreover, she told me a story (albeit in rather rational terms) of a couple arriving in a vampire's castle. A bit later, I referred to her parents' work. She didn't know, apparently, what they did, but above all she added (and this was addressed to me):

"One mustn't be curious", and then, "I don't want to know". When I linked these affirmations up with what had happened between us with regard to her drawings of a few years before, she was troubled and said: "I don't know." Then, as this consultation had been brought forward owing to a cancelled appointment, for the next one Magda took it upon herself to suggest the date of the one that had initially been planned, saying that she wanted to use it. This quite impressed me. The father, still alone, was completely on the defensive, contained, mistrustful, and always polite. For him, his daughter had no problems except in arithmetic. When I mentioned the question of his work, he showed me subtly that the particular attire he was wearing indicated quite clearly what he did: it spoke for itself. But there had been no verbal exchanges on this subject with his daughter. His rise up the hierarchy since then meant that he no longer wore this attire. He told me that children can be curious, except when it comes to their father or mother. Something other than a purely cultural trait was involved here.

During the meeting that took place one month later at the school, I was told that Magda was still causing concern for her teachers in arithmetic. During outings, her behaviour was striking. For example, at the art gallery, she didn't listen to the guide like the other children. She would intervene at the wrong moment to ask questions about another painting, which irritated her peers. Shortly after, I saw her for a consultation. Her attitude was one of "everything's fine". I was the one who gradually re-established the link with the last consultation. Her face lit up for a moment, then her expression became closed for good after she had made the stunning remark: "There we are . . . it's finished . . . a long time ago already." If I tried to make the child sensitive to these two conflictual movements within her, she listened to me but remained at the level of "everything's fine". Afterwards, in front of her father, this process was tragically reinforced. She submitted completely to her father who felt, precisely, that "everything *was* fine". Moreover, she was going to move into the 6th year. She now took part in discussions much more than before, I was told, etc.

During this time, Magda showed me rather pathetically (while her father was not looking) by her gestures, her expression, her rolling eyes, that I had better give up. The father announced, moreover, that in future he would only request a consultation if there was a problem. The process culminated in a discussion about Magda's problem of imagination, of what gets blocked in her at this level. Mr A. reacted by saying to me: "She doesn't have any secrets." When I tried to draw him out in a somewhat psychodramatic, playful mode, concerning his daughter's adolescence, Mr A. replied that there were no secrets. Magda then intervened to tell me that she told her father everything. And at that point I learnt from Mr A. that he would get up every night to make sure that his children were sleeping well. Finally, he added that he was the one who had fed Magda when she was a baby, rather than her mother. So we had come full circle. There was a symptomatic cure (the encopresis), but one that reinforced a structural anality of character in the sense of narcissistic control/mastery at the expense of the erotic impulses that were thus "cured". Until, that is, she had a so-called delusional "crisis" when everything "came out". Then there was an attempt to preserve a situation of homeostasis that was simply waiting to be called into question, if it had not been for the anti-drive influence of the father, an attempt that ultimately became pathetic and in the face of which I was powerless. Except for the fact that I still hope that later on, this child, as an adult, will have retained traces of our meetings and that she might one day seek help, even if this hope remains meagre.

Isabelle, openness to change

The second solution, in direct contrast with the first, is the one found by Isabelle. She was referred to me at the age of nine-and-a-half by her mother's analyst, because she did not feel good about herself and was withdrawn. This was having consequences on her work at school, even though she had average marks in her class. She was the only daughter of parents who had separated when she was a little girl. This separation was immediately linked by her mother to her daughter's difficulties. Mrs B. lived alone with her daughter, while the father had rebuilt his life and had another child. The description I was given of this man was of someone who was suffering. Mrs B., the youngest of several children, was the only one who had done higher studies. She was pretty, intelligent, sensitive and sweet, too sweet even.

When I saw her for the first time, Isabelle, too, had the sweetness, on the face of it, of a little girl, younger than she actually was, with a manner of speaking that was a bit more childish than one would expect for her age. Apart from her fear of making spelling mistakes and of not succeeding in her sport – later, I realised that she took part in competitions, which bore witness to her motor skills – she did not complain about anything, and in particular did not complain about not feeling good about herself. As for the separation of her parents, she was too young to remember, she told me. Her imagination was restricted, but distinctive. She could not imagine anything concerning the future, but she was able to tell me a "simple" dream about a bowl with two tortoises in it, a good illustration of her relationship with her mother. Later on, the two tortoises became fat, a nice condensation. Isabelle preferred to remain a little girl. Otherwise, it would mean leaving her mother. And worse still, it might kill her mother.

The cards were thus dealt from the outset in such a way as to facilitate my potential role as a third party. In front of her daughter, Mrs B. told me that the mere fact of having requested a consultation had led to some improvement in Isabelle. Gradually, she managed to implicate herself in relation to her guilt. In effect, she felt guilty for having been too attentive to her husband when they were living together, especially as she was sensitive to his difficulties. It had been at Isabelle's expense, she added. Mrs B. was catching up with lost time, as it were. She confirmed, humorously, that I was intervening in the relationship thus created between mother and daughter, as if to loosen it. Finally, it is worth noting for the future that Isabelle cried a lot on returning from the crèche where she was during the day. We separated after agreeing on the principle of therapeutic consultations, the only useful indication at this point.

Two months later, Isabelle spoke about the progress she had been making in class, about her recollection of telling me the last time we met about a dream, but not about its content. Nor could she speak about any products of her imagination. She felt that she was doing fine. Although her mother confirmed that she had been making progress since the last consultation, she was struck by a panic attack her daughter had had eight days earlier, what's more, in a triangular context. Her girlfriends were exchanging remarks on their outings and contact with their respective fathers, and Isabelle was seized by panic when her turn came round. This event permitted Mrs B. to talk about the conflict on the subject of the holidays her daughter spent at her ex-husband's home, which was to be the nodal point, moreover, of all the coming consultations. Mr Z., who lived abroad, was in fact not very available during these periods, and his new wife could not tolerate Isabelle's presence. So it was the paternal grandmother, living in another house, who took care of the child. Finally, and this was to occur again often, Mrs B. told me about something her daughter had said to her on leaving the last consultation, namely, her fear that her mother would die, a theme that had already been raised in connection with the dream of the two tortoises.

We saw each other again four months later. The child was doing well and was quite talkative as soon as it involved talking about her sports activities. She mentioned a new dream that was "too simple": in the dream her dog had turned into her daddy. There was no question, moreover, of another man taking her father's place, and she talked about a friend of her mother's as if he did not exist. As far as her relationship with her mother was concerned, everything was fine apart from the matter of the conflicts on the subject of the holidays with her father. Isabelle had spoken to her mother about the dream about the dog, a dog which, in reality, had been at home since the separation of her parents. Mrs B. would not have separated from her husband, she told me, if he had been prepared to do some psychotherapy. Isabelle, moreover, had recently said to her mother that her father ought to see someone like me.

We met again after the holidays. She was now more than ten years old. This time, Mrs B. wanted to see me alone, and her daughter agreed.[4] She needed to tell me how unavailable she had been for Isabelle when she was married. Above all, she was able to tell me that she had been violent when her daughter reminded her that she existed. Of course, more than the content which I already partly knew about, it was the fact of telling me this that had a dynamic value. In addition, I learnt that when her parents separated, Isabelle had suffered from stomach ulcers. By the age of seven these symptoms had stopped, though she had had another bout the summer before on the occasion of the death of a grandparent. Isabelle told me, however, that she had not felt sad about it because "it happened very quickly". We may none the less wonder about the link, on the psychosomatic level, between this somatic expression and the particular and "too simple" quality of the expressions of fantasy, including dreams, which I have described, as well as the link with her hypercathected motor functioning on which subject – the only one – she was prolix. Moreover, Isabelle, who was in the 5th year of primary school and working hard, liked her teacher particularly because she was sportive. She had nothing but commonplace things to tell me.

A few months later, her mother requested to see me alone first. Her ex-husband was not well, and his wife was expecting a child. Mrs B. did not know anymore where she stood in relation to him. She showed me more clearly than usual that she had not come to terms with this separation. Her husband's shouting reminded her of how her own mother used to shout and many other things of her family past. She told me she felt blocked in analysis whenever she was led to talk about her husband; she felt that she was placing the weight of all this on her daughter's shoulders. I saw the daughter afterwards. Apart from the fact that she was always happy in class and that her notes were good, when we touched on the question of her mother's concerns about her, Isabelle told me that her mother worried too much about her, when in fact she was perfectly capable of "getting by", as she put it. Then, when mother and daughter were together, the first, in addition to what she had said about putting a burden on the second, said that her daughter would go through heavy emotional situations as if nothing had happened, and in any case swiftly regained her composure. I then told Isabelle – thinking again for my part about her somatic past and how she functioned – that it was better to be able to express what one feels, on the condition, of course, that her mother could refrain from reacting too strongly to it. Isabelle turned towards her mother with a smile on her face.

At the start of the following new school year, we saw the outcome of what, in retrospect, had taken on the significance of suggestion. There remained one consultation before the holidays. Everything was fine except for her habitual apprehension about spending the holiday period with her father. At a certain moment, Mrs B. replied that she could imagine her daughter later as "tall and beautiful" but could not imagine anything on the relational or social level. Isabelle looked at her mother again. After the summer holidays, Mrs B. requested a consultation as a matter of urgency because her daughter, who had just started Year 6 at school, was having an anxiety attack. Isabelle said she was fine apart from the fact that she told me she had been very anxious when her art teacher had asked her to draw a holiday landscape. You will recall the earlier exchange between children concerning their outings with their fathers. What interested me at the level of fantasy is that, when I asked Isabelle for her associations to this type of drawing, she said she was incapable of drawing *the sea* and of locating it between the horizon and the beach. By way of a triangular counterpoint, she mentioned a visit to a castle in ruins . . . with her mother's brother. For her part, Mrs. B. felt more and more unable to come to terms with the breakdown of her marriage with her ex-husband.

During this time, Isabelle was no longer able to be separate from her mother. She would cry, without knowing why, and say to her mother, before going into class, that she was going to miss her. As if in echo, Mrs B. even had the fantasy of stopping her analysis. One month later, I learnt that Isabelle cried every morning until ten o'clock exactly. "After that, she was all right", she said. Fortunately, this was tolerated in class. She did not feel sad and her school results were good. Mrs B. recalled how her daughter had cried at the crèche. When I reminded her that Isabelle had almost reached puberty, Isabelle listened to me without reacting. On the other hand, she described the film *Abyss*[5] to me in detail, which we can link up with her inability to draw the sea.

One month later, Isabelle had not cried for . . . one week. This pause was linked to her expectations with respect to the consultation, but also to the coming All Saints holidays. She wanted to prolong these by two days in order to see her father who, once again, was not well. This time Mrs B. told me that on two occasions she had, *for the first time*, asserted her authority. In the first place, she had come to fetch her daughter. Next, concerning the coming new school year, she told Isabelle, who was crying, that enough was enough and that at the end of the day she could do as she wished. She, her mother, could not do everything for her. On this occasion, moreover, Mrs B. associated her own gentleness with the victim side of her. Her recent fantasy of stopping her analysis had certainly brought about this change in her. When it came round to the fact that Mrs B., on fetching her daughter at the end of the holidays, had been struck to see that she was trying to help her father who was not well by . . . crying, I intervened to show Isabelle in front of her mother that it was not possible to help her father by putting herself in his place by crying, and by being as badly off as him. She was touched by this intervention/suggestion which, in fact, hystericised symbolically the dynamic between cathexis and identification. After the Christmas holidays, both the mother and daughter felt that everything was going well; Isabelle was capable of standing up to her mother, which she obviously considered to be a good thing, while Mrs B. continued to maintain her newfound authority. She added, moreover, that Isabelle told her frankly what she thought about things and added, "When I think that it took her all this time to tell me about them." Two consultations remained before the holidays. Nothing fundamental needs to be added.

The evolution followed its course and links with the past continued to be made, a process that occurred spontaneously in this woman
who was still in analysis, which was the reason why I had not wanted
to draw her out – in particular with regard to her oedipal history. It
proved more useful to wait and let the opportunities arise. A space was
recreated between mother and daughter, who made me think of the two
tortoises in a bowl. The third function that I represented was the essential element that led to change, but it was also helped by the mother's
analysis. We should not forget, however, that if this new development
occurred, it was nevertheless true that Isabelle's structural functioning
and her unconscious death wishes towards her mother, linked with her
unconscious/preconscious sense of guilt (being responsible for her parents' separation), entered into resonance with her mother's inability to
work through her grief over the separation from her ex-husband.

Notes

1 Translator's note: Throughout this book the term "representation(s)"
   (S.E. *thing-and word presentations*) refers to the ideational representatives
   of the drive (*Vorstellungsrepräsentanz*), in accordance with French usage,
   rather than to more conscious visual forms of representability, as in
   dreams (Fr.: *figuration, figurabilité*; G. *Darstellung, Darstellbarkeit*).
2 A general category introduced by André Green including different types
   of representation (psychic representative, ideational representative,
   affect representative, representative of the drive, etc.) and which implies
   the movement, activity of representation.
3 This passage takes up again the article "Consultation thérapeutique, cure
   de l'enfant. Processus et changement", initially published in *Les Textes du
   Centre Alfred Binet*, 18, Paris, ASM 13, 1991, pp. 1–22. Reproduced with
   the kind permission of the Alfred Binet Centre.
4 When I accept this type of request, it is generally on the condition that
   what concerns the child can be communicated to him/her afterwards.
5 Translator's note: an American science-fiction film directed by James
   Cameron.

CHAPTER TWO

Clinical experience of the movements of psychic life

*From the therapeutic consultation to child
psychoanalysis – two clinical experiences*[1]

T
he two following situations, one involving therapeutic consultations, the other analysis, have the particular feature of having
taken place over roughly the same length of time, four years.
Even though the duration of the treatment was the same, the process
involved was not, as we shall see, including what preceded or followed
each type of indication.

The therapeutic consultations – Alexandre

Ten or so consultations took place over a period of four years, the child
being between almost three and seven years old. He was five years and
a few months when the first indication of psychotherapy was made.
It had taken almost two years, then, to confirm it; otherwise, it would
have been premature, especially for the parents, and particularly for the
father. The father had agreed with the indication following a symbolic
period of learning to write and of the sense of failure that ensued, while
at the same time playing an active role in helping his son. This shows,

it may be said in passing, the importance of the role of the parents in the work of therapeutic indication. Two movements may be noted in this connection. On the one hand, the child's psychic functioning had evolved, with its organising scansions attesting to oedipal structuring, marked by displacement, symbolisation, and triangular dynamics. This was accompanied by an evolution of the symptoms (enuresis, sleeping difficulties, fits of anger) and character traits. On the other hand, there had been an evolution in the parents' psychic functioning, bearing witness both to a degree of progress and to the persistence of certain difficulties. For obvious reasons of confidentiality, I will only give a minimum of historical elements, which will not have any dynamic effects on a contribution that is primarily oriented towards technical problems.

Alexandre is an only son and an adopted child. Both his parents are intelligent and sensitive, and each of them has quite a strong personality. The father is a calm and patient man; his wife is more extraverted, including at the emotional level, without being overwhelming. The child cannot be separate from his parents and still clings to his mother's bosom, while saying "gum" (like the chewing gum that he has in his mouth). I enacted his separation anxiety in front of the stranger that I was for him, by identifying with him and saying to him: "I don't know you; I'm staying close to my mummy." The triangular mobilisation of the boy occurred immediately, because he moved towards his father. As this movement created a space, the child then played hide-and-seek. I accompanied him, just as I did when he moved towards the drawing board, but he did not draw any recognisable forms. He scribbled, but changed the felt pens systematically, putting the cap back on each of them. This pre-obsessional sign of the prematurity of the ego over instinctual expression became clearer in his play. He took some animals out of the toy box and placed them in a line, placed closely against each other, whether they were wild or domestic. I pointed out to him that, like that, there was no risk of them getting separated from each other, which led Alexandre to place a crocodile close to a cow. The child confirmed that the first was going to eat the second. He then undid the line of animals, while uttering the words "death" and "poo".

This time, the anal instinctual expression with its word-presentations was manifested directly. Many other elements in this first consultation could be mentioned, such as those that put the mother in difficulty, and which were related to the adoption. They will be the subject of a later study. We agreed to meet again a few months later, after the summer holidays. Alexandre was now three years and three months old. He followed me this time without any difficulty. This first sign of an evolution was followed by a second on the graphic level. The child wasn't scribbling any more and, after saying to me, "I can't" (draw a man), he agreed, with my encouragement, to draw a house. He depicted it by drawing a circle with other circles inside it, and a vertical line for the chimney. In short, he was developing a certain degree of logic. In view of this progressive movement, he agreed to continue his drawing, adding what looked like a man. The situation of "I can't", with which he started, had thus evolved. Furthermore, this man grew taller as a result of a parapraxis: one leg became longer than the other. His play followed this movement. It was more expansive and joyful, even though he was unable to organise a really playful scenario, even with my help, except for a brief moment when a little calf was described as "nasty" because it was doing "silly things". Alexandre negotiated this movement of projective identification; a crocodile that was approaching the little calf was beaten to death by a "man".

The excitement did not disorganise the child, thanks to his obvious appetite for relating. He made progress at the level of language, even if a certain delayed speech development and enunciation disorders were clearly noticeable. In this connection a speech and language assessment suggested the need for re-education. The parents confirmed that their son was developing well in spite of the qualitative persistence of his symptoms. It was more his character that they found difficult, due to his tendency to be oppositional and stubborn. But, as a whole, they were satisfied with this evolution. Mrs C., for her part, was also evolving with regard to the adoption. Of course, her son sometimes questioned her about it, in a more or less symbolic way, in resonance with his oedipal difficulties. We worked on this, but I cannot give an account of this work here. But, given that things were developing positively, we agreed to continue consultations at irregular intervals.

I saw Alexandre again when he was three years and eight months of age. I noted that he was both more oppositional towards the familiar person that I was becoming and, at the same time, more playful. This was why he described animals in his play as "not beautiful" and "not nice". I interpreted this as being linked to the way he described himself when he was unhappy. He confirmed this interpretation for me symbolically by attributing kindness to a phallicised maternal substitute: a "nice" lion. The parents considered that he was making considerable progress. Their son was becoming more sociable and was not trying to test them so much. The speech and language assessment concluded that "everything was settling down". At four years and three months, his character was asserting itself. In one of our meetings, he said to me – feeling very content with himself – that he would say nothing and do nothing. He nevertheless started playing again, enacting very vigorous fights, without becoming disorganised or agitated. His parents were struck, I would say, by their son's instinctual drive energy. He could be charming, just as he could be impossible. His way of thinking was expressed in a new way in such moments: "Mummy, you know, I have thought about things, I have decided not to get angry anymore." Two days before the consultation, Alexandre had a serious stomach ache, which the parents understood, with my help, as perhaps being linked to our next meeting. This connection led Mrs C. to bring associations to her son's declarations of love towards her in the form of, "I love you Mummy."

This new oedipal manifestation – which at the same time was appropriate for the child's age – had its aggressive counterpoint. He was now able to tell his mother that he didn't want her anymore, that she should go away, which destabilised her position as an adoptive mother. But from now on she was better able to tolerate what was said – and she was also less taken in by it – than what had been acted out in the past. The speech and language assessment concluded none the less, that in spite of the progress made, re-education was necessary for the speech disorders. This began at the age of four years and seven months. I saw the child again two months before that. He began speaking to me immediately – which was new for him – about his friends who were doing stupid things. We thought about the things the calf had done in his earlier play activity. But there was something more, he said: "They had taken pieces of chalk and written on doors!" Recalling that, according to André Green, every conquest is a transgression in the domain of sublimation, I linked this to Alexandre's wish to be grown up, to go to the "big" school in order to write. The child reacted by denying this, a process that was becoming quite familiar for him. His drawing portrayed for the first time a symbolic movement of anal retention, between sublimation and reaction formation. Indeed, after drawing houses, he introduced between them a form made up of strips of colours, an aesthetic but unnameable form. The parents remarked that although their son remained sensitive to separation, he was making progress none the less, as could be seen from the quality of his sleep. After calling out three or four times, he would fall asleep without any further interruption. Alexandre was now five years and three months old; in other words, two and a half years had passed since our first meeting.

This consultation raised for the first time the question of psychotherapy. I will therefore give a few further details about this. Triangulation was expressed much more clearly in it, while at the same time there was a sort of race to find a degree of "equilibrium in the disequilibrium" of the relations between primary and secondary processes. He began talking to me right away, and for the first time about his enuresis. In a discreetly provocative way, he told me that he "wet his bed everyday", something his mother confirmed subsequently, apart from fifteen days during the summer. Then he brought associations to the summer holidays. He had been in the forest where, he said, he had seen some wild boar, in a sort of symbolic evocation of the paternal third party. Alexandre went on to talk about some couples, friends of his parents, telling me their first names, masculine and feminine. He also talked to me about school. He was now with the "big" children; it was the last year of nursery school.

There was a progressive movement in his associative processes, during which he told me that he was learning things and drawing. So I suggested he might draw something. He began for the first time, following on from the dynamics of the last consultation, to trace a series of figures between one and eight. Then he began, in a movement of formal regression involving the process of equilibrium/disequilibrium mentioned above, a figurative activity. He began by drawing a character, which he then replaced with a big butterfly and a smaller house beside it. He indicated the movements of the butterfly inside the house and added a second. I accompanied this movement verbally, which triggered the child's negation, leading him to say that it was a "baby". A movement of "secondarisation", or discursive binding, followed during which Alexandre explained that the big butterfly was the mummy. Then he retracted this saying, "It's not the baby . . . it's the big brother", and added a little butterfly for the baby.

Whatever progress the child may have made, we found ourselves faced with a pre-obsessional process of mental functioning, the prolegomena of which we have seen in earlier consultations. This process did not seem sufficiently hermetic to the point of preventing Alexandre from enriching his scenario. He continued his drawing with a depiction whose meaning I did not immediately understand. "It's not the mummy," he said, formulating a negation, and then added, "It's a boat," which was true. He then drew the sea and the boat's portholes; he began drawing the pilot, but then stopped himself, depicting a female character instead, "the daughter", he said. "Yes, the man's daughter," he said, adding: "He's dead". Alexandre confirmed for me unconsciously, in connection with his oedipal difficulties and the obsessional problem of the "dead father" – here the suppression of the boat's captain – what underlay his latent thoughts. Finally, he introduced another female character, a woman who turned out to be blind and who had no meaning for him. But, in counterpoint, he drew something prominent at the bottom of her dress, which he called "her willy". Then he laughed, displacing symbolically this phallic "willy" and drawing big fingers for the character. Then, in what was the equivalent of a countercathexis, I suggested that he should cover the lady's willy because she would find it difficult to stay like that. "No," he replied, but immediately displaced, symbolised, and "secondarised". He drew a cat, then another one. They were his godmother's cats. He laughed: "She doesn't have two, but only one." Reality was getting the upper hand again. "It was a joke," Alexandre added, employing a very shrewd symbolic expression, while saying in front of one of his apparently abstract depictions: "I don't know yet," (what that represents), thereby showing a good sense of temporality concerning the "unknown relationship" (Rosolato, 1978).

His mother accompanied him alone that day. She felt that there had been a "great change" in her son. He was well integrated in his class and participated actively without showing any signs of agitation. His attempts to test the family had also lessened. On the instinctual level, during a fit of anger, he planted pins into a photo of his mother at the level of her eyes. Thinking about the drawing of the blind woman, I told myself that this event showed that his preconscious was functioning, especially as nothing impeded statements of the following sort: "Little girls are in love with their daddies and boys with their mummies." Later on, I let Mrs C. know how I saw things: on the one hand, he was continuing to make progress, but on the other Alexandre was struggling with, let's say, the pressure that was inside him. She heard what I was saying and associated to the questions related to death which her son was wrestling with. I raised the possibility of a psychotherapy. She agreed that we would think about it together.

I will simply note the main points of the two following sessions and dwell at greater length on the third, which confirmed the indication of psychotherapy. Alexandre was now five years and seven months old. His comments on a drawing made the link for the first time, at the level of urethral symbolism, with his enuresis. At the same time his symptoms had receded noticeably. Oedipal contents came to light in his dreams. Alexandre told me that he was having bad dreams about thieves. Later, his mother enriched Alexandre's account with what he had told her: he was afraid that the thief would take his mother's jewels . . . she was so pretty with them. Immediately after this, Mrs C. reported a question Alexandre had asked her: "Could daddy die?" Mr C., apparently seeing through this, added that his son sometimes had "pistols in the place of his eyes". At the same period, Alexandre moved into the first year of primary school without difficulty and was able to spend a night at a friend's house, something that had hitherto been impossible. As a result, Mrs C. was ready for her son to undergo psychotherapy, whereas her husband preferred to think about it further. After the summer holidays, when Alexandre was six years old, he talked about walks in the forest and wild boar. He then started drawing separate houses for men and women, but stopped himself, as if to redistribute the cards. In keeping with his pre-obsessional mode of functioning, he established orders between the houses he had drawn: a hospital, a police station, and a fire station. Then, a manifestation of another order emerged, that is to say, writing. Although the word he had written was incomprehensible, Alexandre, shrewd as ever, "found" a symbolic solution to this conflict: he cut up the "word" and attributed each part to one of the above orders (police, firemen, etc.).

In other words, his mode of functioning did not exclude modes of functioning linked to the Oedipus complex, to *infantile neurosis* with its pre-obsessional elements, thereby attesting to the presence of symbolic associations, triangular movements with expressions of the superego, including the collective superego. The parents told me that Alexandre was participating a lot in class and that the teacher had not said anything particular about him. Apparently, he was still sleeping well. At the level of the (individual) superego, he was showing feelings of guilt, allowing him to describe himself as a monster when he "made scenes" with his mother. At the end of this consultation just before the beginning of the new school year, there was still a discrepancy between my point of view confirming the indication of psychotherapy and that of his parents who preferred to wait for things to improve at school. I saw them again when Alexandre was six years and seven months old. This time the indication was accepted and confirmed. The child told me right away that he was feeling better, an improvement he attributed to work at school and to the sessions of speech therapy. As for the other things, "it's not very nice", he said, without being able to say anything more about it this time. I reminded him about his dreams. He told me that he only had bad dreams sometimes. This was especially the case when he closed the door to be able to go to sleep. Was there anything else that was not nice? He mentioned his bed-wetting, this time with an air of concern. It occurred less frequently, and it had even ceased completely once for a week, but had then returned. "Unfortunately", he added, laughing a little.

He none the less anticipated the future, foreseeing that gradually he would wet his bed less. It was a drawing that would help us get to the heart of his fantasy life. Alexandre portrayed a character in red. It's "because he's bleeding everywhere . . . it's because he was falling over everywhere", and he added, "He's dead." Around the character he traced a coffin, and tried to write the name for it. Alexandre had difficulty in writing, especially in such a fantasy-based context, even if his attempt was more legible than the time before. His parents confirmed, moreover, their son's difficulties in this domain. He continued his drawing with a flower and a yellow "streamer", half-animal, half-abstraction, probably symbolising the urethral penis. He then introduced a second character, the butcher. Yes, he said, he would take the animal; then, he added a "barbecue" for the steaks cut up by the butcher. Alexandre then reintroduced the first character who was bleeding, saying that he was dead because he had eaten everything, the barbecue included. He had burned himself to death, but he would live again by eating his coffin. The child finished his drawing with a great spiral, which he baptised "snail". "That's the daddy snail", he said, but then corrected himself, and said: "It's the mummy." As far as the hermaphrodism was concerned, however, he was not wrong. He then drew two eggs that were going to be laid.

This brings us back to what I was saying earlier about the relations between primary process and secondary process, except that here there is no disorganisation of the narrative, drawing or behavioural expression. However, the pressure of the instinctual drives, which regressed to the level of oral sadism with its correlative manic defence, obliged the child to "run" after the secondary organisation of his narrative. But my purpose is less to comment on the contents of such a sequence than to show how it was resolved for each of the protagonists of this "adventure".

The exchanges with the parents were more favourable this time thanks to the symbolic dimension of the transition to the primary school, implying the challenge of learning to write. Alexandre's difficulties on this level were, moreover, not helped by the discontinuous availability of the teacher who was very involved in trade union and training activities, which led to replacements during the course of the year. But it was Alexandre himself who was going to help settle the question of the indication of his psychotherapy. Indeed, as I was going over a certain number of points again with the parents concerning their son's psychic functioning, Alexandre, who had preferred his drawing to be placed face down so that it could not be seen, turned it over so that it was visible, and then said a few things about it quickly, while asking me to give a more detailed account. In a certain way, Alexandre helped me to concretise what I was reporting to his parents and to confirm the indication of psychotherapy. His parents agreed with us. Mrs C. referred to a woman friend of hers who had told her that Alexandre was fooling people when he gave the impression of lacking confidence in himself. Mr C. thought again about the time when his son had started primary school, the first few weeks of which had been quite turbulent; in his view, this was no doubt a sign of his uneasiness. As a result, this time all three of them were agreed on the indication of psychoanalytic psychotherapy.

Owing to a lack of an available place, the work only began after the summer holidays, in October, on the basis of two sessions a week for reasons of feasibility. Consequently, I saw Alexandre once again when he was aged seven and had just entered Year 3 (in France, *cours élémentaire*, CE1). Although he still had a lack of confidence in himself, to the point that he anticipated failing his Year 3, he still seemed to be quite well. Interestingly, he told me right away that he was no longer having nightmares, which was a significant development. Moreover, he was drawing a lot more like a child in the period of latency. He portrayed Tintin and Milou, though he felt he had got the latter wrong.

He did not react with a denial, as he usually did, when I linked this up with his lack of confidence in himself and his tendency to anticipate failure. He then did a successful drawing of Tintin who was in prison, and who, in a "bubble", expressed the thought of being freed by Milou, thereby seeming to cathect the normal cultural interests of a child of this age. He was still ready to begin a psychotherapy and added that he would "also" like to have some sessions with a woman. Beyond what at a latent level referred to his relationship with me, this meant that he did not want to stop his sessions with his speech therapist. I told him that I could understand this, since he had a mother who had given birth to him and a mother with whom he lived. "I don't know the story," he replied, an answer that had an associative function, for he had heard the story during a consultation.

During the fifteen days to three weeks that preceded the beginning of his psychotherapy, Alexandre reactivated his symptoms but, "just like in books", Mrs C. told me, everything settled down again as soon as the sessions had begun. A few months after the beginning of his new treatment, he decided of his own accord to separate from his speech therapist who felt that she could not do much more for him. As for the transition between his meetings with me and his sessions with his analyst, Alexandre resolved the question himself by making a compromise. In effect, I continued to see the parents alone from time to time. For the first time since the beginning of the sessions, he was present in the waiting-room.

Faced with the different possibilities that I offered him with regard to his presence in my office, he chose the best solution, which was for me to see him with his parents. I will only sketch the broad outlines of how things evolved during the first year, as this was transmitted to me by his psychoanalyst, the purpose of the first part of this book being to illustrate a process of therapeutic consultations. Alexandre settled down quickly into the process, the sessions being nourished with his infantile sexual theories concerning birth, comparing the respective roles of the mother and father, both in animals and humans. The displacement of this material in the transference led, as one might expect, to an anal regression, sometimes expressed in crude terms. Thus he identified himself with an animal emitting wild noises, referred to his "farting asshole", and said a few dirty things to his analyst on leaving his sessions. He also spoke about his fear that a spider with black eyes would come and bite him in his "poo".

Interestingly, his analyst did not choose, in her interpretations, the classical direction of the "pregenital" or "archaic" mother, as we say, but linked this fear to his fear of the thieves (those in his dreams) who might come to his bedroom and take him away, as well as to his difficulty of being alone with his analyst. This triangular interpretation led Alexandre to represent a male character at the wheel of a complicated machine that was making flowers. The question of in front/behind, concerning the orifices of the machine, introduced an element of castration anxiety following the interventions of the analyst, followed by a displacement in the transference accompanied by a number of significant transgressions. A degree of calm then returned thanks to the introduction by the child of an imaginary third party, an "elder brother", who put some order between him and his analyst.

A child analysis: Jean-Éric and self-evaluation

The situation I found myself in with this boy contrasted with the case above. Jean-Éric, who figured in the last chapter and whom we will come across at other moments in the book, had already been seen in a consultation by the colleague who had referred him to me. As with Alexandre, it was the work both with the child and the parents that enabled us to undertake Jean-Éric's analytic treatment. In order to highlight better the difference between process of consultation and process of analysis, I will gradually be led to identify the process that characterises the *self-evaluation* of the treatment by the child himself, the major indicators of which, referring both to the potentialities and concrete expressions of the child, lead to insight as well as to identification with the interpreting function of the analyst. These qualities, extremely rare in child analysis, must be examined in the light of the standard process and in analogy with the model of the standard treatment insofar as they are not free of conflictuality any more than others are, putting in tension the dynamics of the transference and countertransference.

This analysis lasted four years. Jean-Éric was the same age as Alexandre when it began, that is, almost seven-and-a-half years old. Though initially he had suffered from repetitive and violent nightmares as well as death-anxiety, his symptomatology, the quality of which persisted none the less, had diminished in its intensity during the course of the therapeutic consultations. His parents, caught up in their own difficulties, were able, thanks to the work they took part in with the consultant, to convince themselves that their son could benefit from an analysis. This was undertaken on the basis of three sessions a week for almost two years, then reduced to two sessions a week due to a move. This modification of the frequency of the sessions did not have any fundamental effect on a dynamic that seemed to be well established.

Remember that at the beginning of this analysis, the child, who had excellent verbal capacities in comparison with his graphic abilities, depicted a scene with diverse transference connotations that was of fundamental value for what followed. A lion, enclosed in a coffin with a witch, was urinating and defecating. As a result, Jean-Éric gave up any kind of drawing for a long period, preferring the motor sphere (various physical activities, paper-folding, aeroplane and rocket flights). Noticing what the formal regression had led to, I introduced a psychodramatic technique. Sufficiently symbolised psychodramatic contents, similar to fairy tales and myths, could be linked up with possible scenarios. The fundamental scene, which was gradually reintroduced, was then decondensed and enriched. I will now turn to a session that took place after two-and-a-half years of analysis. Jean-Éric was nine-and-a-half years old.

Recently, he had developed a repetitive form of behaviour, namely, of leaving the session to urinate in the toilets (just as he had "left" the office/coffin). This behaviour was often analysed in relation to each context, which could be linked either to a urethral discharge in connection with *sexual co-excitation* at this or that moment in the session, or to the need to verify the integrity of his penis following the excitation. One of the main contexts involved emerged in connection with the movements of sublimation that occurred during the analysis. The psychical working-over that followed had the effect both of attenuating the frequency of discharge and eventually of anticipating it. It was a new context (the occurrence of a movement of sublimation) that was likely to reactivate the urethral discharge (movement of regression): a "retroprogression", to use André Green's term. Prior to the session that I am going to describe, on several occasions and in the form of a game, Jean-Éric had crawled through a tunnel built with the chairs from my office. Having suffered from bouts of bronchitis, it was a sort of respiratory test for him, in addition to the sexual connotations that this game implied symbolically. This time he did not leave the room to go to the toilets. In the following session, Jean-Éric reversed the situation by making me play a guessing game with felt-tip pens the caps of which he had switched. I had to guess, on the basis of the cap, which felt-tip pen he had hidden in his hand. Now while this was going on, he touched his genital organs briefly on several occasions, while the felt-tip pens were pointing upwards in this same area. At the height of this movement, he declared: "I'm going to say something that you know about . . . the toilets!" Clearly, I did not make a homosexual transference interpretation but, given what had been said about the toilets, I simply said to him: "This time, it's the felt-pen willy." "Exactly!" Jean-Éric said, and added: "I'll tell you afterwards." He left the room and as soon as he returned, he continued: "You've taught me something, Dr Ody, which is that there is a relationship between going to the toilet and emotions."

After this example of a *trajectory towards insight*, he changed register and showed me a more desexualised, more socialised "erection", linked to certain judo exercises that he had learnt. It was during this period, at the beginning of his third year of analysis, that Jean-Éric referred associatively to an artistic activity of his father, while he himself was in the process of drawing a devil, extremely well, moreover. A lot had been said about the devil, but this time it seemed to have its place within a sublimated register (Ody, 1998) with reference to the paternal third element, which was generally absent in the material. In the following session, and apparently related to what had just happened, his mother told me what he himself was unable to tell me, namely, that her son did not understand what I said to him in the sessions. I did not feel too destabilised by this particular triangular movement because I recalled certain elements which suggested the contrary, such as the time at the beginning of the analysis when Jean-Éric had said to me: "I know how you think." In passing, Mrs D. added that her son was doing much better, particularly where his sleep was concerned, except when he watched a film that was too exciting. Meanwhile, Jean-Éric had drawn another devil which, he told me once he was alone, was much better than the last one. It was as if, via this movement, he was introducing paternal intelligibility thanks to the artistic identification with the devil/father, but under cover (in the transference) of its opposite in the form of a negation, namely the statement, "I do not know what you are saying", communicated by his mother.

In the following session, Jean-Éric managed to speak to me about his fears in a way that he had never done before. Then, as if moved by a violent impulsion, he started beating a rag doll at length – it made me think of Freud's (1919e) text "A child is being beaten" – without however lapsing, owing to the increasing state of excitation, into the disorganisation and frequent eruptions of acting out that he had manifested before. The analyst was thus able to associate to the unconscious fantasy of the child beaten by the father. This fantasy, a structural one insofar as it arose from the conflict of identification with the father, was recognised this time via the father/devil/psychoanalyst, including the latter's interpreting function. This movement as a whole seemed to be an integral part of what was to lead the child to self-evaluation and insight, in analogy with the process, described by Freud, which leads to increased awareness through becoming conscious, *Bewusstwerden* (Freud, 1915e, p. 173). Such a process characterises the hypercathexis of thing-presentations by word-presentations, which Freud differentiated from the so-called "symptom" which consists in "being conscious", while considering it as indissociable from working-through, *Durcharbeitung* (1914g, p. 155).

From this period onwards, thought games of a sort emerged. Faced with the question of "understanding", Jean-Éric would reverse the situation by putting to me what he called an enigma. He drew a sort of stick, which, given the context of the earlier productions, could make one think of a penis (he showed me in passing that he knew the words penis and *vergue* (*sic*)).[2] In reality, it was a ruler and, understanding the polysemy of the word, he concluded that he had never had so much fun as on that day. Along this trajectory, he turned more and more towards the unrepresented, the unknown, indulging in graphic activities without knowing in advance where they would lead. If we return to the problem of "evaluation", we can compare this to the beginning of the analysis, when the drawing of the lion, with its impact on the content of his nightmares, had led him to stop drawing of any kind for a long time.

This new type of movement gave rise for the first time to an imaginative narrative in which, after various adventures, a little boat was rescued by a sailing vessel even though the big boat sank. Jean-Éric was unable to evolve linearly in relation to this peculiar oedipal symbolism, for he had to bolster his identification with the father regardless of the latter's possible "failings", a mode of functioning that he gradually introduced into his associations. This movement of identification was able to take place along the trajectory of the sublimations of the father.

A dialectic thus occurred from the moment the *negativation* of the father prevailed, for it was followed by a return to disquieting maternal themes of the witch-type, without the repetition being identical. He gradually portrayed a witch who gave birth by caesarean, something his mother had also had, thereby marking an attempt to decondense the initial witch. When, in a state of ambivalence – ambivalence that was being worked on and elaborated – the positive cathexis of the father came to light, Jean-Éric became aware of the fact in the aftermath of a success. He executed a fine drawing, for which he then built a frame, as his father had taught him to do. The sexual co-excitation manifested itself at the height of his success thanks to a progressive surge of energy, and he even anticipated it with humour. "It's the emotions, as you know well!", he said, before leaving the room to go to the toilet. At the same time, he was enriching his anatomical knowledge of the kidneys and urinary canal, the urethrality being sublimated with the help of the description that he gave me of the rivers of France. But the primary process reasserted itself from time to time when faced with the risk of an excess of desexualisation inherent to the sublimatory movements. Jean-Éric associated the drawing of France he had made with a head that he was going to make a hole in, though his narrative resisted this instinctual drive defusion. They are bombardments, and it is the head of the President of Iran that is being bombarded, he explained. "Why?", I asked. "To take his place," he replied. I had not expected so much. Jean-Éric had reached the age of ten.

This was an opportunity for him to oscillate between fantasised contents, where getting younger would be the equivalent of remaining his mother's baby and where getting older would be associated with death. With the help of a potion, whose characteristics he gave details of, he became a man, a great king. We were nearing the end of his third year of analysis. He continued to enrich his knowledge, in relation to which the sexual co-excitation had become more moderate, while at the same time the *instinctual drive defusion* was being expressed in more processual terms. So it was that at the height of a familiar success, such as building increasingly sophisticated aeroplanes, he would sometimes destroy them, saying afterwards that they had been destroyed by "crushing hands". I realised that this movement of destruction emerged when Jean-Éric was unable to master the sexual co-excitation in a familiar context, although he was able to anticipate it humouristically, as he had become accustomed to doing.

Thus when he had made a successful paper aeroplane – which was part of a more regressive movement compared with what had gone before – , the success resulted in a formulation anticipating (even with humour) leaving the room to go to the toilet following a moment of sexual co-excitation, which was itself a sign of progress. It was then that he destroyed his aeroplane. I was then able to say to him that he was unhappy and disappointed about this excitation that he had been unable to master. He listened to me attentively – which was also a sign of how he was developing – and said to me, as proof of the difference between a session of psychoanalysis and a socialised, school-related performance: "I'm fourth in my class".

We were approaching the last sessions of the school year and, for the first time, Jean-Éric raised the question of the end of the analysis. A quarter of an hour before the session ended, he looked at his watch, a gesture that I interpreted as prefiguring the holiday break. "Precisely," he said, and he talked to me about his wish to end the analysis. "I have no more problems, no more nightmares, no more worries." I thought about the fact that he was still being followed medically for his bouts of bronchitis, which now occurred less often. "So," I said to him, "if there is still a reason to continue, it is the problem of excitation when you have success." He kept silent. During the following session, his mother confirmed her son's *self-evaluation*. The only problem that remained for her was Jean-Éric's excessive sensibility concerning his school results. He intervened to say that his brother had more problems than he did, and then – evoking familiar memories – that he didn't understand what I said in the sessions. He added, "You don't answer questions." All this allowed me, more easily than a year before, to compare what he had just said to us with the ideas expressed here and there following certain things that I had said. His face lit up and he said, "Yes!" Of course, it sometimes happens that we are incomprehensible for a child, and one generally realises it quickly, if only when faced with an absence of asso-ciative working-through.

Something else was involved here, namely, the emergence of a movement of *negativity* in a precise context, one where the child con-siders for the first time the perspective of the end of his/her analysis, a movement of progression that necessarily involves an element of con-flictuality. I was led to differentiate such a movement from those that had occurred before, when Jean-Éric had attacked my analytic func-tion, whatever I said. One can imagine, therefore, how another analyst who questions a child about an earlier period of analytic work, including when he or she was seen again in adolescence or adulthood, can well appreciate the progress that has been made.

At the following session, the last of the year, Jean-Éric said to me on arriving: "One more year, and that will make four years of analysis." This is, in fact, what happened. Then we talked about what had happened during the last session. He had "forgotten", but quickly recovered his memory. "Ah, yes! I'm going to tell you a tale that I have made up about intelligence. You'll see, it will remind you of something." It was about my Lord the tiger, the buffalo, and the farmer. The buffalo, coming back from its bath, heard someone behind it saying, "Good evening!" It was the tiger; the buffalo was afraid, but a discussion started up between them. "Why are you a prisoner of man, man is tiny?" said the tiger. "But he has intelligence," the buffalo replied. The farmer, who had arrived in the meantime, offered to go to his house to search for intelligence but, not wanting the buffalo to be eaten, he tied up the tiger, who accepted this. The farmer came back with glowing coals, which burned the ropes. Hence the origin of the tiger's stripes. In connection with the words, "It will remind you of something", this tale attested to the latent self-evaluative process in Jean-Éric, as well as to the gap between this tiger "caught up" in a cultural elaboration and the lion with the witch in the original scene. As it was the first time that the child had produced such a tale, it was not very surprising that he needed to go to the toilet immediately afterwards, which I pointed out to him by making a link with the success he had had in this last session of the year, which made Jean-Éric smile.

After the beginning of the new school year, signs gradually emerged relating to the trajectory of identification with the analyst's interpreting function. Thus, in one session, Jean-Éric threw himself into building aeroplanes, a familiar activity, admittedly, but one that was increasingly successful. He had already told me, moreover, that it was his father who had taught him how to do it. I told him that "in a way he was like an architect of aeroplanes". He was surprised, and for the first time talked to me about his wish to become a physiotherapist. Undoubtedly, this had something to do with an old tendency towards sprains, as well as with his increasing knowledge about the human body. But above all, as Jean-Éric put it: "It's because I very much like to explain things", which seemed to suggest a certain relationship with the work of analysis. It is also worth noting a detail following the fact that I had used the expression "in a way". A little later in the session, he confirmed this by saying – returning to the problem already mentioned of his sensitivity about school results – that he had noticed he felt afraid before tests in class, though during the tests he was much less afraid. He then started drawing, gave up and "came back" to aeroplanes. I then linked up as part of the same movement the regressive dynamic, the defensive dynamic, and the signs of the progress he was making, which he had just told me about. "In a way," Jean-Éric replied, marking his identification with his analyst.

But this gain subsequently became conflictualised in a triangular context, which was metapsychologically coherent. In effect, shortly after, his mother told me the same thing concerning the two phases of his school tests. Jean-Éric "took advantage" of this, once again in a triangular context, to say that he did not understand what I said to him in the sessions. In the following session, he did not want to speak about that again, and instead played at shooting in the dark with a headband over his eyes. Inevitably, after a moment, he anticipated that he was going to leave the room to go to the toilet. So I said to him that we had a good example here concerning "making connections" and "understanding". He was ready to listen to me. I showed him that, in the context of his progress, he was playing at killing me by chance, with his eyes blindfolded, but that this triggered the excitation he was familiar with, accompanied by the announcement that he was going to leave the room to go to the toilet. He remained attentive, and said to me: "Perhaps, I don't know if I have understood everything." Immediately after that, feeling a bit "tired", as he said, he lay down on the couch and stayed there calmly for the few minutes that remained. The session after, Jean-Éric gave me a little guessing game to solve, rather like the "enigma" that he had put to me previously in a comparable structural context. I had to discover that his drawing represented the eye of an eagle, which, symbolically speaking, I did not have too much difficulty in guessing. I added: "Today the situation is reversed, it's for me to understand or not understand". "Yes," he replied, with a smile on his face.

These games of reversal, these thought games, linked to the conflictual problem of identification with the analyst's interpreting function, seem to me to be essential to the analytic process with a child; they are part of the dynamic of the self-evaluative process. During the rest of the session, Jean-Éric changed register – something he did quite frequently – in the sense in which he shared with me his regret that the house where he usually spent his holidays was no longer available. At the end of the session, he put all his felt pens away except for one which he pushed a bit violently against the wall to "see" if it would fall between the table and the wall. I suggested to him that there was a connection between his violent gesture – he agreed with this description of it – and his disappointment concerning what he had told me about the house that was no longer available. "Nostalgia," he said, – or interpreted, one might even say. In the middle of the last year of analysis (he was ten and a half), both his parents came to see me, with their son's agreement and in his presence, while they themselves remained in contact with the consultant. For some time now the sessions had proved to be a bit "flat", which I understood as having to do with the question of switching to one session a week, a request the child had not spoken to me about. The father said, "It's going well, more than well, even, on all levels." He added, "Jean-Éric analyses all the situations well." His wife agreed, which meant that the process was underway again, at a new rhythm.

During the following sessions, Jean-Éric recapitulated, one could say, many of his previous games, including his constructions with the chairs in my office. It was probably not unrelated to his earlier sense of nostalgia, anticipated this time, and also to the approaching end of the analysis reactivated by this switch to one session a week. However that may be, at a certain moment in the resumption of the games, there was mention of "noises" and "rubbing", which I linked to those that he heard at home. He said to me in a quasi-hallucinatory mode, in relation with the underlying primal scene phantasy: "The light is not the same as it usually is." I reminded him of a previous sequence "night, day", which had been represented psychodramatically, in which certain themes of his nightmares had been played out by switching the light in my office on and off repeatedly. He laughed, lay down on the chairs, and then on the couch. I said to him that the noises and rubbing were perhaps linked to what went on between his parents when they were in bed at night. Jean-Éric replied: "They don't do anything; I keep an eye on them," adding that he had already got up in the night to listen. He was "certain that they didn't make love".

In the following sessions, the history of the sperm cell, which we had already talked about in his sessions, came up again. A little bit dreamy, with a bit of putty in his hand, Jean-Éric attributed this meaning to what he was modelling. And, as soon as the word had been pronounced, Jean-Éric severed the flagellum. I said: "So, no possibility of a child." Half-astonished and half-humoristically, he replied: "You think?" At the next session, he brought a little Colt revolver key-ring. Jean-Éric was somewhat surprised when I likened the sperm cell with the severed flagellum to the Colt without bullets. He "re-established" the situation by saying: "What does that make you think of?"

At the same time, next to his colt and his chain, he drew a sperm cell and its flagellum. But he didn't stop there. He then drew a pair of testicules in their scrotum, while at the same time associating to a "a slightly dirty" joke, as he said. At a restaurant called "The Corrida", a client was fond of bull's testicles. One day, he had some testicles on his plate that were much smaller than usual. "What's going on?" he asked. The waiter replied: "What do you mean, it's not always the toreador who wins." Of course, the homosexual transference was once again involved, and correlatively, as in this whole sequence, paternal castration with its possibility of reversal. But beyond the fact that reaching this level had a structuring value, what I want to emphasise is the fact that it was possible for such sexualised material to be integrated within *symbolised* sequences, and that it did not become disorganised through contact with the excitation that it certainly triggered. It is worth recalling that previously, when faced with any kind of sexual content, Jean-Éric would "resolve" the excitation connected with it through forms of acting out, even if it was possible to channel them. Here, as he was telling his joke, he did not even anticipate going to the toilet.

After these sessions, Jean-Éric left for a few weeks on a school trip to the seaside. On his return, he took up his "speciality" again, as he called it: drawings of skeletons transformed into pirates. The link was made with his school trip to the seaside, and also between a knife that went through the skull of the skeleton/pirate and the dental apparatus that he was wearing provisionally. He then moved the knife so that it was now lying flat on the pirate's sternum and announced . . . that he wanted to go to the toilet. Jean-Éric certainly seemed to understand that the knife was the equivalent of a penis, as well as my comparison between a big penis and a little penis (which he reacted to by laughing) formulated after he had executed a drawing of a "shrunken" skull. In the following session, he was able to talk to me spontaneously about the end of the analysis, thereby confirming the link between these themes of death, albeit "stylised", and this other "end". He told me he had "no problems at all anymore" and "everyone" agreed with him about this. Immediately afterwards, he drew a skull, a cast of Picasso, he added. I linked this up for him with the end of the analysis (and of the analyst), which led him to say to me: "No, I'm not going to drop you!" and imagined coming back to see me sometimes.

During this last session, Mrs D. was alone with her son but insisted on telling me that she and her husband were both in agreement. She was feeling positive because Jean-Éric was going to enter the first year of secondary school. There would be no more problems. The only thing she noted about him, apart from his tendency in class not to read his work through, was that he hypercathected speech in the conflicts that he had with his schoolmates. The difference of level that he often displayed in comparison with them in this respect led them to react physically, resulting sometimes in a certain number of fights. He did not like fighting but stood up for himself if necessary. During this time, Jean-Éric drew skulls, always very successfully, but he said something else that day in front of his mother that was linked, I would say, with the question of "understanding". He said he had noticed that since he had been drawing skulls he was no longer afraid of death, which clearly went beyond the question of drawing. This supplementary sign of his capacity for self-evaluation was part of the process of ending the analysis. Mrs D. intervened to say that her son was now able to draw "with a single stroke of the pen" in comparison with the way he had drawn before, which equally went beyond the question of drawing. Jean-Éric intervened one last time, in a triangular mode. He referred to his father in connection with the latter's graphic capacities, thereby underlining their similarities and their differences. As the time of the analysis had now come to an end, we separated, believing that it was possible to do so.

Recapitulation

The manner in which the case presented above unfolded makes it possible to appreciate the similarities and differences between the processes at work in intermittent therapeutic consultations and regular psychoanalytic treatment. It is essential in both situations that the the parents' participation is "good enough". We are only too familiar with the eventual situation in which a psychoanalytic indication for the child

turns into a counterindication or, at the very least, is postponed indefi-
nitely after a meeting with the parents. Though it is difficult to count
from the outset on the sensitivity of the parents to the existence of the
unconscious and infantile sexuality, it is still often possible to share
with them certain aspects of their child's mode of functioning. This was
very quickly the case with Alexandre concerning his separation anxiety
during the first consultation, and also later on once the question of analytic treatment had been raised.

While I tried to make the mother more aware of the instinctual drive
pressure at work in her son, she was able to associate to the questions
that Alexandre was asking on the subject of death (questions that were
expressed in an oedipal context). On the other hand, for Jean-Éric,
because the work with his consultant had advanced on this level, I only
needed to see the parents in precise circumstances, which always had
a dynamic function. The therapeutic consultation, whether or not it is
followed by an analytic indication, makes it possible to evaluate the
degree of the parents' associative capacity, not only in the sense that
I have just referred to, but also in relation to contents relating to the
parents' history, particularly their childhood history. They may thus be
surprised when observing certain repetitions, which makes them more
aware of the existence of the personal psychic space of their child who,
up until then, had been "caught up" in the repetitive spiral.

This type of work can be facilitated by meeting the parents and
the child together, thereby creating a specific space in which the inter-
cathexes involved can facilitate this type of emergence. This was the
case in both the situations presented, even if, for reasons of confidentiality, I was unable to dwell on them further. To sum up, one could say
that everything on the parents' side that favours their associations, both
in the present and with reference to the past, is an auspicious sign of the
possibility of continuing work of processual value with them and their
child, whether in the context of therapeutic consultations at irregular
intervals or of child psychoanalysis. On the contrary, everything that
goes against these associations makes the decision to begin a psychoanalytic treatment difficult, if not impossible.

There still remains the possibility of continuing to see the parents
and the child until the situation acquires the dynamic I mentioned
earlier. A mediation therapy with the child, when it is indicated, may
help to obtain therapeutic effects that go beyond instrumental consequences.[3] As for the child, it is still necessary to evaluate what will orient him or her towards a series of consultations, or towards an analysis,

or alternatively towards a psychotherapy. The common denominator remains the same, namely, the associative capacities of the child, and the interpretive act always has its origin in the preconscious minds of both protagonists. The work may suffice, after a few consultations, to get a process going again that had been hampered by a context of events (trauma, bereavement, birth of a younger sibling, etc.) in a child who does not present a psychopathological structure that is already organised. It may also pave the way for beginning a psychotherapeutic treatment. This was the case for Alexandre, which lasted several years. It is when, and in spite of the work accomplished, the imbalance of the elements of the relationship between primary process and secondary process repeats itself, that the analytic indication becomes clear. The example of Alexandre is enlightening in this respect, even though it took time for his parents to be convinced, and it may be said that it was he himself who made the indication. Of course, there are situations in which the different factors present make it possible to begin an analysis in the first consultations. From thereon, if the interpretive work arising from the preconscious still has its raison d'être, the frequency of the sessions, with the regression that goes with them, allows for the interpretation of conscious fantasies at certain moments, as we have seen.

In short, the expression of infantile sexuality and its theories with the defence mechanisms that go with it in analysis requires the setting of analysis. It represents what may be described as a specificity in comparison with what unfolds in spaced therapeutic consultations. The analysis of Jean-Éric permitted something more, in the sense that it was possible to conduct it until its end, with what seemed to me to be a real work of termination. This work revealed what I have formalised by the expression "self-evaluative process", with a trajectory towards *insight*, towards becoming conscious, towards working-through, etc., a process that was progressively put in place during the analysis. It is a truism to say so, but the opportunity for doing this work only presents itself in analysis. It is none the less true that the limits of the end of a child analysis lie in the fact that certain contents, a certain dynamic, can only find their place in the context of an adult analysis.

The "pre-psychotic" states of the child[4]

In the series of articles by René Diatkine concerning pre-psychotic states, spanning the period from 1963 to 1974, including the well-known article "L'enfant prépsychotique" (Diatkine, 1969), we find in the context of a longitudinal study preoccupations and reflections concerning the relations between borderline states and psychoses in the adult and pre-psychotic states in the child. In general psychiatry, the dismemberment of the categories of classical nosography introduced the notion of borderline state, a category with an inflationary risk as far as its content is concerned. The category of the pre-psychotic states of the child is derived from the same historical dynamic, except that if the borderline states of the adult have a certain specificity in Green's (1990) sense, it cannot be applied directly to the child, and this is for two reasons.

First, and in analogy to the history of the notion of infantile schizophrenia in relation to that of schizophrenia in the adult, the borderline state has a quality of organisation that cannot be established before adolescence. Secondly, psychopathological "states" in the adult, apart from acute states, have a certain stability that those in a child do not generally have, except in autism. Why speak of a "pre-psychotic state", a term that is reminiscent in other authors of that of developmental dysharmony, parapsychosis or paraneurotic states? It seems to indicate above all the interest that Diatkine took in psychic states that may have existed in the childhood of schizophrenics, even though he was not oblivious to the limits that this notion had. And it was in the light of clinical studies based on retrospective material that it appeared that the sky had not been as calm as all that before the "clap of thunder".

Conversely, when treating certain children, one may be alerted by signs of an evolution towards psychosis that are not pathognomonic, yet at the same time are compatible with the eventual *risk* of such an evolution. The paradox is only apparent if one reasons at two levels, namely, at the symptomatic or syndromic level and at the level of the dynamics of psychic functioning. In the first case, it is known that certain diffuse or atypical phobias of the latency period, such as invasive obsessional manifestations, a prevalence of manic defences, false-self organisations, massive inhibitions, character pathologies, and a prevalence of behavioural disorders, etc., may be indicative of pre-psychotic states. But the essential point – and this was Diatkine's major contribution – concerns the clinical manifestations, that is, the particularities of the dynamism of psychic functioning.

They boil down to one fundamental fact, which is still of relevance today, namely, the repeated imbalance between the expressions of the primary process and those of the secondary process. Put in other terms, this means that, faced with the danger of a psychotic reorganisation, the latter risks manifesting itself "each time that the primitive cathexis of the internalised objects is insufficiently balanced by other sources of pleasure of a secondary nature, and by sufficiently efficient neurotic counter-cathexes" (Diatkine, 1969, p. 422). The result of this is that the dynamics of psychic functioning necessarily involve the dynamics of the relationship between a family and the consultant, in other words, a clinical understanding of the relationship along with what is indissociably linked to it, that is, the modes of intervention or interpretation of the consultant.

It is worth recalling that "ordinary" so-called "normal neurotic" associativity unfolds through play, drawing, verbalisations and certain forms of acting out. It produces solutions to conflictuality that are sufficiently symbolised and displaced, even when the transference connotations are very close to consciousness. In other words, any tendency towards a disequilibrium in the relationship between primary processes and secondary processes is *constantly balanced by a movement back towards its equilibrium*. The processes of symbolisation, which may be completed by those of sublimation, support, and I would even say underpin, the process of "secondarisation" (discursive binding) in the face of the surge of primary processes, that is to say, of the mobilisation of the instinctual drives, which is itself stimulated and catalysed by the child/consultant relationship. The equilibrium between the two processes thus has nothing static about it; it translates a resultant of forces. This is how a child functioning in this way, that is, according to a certain form of equilibrium within a disequilibrium, will move closer to the "narrative" model of a story or narration, which in turn will approximate to the millennium-old model of tales and myths, and so on.

This means that the language of the narrative – which the secondary process exerts its function of binding – unfolds, if not without ruptures, in any case without disorganising ruptures. On the contrary, the prepsychotic process is studded with movements of disorganisation at the level of associativity. While these may be sporadic and not necessarily large in scale, the essential point is that they are subject to *repetition*. Such breaks in associative sequences seek discharge via the short paths of the primary process, or of primitive, narcissistic and anti-traumatic logic (Neyraut, 1997, p. 180). They seek here to discharge the drive excitation mobilised by the child/consultant encounter. These breaks may be expressed in various ways: either through informal scribbling or in the more formalised way of a fire or of an outburst of violence, etc., which suddenly erupts in a drawing, possibly after an initial stage of inhibition, through correcting the movements of a barely outlined disorganising excitation, expressed through abstract and non-narrative graphic productions, far removed from any kind of visual represent-ability (*figurabilité*). It is as if containing the potential excitation prevents an associative rupture, at the price, however, of being *unrepresentable*. The disorganisation in play or in drawing, as well as in the account given of them, when it is manifest, can even go as far as to endanger the setting by passing along the ultra-short paths of motricity. It mobilises forms of acting out, directly or indirectly, towards the consultant. Once the discharge has occurred, a *new equilibrium* is created thanks to an associative process that is represented through immediate or progres-sive figuration, until a new movement of disorganisation occurs. As an illustration of this, I have chosen a situation that took place a long time ago.

Sylvain was four years and nine months old when I met him for the first time. He was an inhibited and angry child who presented a significant language delay. The inhibition reoccurred during our meet-ing insofar as Sylvain, who smiled a fair amount, did not respond to anything I said, except sometimes with a nod of the head. His draw-ing turned out, on the other hand, to be more dynamic, but in a par-ticular way. Sylvain finally took hold of a black felt pen with which he drew two symmetrical oblique lines joined at the top, which made me think of the roof of a house. He neither confirmed nor rebuffed the idea that I put to him. Under the purported roof, he drew a series of more or less geometrical lines, still without saying a word. Then, by drawing another line that followed a similar path to the one before, he depicted some smoke coming out of what I imagined to be a chimney. We found ourselves faced with the scenario already mentioned, that of being contained by the unrepresentable, and, at the very least, by the unportrayable (*non-figurable*). That is to say, the risk of disorganisa-tion was contained by excitation, as if ideational representatives/thing-presentations were too close to the drive contents, which in turn were too charged economically, too close to the "drive impulses". However, on the condition perhaps of this long graphic preamble, Sylvain told me that there was someone, and he depicted a man with a sword, this time sufficiently recognisable. When I asked him who would be attacked by the man, Sylvain did not answer verbally, no doubt because of the transferential connotation that was inevitably involved. On the other hand, at the end of the other arm of the man he drew what he called a "little sword" touching the line that started from the chimney of the house, something I drew his attention to. He confirmed this and then introduced a friend of the first man, who also had a sword.

There was, however, no organised scenario. A break in the associative flow followed, Sylvain changed felt pens for the first time, and it was with a yellow felt pen (I should point out in passing that this boy was enuretic) that he drew a long line similar to the one before, starting from the chimney. At a given moment, this line passed just above the head of the first character. Sylvain then confirmed that this line would be "the thing" (*"la chose"*), as I say (originating in Freud and taken up by Lacan (1986) for the chapters on *das Ding* in his seminar *The Ethics of Psychoanalysis* at the end of 1959), the thing that the first character would attack with his sword. The child depicted this by reversing the line, making it go in the opposite direction to the man.

The theory that I formulated was that Sylvain found himself faced with a maternal imago that was impossible to attack, to touch, to name, and even to represent, except in a clearly indirect way, the symbolism of the house probably being too close to its maternal meaning. In counterpoint, the only means of protection available referred to unconscious homosexuality (the friend), which proved, paradoxically, to be representable and symbolically portrayable. It is interesting that in the game that followed – which contained "inevitable" depictions (animals and characters) – Sylvain this time organised a scenario. The key moment represented a scene in which a nice lion, a "friend", fights against a lioness, not named as such, and even not named at all. The lioness is in league with a monkey, both being the nasty animals, whereas the nice ones represent a world composed of all the humans and the rest of the animals. Twelve years later, Sylvain, became clearly schizophrenic. Does that mean that the schizophrenic evolution of this child was already present in the prolegomena of this first consultation? It would certainly be difficult to say that. Conversely, it seems clear that a psychosis never erupts in a "calm sky".

What I would like to stress, however, is the fact that circumstantial elements that were capable of reorienting the risk of a psychotic evolution did not suffice to avoid this evolution. Among these elements, and not the least important, was what gradually led Sylvain, after a therapy conducted by a female psycho-motor specialist, to enter psychoanalytic psychotherapy for four years. It was broken off by the parents, who were satisfied with the way things had evolved, but who, above all, had "taken advantage" of Sylvain's move into the first year of secondary school (in France, *6ème*), whereas his analyst was quite rightly more pessimistic. In this connection, I will simply give one example, taken from the last lines of the analyst's report before the end of the treatment. Sylvain was eleven-and-a-half years old.

Death and castration anxiety continued to appear in a condensed way; the problem of bodily changes and of masturbation were touched on, for example through the interpretation of an act, where Sylvain, protecting his index finger with the modelling clay, and banging it on the desk, asked his analyst if she thought this could hurt him. A little further on in her report, the analyst wrote: "In our last sessions a dangerous paternal image emerged, a father eagle that wanted to seize the little bird from the mother in order to eat it. The mother had to flee from the father in order to protect the child. Then he talked about a child eagle which, after flying over the Himalayas, fell to earth and died." Sylvain then wanted to throw the modelling clay, symbolising the "dead bird" back and forth between himself and the analyst. The tone of the very last lines in the analyst's report was somewhat depressed: "It would seem that there is no other solution to his phallic movements apart from a repetitive game between us in an affectless mode, repetition being Sylvain's way of extinguishing his instinctual life."

At the same time, there is no better way of saying, in effect, that this did not indicate the end of the treatment. Of course, I could say more about the subject of Sylvain and his parents, about what were undoubtedly failures during the treatment, and about what could only be elaborated, in particular with the parents, once their son had become schizophrenic. I can say this all the more easily in that they were high-quality individuals. I saw Sylvain and his parents once a month for several years, in addition to the institutional work. During these years I learnt a great deal; we all learnt a lot. In the family history, there was not just one life event but several, spread out in time, which had never been possible to put into words. The psychic burden of these events cannot be attributed here, any more than elsewhere, to a linear causality, with regard to what we are bound to call Sylvain's illness.

But, on the other hand, these events, with their respective psychic translation, necessarily had a major impact on the conscious and unconscious history of Sylvain's relationship with his parents. In what has just been reported I have tried to define the general framework of pre-psychotic states in the child, illustrating a moment of childhood which echoed, twelve years after, a schizophrenia in adolescence. In this scenario, the pre-psychotic state preceded the psychosis, a precession that occurred in a non-linear mode.

The time of understanding/misunderstanding[5] in the space of the family consultation[6]

The psychoanalytic treatment of the adult is a model of reference when one tackles the issue of *understanding/misunderstanding* in the parents of the child we are following. An indication close to the model of the standard treatment in the adult presupposes that the problem of his/her evolution since childhood, enabling him/her to benefit from such an indication, has been resolved. It will then be sufficient for us to become acquainted with his/her parental imagos. We must keep this situation in mind as a theoretical limit and ask ourselves about the degree of parental psychic reality that is present in the subject's imagos. The compulsion to repeat at work in the subject leads the analyst to be not only the projective support for his/her patient's imago, but also the ideational representative thanks to the countertransference.

In such moments, the subject is no longer the subject of his/her own instinctual drive movements. What characterises child analyses, however, is the fact that the analyst is also dealing with the child's real parents, with their physical and mental presence, their psychic reality, their personal history as well as that of which the child is a part. It is with this ensemble and with its psychic "imprint" that the analyst will be faced before undertaking and continuing an analysis with the child. Another scenario deserves our attention, namely, that of synchronous parent(s)/child consultations, currently called family consultations. The specificity of such a setting is defined by the exercise of *understanding/ misunderstanding* which is played out in the presence of a third party, and the interactive quality of the participants. The economy and dynamics of such a situation multiply the countertransference demands and the risks of counter-attitudes in the consultant.

Evoking a psychoanalytic concept such as that of countertransference in a setting other than that of the psychoanalytic treatment and its process, obviously poses a problem which is only possible to understand if we accept that as the consultant is a psychoanalyst he/she cannot leave his/her identity in the cloakroom of family consultation. Even if one cannot really speak of the countertransference as a response to the transference, it is still true that the consultant experiences sporadic countertransference movements. Rather than introducing new concepts that would be specific to the family setting, of a systemic type, for example, it is preferable to conserve as much as possible those of Freudian psychoanalysis and applied psychoanalysis, while remaining vigilant with respect to the limits that are imposed on us. We will keep in mind the concepts and their utility, including their metaphorical value, from the moment we are dealing with at least three psychical apparatuses in interaction.

It is thanks to this encounter with the parents who have been referred, for example, by the social worker of the team, that we are able to form a picture of the child. Even before seeing someone, we are faced with psychoanalytic concepts such as representation and construction, which are part of Freudian metapsychology. Yet, there is a mind that is already functioning, namely, the consultant's mind functioning as countertransference precession, to paraphrase Neyraut (1974). What I mean by this is that the theory of the case that is formed by the consultant from listening to the interview with the parents conducted by the social worker is represented, portrayed figuratively and charged with affect, and will function in a similar way to an infantile sexual theory. It will become fixed in us and become a tool for interpreting what is going to happen between us and those who consult us, while impeding at the same time any form of transformation or temporality. In other words, a psychopathological construction will function in us as a manifest purposive idea (représentation-but).

This theory, acting in the place of countertransference, is essential. But it is by letting oneself be inhabited by it, without succumbing to the "reflex arc" of the counter-attitude underlying the appropriation of the two phases that accompany the inner movement of the countertransference, as well as by the period of latency necessary for all elaboration, that we will be able to take cognisance of this "idea/theory" and make it transformable. In the situation of the family consultation, the crucial moments of the process take shape around interactive phases that develop between the various participants, including the consultant. I will illustrate these introductory considerations with the help of eight consultations which took place during a period of a little more than a year. I will only use material that is relevant to the subject I am discussing.

Mrs E., the mother of two children, requested a consultation for her youngest son, Marc, aged ten-and-a-half, because he was repeatedly failing at school. What appeared to be a symptom in a child who worked willingly when he was at home but who could not remember anything when he was in class, was complicated by what had been communicated *in extremis* to the social worker in the interview that preceded the first consultation, before the summer holidays. The head of the school had apparently written to the mother, after the child had been excluded from the canteen for 48 hours, to say that the boy had been lifting up the skirts of little girls for . . . two years. Mrs E. said how shocked she had been both by the content of the information and by the fact that she had been informed so late in the day. She was also wondering about the emotional reasons for her son's difficulties at school, which might be linked to divorce proceedings that were underway, following a separation three years before. We learnt, however, during this interview that Marc had never been interested in school, crying each time there was a change of setting, reactions that had already been present when he started going to the day-nursery at the age of five months, because his mother had taken up her job as an office worker again. Mrs E. finally touched on the complex history of her mixed-race origins and insisted on the fact that she had been informed very late in the day (once again) about her maternal filiation. She had learnt the truth from her paternal grandmother following her father's death a few years earlier. As a child, she had already asked herself questions about her mother, who was in fact her step-mother. Her ex-husband was also of mixed-race, and she described him as having been unstable and as a fantasist, driven by professional projects that never got off the ground.

From reading the report of this interview, the idea/theory – an anticipatory idea – formed in me of a boy driven by the contradiction between a symptom, failure at school, and a mode of behaviour, repeated sexual acting out, which united him, in the mode of identification, with a father presented by his ex-wife as dominated by acting out. The picture that I formed of the mother was one of an intelligent woman who asked herself questions, and who, irrespective of the questionable aspect of the way the information concerning her son's behaviour towards the girls had been communicated to her, displayed a critical attitude of vigilance towards a man, the head of the school, that was commensurate with her critical attitude, this time for the opposite reasons, towards her ex-husband. In short, I sensed in her a fundamentally critical attitude, particularly as certain men exposed themselves to it.

Gradually, a sort of "psychopathic model" formed itself in me, at the risk of becoming a purposive idea, with which I was going to have to work. My first meeting with Mrs E. and her son, at the beginning of the new school year, confirmed this impression of a preliminary construction to which elements were later added some of which were discrepant with this preliminary construction. As for Marc, I would say that what he communicated was swiftly caught up in a process of distancing and trivialisation, both with regard to his symptom and to his character, to such a point that his only "demand" was at the level of pedagogical help, expressed reluctantly. As for his mother, her finesse was confirmed, while at the same time I felt I was being quietly evaluated. Each intervention I made was received silently, first with a discretely impenetrable look on her face, and then by means of a reaction that was expressed either in a questioning mode or in a mode of perplexity suggesting that she was thinking about what I had said.

Concerning the psychological and speech therapy assessment, Marc primarily communicated his failures, his impatience and his concerns with female specialists, without however expressing a wish to be helped. He wanted to succeed, but by himself. When I saw Marc two months later, the mobilisation of his economy of character was henceforth directed towards the man that I am. Everything seemed normal, as he said, but although the situation seemed to have eased, his tendency towards negation and trivialisation was still predominant. This led me to see the mother alone in order to talk to her about the contradiction between what her son said about his problems and how he dealt with them concretely. She reacted by describing essentially the symptoms and the various inhibitions of her son. But, above all, she told me what she thought about it: she absolutely did not want him to avoid facing up to reality. She added, following my intervention, that he would end up like his father, something she absolutely wanted to prevent. I thus became aware of the importance of the narcissistic infiltration of her relationship with her ex-husband, whom she had married because he was above all of mixed-race like her, thus becoming the first man to recognise her.

It was the gap between this narcissistic dimension and the evolution of their relationship that had led her to wonder about the past of this man. She had become aware of how his mother had overprotected him because he was born between two boys, who had died shortly after their birth, and a younger sister who had also died at the age of two. Though Mrs E.'s questioning attested to her finesse, at the same time it was accompanied by an urge for mastery. Indeed, her understanding and thinking prevailed over the expression of feelings. This made me think of the history of her maternal filiation precisely because it had escaped such questioning during her childhood.

After the Christmas holidays, during the third consultation, Marc's determination to manage his difficulties at school (the only ones he acknowledged) without help, became even more pronounced. Faced with what seemed to me to be an impasse, I then decided to work on the mother/child interaction, as the only remaining possibility. I put the contradiction that was facing us to Mrs E., this time in her son's presence. Meanwhile, Marc was playing with the felt pens, so I suggested that he did some drawing. He depicted in broad outlines, without saying a word, while at the same time discreetly watching his mother, a series of heads of increasingly sinister characters. As his mother expressed her incomprehension at the sight of such drawings, I led her to express what she was feeling. She began by defending herself in a humouristic fashion, then changed tack, saying that what she had seen had no effect on her. I contradicted her by saying that these were certainly the kind of images that she could not bear, which she confirmed. I added that I understood better now why her son insisted so much on managing things by himself, for this was what she did with her own emotions. She immediately broke into tears. I recommended that she should get herself into psychotherapy, which she did for several years. As the psychopathic model eased up, we separated with a new consultation in view. It took place a month and a half later.

Initially, Marc, who was alone, was still acting as if "everything was fine", but said for the first time that he had obtained good marks at school. He clearly did not have much else to tell me. So I asked his mother to come in, with his agreement. She spontaneously confirmed this improvement and added that they were now having more conversations together. But she also added that though Marc was becoming interested in more and more things, he did not explore any of them in depth. Marc now began walking around in my office, which resulted, like the time before, in a drawing which explored things in more detail. He depicted, very skilfully, what he called a Dracula, a vampire with bloody teeth. This time, Mrs E. felt that what her son had drawn was "dreadful", an impression that Marc reinforced by introducing a female victim, an ally of Dracula, whom he transformed into a robot. Marc was plainly satisfied with this triangular situation that we were in, for when I challenged him countertransferentially by suggesting the possibility of doing a psychotherapy, he replied that he preferred to manage by himself and added: "I'm fine as I am". I then asked his mother what she imagined as far as her son's future was concerned. In contrast with what Marc had just said, Mrs E. replied that she never tried to imagine his future. Marc immediately felt the need to go to the toilet and, almost inevitably, in her son's absence, Mrs E. began thinking about the child's father.

When I pointed this connection out to her, she confirmed that Marc's future could only be one of becoming like his father, which led me, once Marc had returned, to say to him, as if by chance, that in his absence, we had begun to speak about his father, while taking the opportunity to raise the question of the latter's presence during the consultations. Mrs E. was immediately concerned, mentioning the conflicts that always arose with her ex-husband, particularly concerning the children. For instance, he had a tendency to say to her: "I like annoying you," and was opposed to everything psychological. As for Marc, he intervened on her behalf, saying: "Leave him out of it". I pointed out to him that this was paradoxical insofar as a father is generally expected to protect his son rather than vice versa, a comment that clearly touched him. We made another appointment during the Easter holidays. During this meeting, Marc, who was initially alone, told me that he had not spoken to his father yet about the consultations.

I suggested enacting a psychodramatic sequence in which he would play the role of his father. What is interesting is that he played a father hesitating over the prospect of a meeting at the Centre: "I don't know . . . perhaps", he said, and stuffed an imaginary piece of paper that I handed to him with our telephone number on it into his pocket. But as soon as the sequence was over, he once again assumed his stubborn look. Once Mrs E. was present, she confirmed her son's improvement at school, adding that things had also improved between them. She linked all this to the fact that she was helping her son with his work. However, I learnt that this went on in Mrs E.'s bedroom, at the child's bidding, though he also asked to share his mother's bed, which she refused, "except sometimes on Saturdays".

Faced with this situation with unconscious incestuous connotations, I reacted by asking Mrs E. to imagine how such a situation might develop in the future. Her response was peculiar because first she said that she had thought about this, and then that she had explained to her son that this could not go on like that because, if she remarried, there would be a man in the house. In short, this was the first time she had shown me her unconscious seductive side vis-à-vis her son. My former psychopathic construction was now taking hold of me again. At the same time, attentive to the risk of adopting a counter-attitude, I sought to mediate by identifying myself with a little boy who was prey during the night to anxieties, which was what led him to want to sleep with his mother, who found herself in difficulty because she was separated from her husband. In sum, I recounted the *story* of this little boy to Mrs E. and her son, and they listened to it.

I finished by saying that this brought us back to the question of the father's presence at the consultations. I added that I remembered very well Mrs E.'s concerns, but that it was better for Marc to be faced with the reality of his father, whatever it might be, than with his mother's concerns alone. In this case he could only prohibit himself from speaking to his father about the very existence of these consultations. I asked her to think about it until the next time. This period of latency that I introduced allowed me to distance myself a bit from a dual oppositional countertransference movement, namely, that of appealing to the father in the face of an unconscious incestuous situation, and that of perpetuating the situation in which I would satisfy myself with being the one he needed, while keeping the real father at distance.

Two months later, a new development occurred. Marc was still getting good marks, but he said he had taken part in a rumpus during a "nature class", of which his mother had been informed by telephone, which had led him thereafter to behave himself. But today he remembered that a month ago we had spoken about the participation of his father in the consultations. When I brought his mother in, Marc left an empty chair between her and him, which made me say, "someone's missing". After the manifestation of different emotional impulses in mother and son, I learnt that the father had indeed been informed of the existence of these consultations by his son. He had apparently replied by saying "I don't know" at the prospect of his coming to the centre, recalling the terms used by Marc during the psychodrama sequence. What followed, almost associatively, led us to the episode of the nature class and to Mrs E.'s incomprehension concerning the fact that it had sufficed for the teacher to telephone her for order to be re-established. She compared the teacher's attitude with her own past experience with children, where the adults dealt with their difficulties alone.

When I asked her about this, she informed me that she had done some training with children in France, but had not been able to make use of it professionally on account of her marriage. This desire for training had been the subject of a conflict between her mother-in-law and her, and it was only due to the intervention of her father that she had been able to fulfil her project. I pointed out to Mrs E. that "order" had thus been re-established, which surprised her. She went on to speak to me about her father as an authoritarian man who would come home late in the evenings after spending time at the café with his friends. This certainly played a part in her intolerance of having to act as the third party re-establishing order for her son, through a movement of identification with a man who reminded her of her father who had been both authoritarian and absent. Her ex-husband reminded her of her father's absence and the headmaster of Marc's school of his authority. For my part, I established some "order" by proposing to write a letter to the father, an offer both mother and son immediately accepted.

At the time agreed upon, Mrs E. and Marc arrived without the father for the consultation. A misunderstanding had occurred with the father about the location of the appointment. Not long after, I received a telephone call from him; he had lost the address of the centre, but not the telephone number (a situation that had been enacted with Marc in the psychodrama sequence). His arrival was spectacular: "Good morning! How are you?!", etc. Immediately, in a long-winded manner, he expressed a series of opinions which he retracted no sooner than he had expressed them, only to continue again a moment later in the same direction or to express his opinion more strongly in an exaggerated manner. He complained that he felt that he was not given any information about the children. Mrs E. contradicted him at one point, mentioning a telephone call about this consultation. He replied: "I've forgotten about that, and why not, after all, I have the right to forget!" It is clear that he was using the distance put by his ex-wife between them to justify his behaviour, as well as his refusal to provide a maintenance allowance for the children, his argument being that if Marc or his sister needed something, well, he was there. Moreover, he did not accept his son's word. As he was still caught up in his ambivalent relationship with his ex-wife, he could only accept information given to him by Marc if he had first verified it with her, as, for example, when his son told him that he was moving up into the 5th year of primary school. Marc intervened, moreover, for the first time, by saying to him: "So, I lied?!", which Mr E. did not hear.

Faced with this totally unpredictable, in other words "psychopathising" father, I was inevitably stimulated by counter-attitudes. I tried to mediate by insisting that it was not possible to ask Marc to choose between his parents, which Mr E. acknowledged, before immediately belying this by adding, "with us it's not like that" (i.e. the relationship between the parents). I questioned him on this subject, but he found it all the more difficult to speak to me in that he was of mixed-race, the "with us" implying three continents down to the third generation. I drew attention to this difficulty as being understandable, for it had certainly been difficult for him to find his identity. He replied that this had nothing to do with it. We parted soon after – once I had drawn his attention to the fact that, in spite of everything, he had in fact come to the consultation on that day – with his agreement in principle that he would come again. He made it clear right away that he would certainly not be there after the holidays, alluding to his plan to leave France, a plan that had been on hold for a year.

At the next consultation in October, mother and son were alone. Marc had only seen his father for one weekend since the month of June. His school work remained satisfactory. The children had been on a summer camp, and Marc had even received compliments. Mrs E. was obviously pleased and, retrospectively, was able, for the first time, to speak about how previously she had often felt lost without her children. At the same time, she told me that she had not been able to stop herself, when leaving the last consultation, from asking her ex-husband whether he had come to the consultation because of his mother, who would have advised him to attend; he acknowledged as much, before adding immediately that he would not come again. She had treated him as a child (which he confirmed) – the same situation in which he had put his son during the consultation. She added, finally, concerning the father's promise that, the following summer, he would take his children on holiday abroad, that if he did not keep his promise, she would bring the children to his home to force him to keep it.

As for Marc, who had remained silent up until then, he intervened to say: "If he doesn't keep his promise, I will never believe in his fibs again". In Marc's case, the issue of the understanding/misunderstanding between his parents was present from the outset. A situation which seemed as if it would lead to an individual child treatment, as is often the case, was transformed, insofar as, in the third consultation, it was suggested that the mother herself should enter psychotherapy. It became pointless, owing to his increasingly determined position to "manage by himself", to offer anything else to the child other than to see him periodically in his mother's presence; the indication of an individual therapy would have been artificial for him. Of course, the question of the father's participation ran like a red thread throughout this work. Mother and son were unconscious "accomplices" in reinforcing his absence, the "school homework in the mother's bedroom" being the exemplary outcome of this process.

Each significant moment in the unfolding of the consultations involved both the image of the father and the real father. It was by virtue of the countertransference movements, where I had the role of the potentially intrusive or excluded third party, that the father's mental presence could be taken into account in the register of the interactions between mother and son, bearing witness thereby to their inter-cathexes. The overall constellation, with the vicissitudes of triangulation, made a psychopathic evolution more or less possible for Marc. At the same time, it is clear that this was not the only thing that was mobilised by mother and son, otherwise their relationship with me would have broken down long ago, as I have experienced in other situations. As the "system" had remained open to its neurotic part, the possibility of coming to a better *understanding* was maintained; but equally there was just as much possibility of *misunderstanding*, given that each new consultation brought a new element to the edifice. It is worth noting that when the father came to one of the consultations, his attitude exceeded anything I had anticipated. Certainly one should not minimise the fact that he found himself in a difficult situation inasmuch as he had come after a lot of work had already been done without him. But I have seen many other fathers getting involved at a late stage in difficult situations, with whom it was possible to do a certain amount of work in spite of everything. At the same time, mother and son, each in their own way helped to preserve the father's misunderstandings through their reluctance to encourage him to participate, quite apart from what unconsciously made them "accomplices" in an oedipal register. This was not because this father corresponded to something other than what mother and son said about him, but because, on the contrary, he corresponded to what they said about him only too well, which could not fail to be the source of a narcissistic wound.

What I wanted to emphasise with the help of this illustration, is the impact of an exclusion/self-exclusion of a parent, in this case a father, marking in a particular way the dialectic between understanding/misunderstanding with which we are faced when we meet both parents. In such situations, it is the history of the relationship that they form with us, through the retroactive effects that are established, which will succeed in reducing the gap between the construction, the representation/theory that they evoke in us – a theory inspired by our countertransference movements – and their own history in their conscious and unconscious dimension. In the case presented above, the moment of the father's introduction could only have meaning if it was linked up with, and found its place in, the temporality of the economic and dynamic process involved in the continuity of the consultations.

Disorders in the activity of représentance *in a child of homosexual parents*[7]

We are certainly more attentive nowadays, concerning the method we use, when we venture into the domain of homosexuality. It is undoubtedly useful to ensure that the approach used is not infiltrated by ideology, even in a subtle form. This links up, more or less, with the old debates in our society aimed at distinguishing between norm (changing, because evolving) and normativity (unchangeable). Thus, for example, the pressing evolution of the demand by certain homosexuals of both sexes to obtain rights to parenthood leads us to define differently the limits of the favourable response to this demand. In effect, previously, the limit was reached if one disclosed one's homosexual identity. Nowadays – and obviously only in certain Western countries – though this limit has not disappeared, it is none the less true that it is beginning to shift as far as the quality of the desire to be a parent is concerned. One factor has played a part in this evolution. It was becoming daring to claim that there would be more psychopathology in children of homosexuals than those of heterosexuals. It is a fact that the heterosexual condition guarantees nothing, even if one tries to get round the difficulty by saying that it is a necessary but insufficient condition. It is thus problematic to superimpose anatomicophysiological reality on ideals.

Plenty of studies, mainly Anglo-Saxon, and more precisely socio-psychological studies, have shown that, contrary to what had been claimed, including by certain psychoanalysts, there is no more disturbance of gender-identity or behaviour in the children of homosexuals than in traditional families. More precisely, no difference was found in items such as cognitive functioning or behavioural or emotional conduct. It is not my intention to pursue this line of inquiry here, my interest being to stay as close as possible to what is psychoanalytic. If one wants to adhere closely to this way of thinking, then the only possible solution, since Freud, is to choose the monographic level, which is the only basis that potentially allows for the emergence of a certain singularity that is useful for our considerations.

When we turn towards the monograph, the reality or realities that it comprises, psychic included, show us that there is a correlation between complexity and singularity, especially as the distance and hindsight offered by the longitudinal method is essential. It follows that any extrapolation based on situations presenting a certain analogy requires us to take certain precautions. Such problems appear from the outset, beginning with the definition of the family context, where we are led to wonder about the meaning of the formulation employed: child of homosexual parents. Is this child, whether a boy or a girl, the child of a homosexual father or of a homosexual mother who had already lived out their homosexuality already before his/her birth? Is he/she the offspring of parents who have since separated because of this homosexuality, and in this case how old was the child at the time? Is he/she the adopted child of a gay or lesbian couple? Was he/she born to a surrogate mother or following an artificial insemination and its various configurations?

Having recalled the above-mentioned methodological issues, it seems necessary now to say a few words about what led me to venture into a field that presents so many pitfalls. On several occasions, I have found myself faced with situations in my practice where one parent was homosexual, usually the father. In all these scenarios it was the open affirmation of homosexuality that had led to the breakdown of the parental couple's relationship, even though the couple had had several children. I do not personally have any experience of a child brought up by a gay or lesbian couple.

However, a well-documented study by a colleague from the Anna Freud Centre, Jennifer Kaplan-Davids (1999) seemed to me to be in line with my own thoughts on the subject. This colleague had a boy in analysis who was brought up by a lesbian couple, one of whom, now separated from the boy's father, was the biological mother. What attracted my attention, given my own experience of such cases, was the fact the children presented in the context of the clinical investigation, and independently of the variability of their symptomatology, disorders in *représentance*, to use André Green's term.

These disorders, already noticeable at the level of the expression of figurability or visual representability, revealed themselves, not surprisingly, in the context of gender identifications and psycho-sexual cathexes. In other words, these children presented a great sensibility towards any form of difference as soon as it had gender and sexual-related connotations, because they were thereby confronted with the universal problem of the difference between the sexes and the generations. From a psychoanalytic point of view, this sensibility manifested itself in the associative process which was caught up in a complex mixture of avoidance and confusion, with or without excitability, and where any attempt by the subject to anticipate the confusion simply reinforced the dimension of avoidance. The particularity of analytic work with children is that it enacts iconographic forms based on situations of play or drawing, which means that any potential disorders affecting the processes of figurability appear clearly in the foreground.

This should come as no surprise to us, once again, since figurability implies a close connection with the body, which includes, among other things, sensoriality. Thus, in the case of a gifted child who does not present psychic disturbances of too much concern, but who, while being a virtuoso with words, has obvious difficulties in situations of figurative graphic expression, which could in turn have an impact on learning to write. Many other registers could be evoked concerning this "sensitive zone", for instance, those of infantile sexual theories in connection with the difference of the sexes or those of the family romance in connection with the difference between the generations. One of the situations I am thinking of is that of a boy whom I followed as a consultant for fourteen years.

This longitudinal factor certainly adds to the complexity and singularity mentioned above, hence my wariness of making any generalisations. I will simply report certain stages of the beginning of the treatment of this boy who had a homosexual father in order to appreciate the consequences of such a family configuration at the level of the dynamic expression of his cathexes and identifications during the analytic process. Louis was four years old when I first met him. He was the youngest of a family of two children. His parents had separated "on account of" the father's homosexuality. His mother had recently been living with another man. Shortly before my meeting with Louis, I had met his elder sister Elise, whose behavioural problems and nightmares were apparently the primary reason for the mother's wish to seek help. Let me say right away that the evolution of the consultations with this little girl led to an indication of psychoanalytic psychotherapy, work that was carried out and brought to a satisfactory conclusion. It seemed, then, that Elise was managing better than her brother, most probably because she was a girl and the elder child, thereby favouring her identification with her mother.

The mother was an intelligent and active woman, even though she sometimes came across as being a bit "pushy" to anyone who had dealings with her. I should point out that, once she had overcome her anxieties, Elise, after our very first consultations, developed various graphic scenarios with alternating movements of anxiety, manic defences and defiance, the evolution of which gradually led to agreeing "calmly" to continue this kind of experience with an analyst. But before this indication could be shared with the two parents, a certain amount of work had to be done, which brings us back to Louis. When I saw Elise for the second time, her mother asked me if I could also see her son; the father was present this time. From my point of view, Louis was the child that posed the most problems. His school confirmed the presence in Louis of a non-focal inhibition because it was massively pervasive. The father was of the same opinion, which caused a conflict with his ex-wife concerning the child who ought, in his view, to benefit from a treatment as a matter of priority. Once this conflict had been overcome, it was decided that Elise would do a psychotherapy and that Louis would initially do a group therapy. During my meeting with the father, I learnt about an important element in his history. When he was little, he had lost a brother. Their mother had never been able to get over this loss. He said that when he was a child he was not interested in school, that he isolated himself and played "dead".

Having made the connection with the dead brother, Mr F. said he had never thought of that, before adding immediately that he had changed since then and that now he knew a lot of people, and so forth. In terms of repetition, it was none the less difficult to imagine that such a problem of identification had not played a role in his son's difficulties. Louis, who was four years old, and whom I had been able to see alone this time, had overcome his inhibition thanks to the introduction of a psychodramatic sequence involving a box of toys, as his graphic abilities were limited to the repetition of a few more or less rounded forms, with an absence of narrative, even in a *squiggle* style. There remained play activity, which, even if it had a dynamic role to play, did not make it possible to "deduce" that the father was homosexual. As I was accompanying Louis' play, a scenario took shape involving a mother kangaroo that was being chased with its baby by a crocodile, which he called a snake. Louis made a soldier intervene, who killed the "snake", which promptly came back to life again. This required the help of a "monster", represented by a gorilla, to bludgeon the reptile. I then placed a lady near the soldier. Louis took great pleasure in reintroducing the crocodile each time I played the role of the lady in symbolic versions of the primal scene with the soldier. When I played the role of this lady, to show that there was really no way for the good man and me to stay together, Louis expressed something rather inaudible in which I distinguished the word "darling", a word that it is rather unusual to hear in a consultation with a child of this age, all the more so in that he was seriously inhibited. This was no doubt the only moment when the question of the father's homosexuality could, in my opinion, be raised, even if only at the level of my countertransference, in terms of an association of ideas caught up in indecision or condensation concerning the sex of the darling: at one level, Louis identified with the soldier, since I was the lady.

The problem was that the future course of the treatment did not lead in this direction for, at the level of the countertransference, I had the impression that if, as a man, I was playing the role of a woman who was going to go out with a man, it was no longer the playful reality of the sexes as portrayed in the play activity that defined the subsequent course of psychic events, but rather the physical reality, the "actual" sex of the consultant and of the child/boy. Under these conditions, it could be a scene between homosexual "darlings", hence the use of the word by Louis. The next consultation took place four months later, owing to the summer holidays. Even if his capacity for graphic representation had evolved very little, it was nonetheless possible to end up with a narrative thanks to the more or less symbolising dynamic of our relationship. Louis drew a sort of spiral-shaped line, which he called a plane. The plane moved backwards because it had seen a ghost. He portrayed the ghost's head, but the rest was erased by scribbles. But its eyes were visible, and Louis told me that the ghost could see that it had made the plane withdraw. He then made one of the ghost's friends appear, then a vague shape that he called a mushroom, which the ghost ate. The friend then attacked the ghost for having eaten "his" mushroom. Faced with such a sequence, it is obviously difficult not to think about the unconscious force of homosexuality and of its vicissitudes, both in terms of the part-object cathexis (the eaten mushroom) and in terms of identification (the ghost is more or less erased by the scribbles).

One year after the first consultation, and after eight months of group therapy, Louis' therapists evoked an evolution of the identificatory movements in three phases: a phase of passivity, "playing dead"; a phase of repeated identification with a woman in the interaction with another boy; and a phase of identification with powerful heroes in comics such as Goldorak, Spiderman or Starsky . . . in order to become more virile. Moreover, it was Starsky that he wanted to draw when he claimed that he was six years old, and it was also Starsky that he said he wanted to be like later on, when he admitted his real age. Louis had made progress from the graphic point of view, even though the quality of his drawing was below his age, while maintaining a comparable structural dynamic. He portrayed Starsky, then, detailing the different parts of his face, arms, and even the fingers of his hands. The problem began at the level of what the child called the belly, a belly without limits, open towards the bottom, unrepresentable. Then, as a counterpoint, he added a big ear to the character. I realised at that moment that I had just spoken to him in a rather loud voice, probably in order to stress the problem of this peculiar "belly". For the first time, Louis answered me in the same tone of voice.

This brief interaction between us gave rise first to the drawing of the ear, and then to the fact that Louis said that the character "was changing his stomach". He drew Starsky's ribs, and then a "belt", a word Louis took from me as I had initially thought that the rib was a belt. Thus, through these transference movements, Louis was on his way to making a *symbolic* representation of a man with a penis. He even went as far as to draw the character's tie. Then, once he had done this, the scenario was enriched by varying the primal scene, but only after having changed the colour of the tie from black to blue and after I had said to him: "It's more colourful like that; otherwise it would have meant that he had lost someone, wouldn't it?" Louis then introduced Hutch. Hutch was crying, "It's because his wife is not there", Louis told me, and then drew her immediately in the position of an absent third party caught up in a scenario that was potentially evocative of the separation of his parents. But this was not enough to stabilise the situation. Louis realised that Starsky's arm was going to touch the woman (a movement that seemed to introduce Mrs F.'s friend with whom the child identified).

But what matters here, as always in psychoanalytic work, is not the hypotheses about the meaning of contents, but what has a bearing on the *singularity of the process*. Faced with this new destabilisation produced by the unconscious, Louis split Hutch in two, beginning with the head, which was transformed into fog (a new erasure), while red rain was falling more and more heavily on all the characters.

Louis could then be heard tapping on the drawing board increasingly hard with his felt pen. Curtain! "It's finished," he said, and stopped drawing. It was during this consultation that I learnt that Louis had suffered from asthma from the age of nine months, and that he continued to have periodic bouts. Recently, other symptoms of this kind had appeared which his mother attributed to the animal his father owned. This somatic parameter added complexity to the situation insofar as its evolution contributed to throwing light both on its determinism and on the reality of its disappearance during the therapeutic process. For understandable reasons, I cannot go more deeply into the history of each of the parents, especially as the most decisive elements only acquire significance in the context of the consultation. However, this longitudinal trajectory of fourteen years showed that there was always something to learn that had not yet been said.

This was the case with the limited number of elements I was able to glean about the parents' history. When Mrs F. married Mr F., she knew that her future husband had homosexual tendencies, but she did no more than think about them. However, during his wife's first pregnancy, he lived out his homosexuality. She did not separate from her husband. When, subsequently, they had Elise, she felt that her husband took care of their little girl very well, but when they had their son, Louis, he apparently sank into passivity (no doubt partly owing to the shadow of this father's dead brother). And this was what had driven her to separate from her husband, whose homosexuality she might have been able to tolerate under other circumstances. We can add that in terms of identifications, the father felt that his son resembled the child that he himself had been. The mother, for her part, felt that Louis resembled the father's brother, who had made a success of his life. Repeatedly, and even violently, and in spite of the evolution of his functioning, Louis stumbled when faced with the masculine and virile figurative image of the father, even if the omnipotent maternal imago played a complementary role. The question that remained unresolved was that of the transition from the therapeutic group to analysis. In fact, the mother "resisted" this indication, considering that her son was developing sufficiently, and was supported, moreover, by her friend who felt he had no problems with Louis. The father, for his part, was participating less in the consultations.

However, as often happens, entering Year 2 (in France, *cours prépara-toires*) served as a catalyst, particularly on account of the child's graphic difficulties. Mrs F. was *then* able to tell me that, if she had resisted the indication of psychoanalytic work, it was because she had had the impression that I was particularly interested in caring for a child whose father was homosexual. The analysis could now begin with one of my colleagues. It lasted six-and-a-half years, on a three-times-weekly basis. In the course of the first six months, during one session, Louis drew the elliptical trajectory of a bullet coming out of an enormous revolver. "A strange bullet that comes back to its starting-point," his analyst commented. Louis commented: "Yes, it's always like that."

A short time after, during a session that followed the one in which he had put a riddle to his analyst, where everything turned out to be false, rather like what he felt during his attempts at virile identifications, Louis pretended he was a cowboy with a horse and lasso. He stood on the table, with a cigar between his lips, and said, "I'm the daytime cowboy". Then, he lay down on the couch and added, "That's the night time cowboy". He had a dreamy expression and at the same time had his thumb in his mouth. He turned towards his analyst and said to her, "And you, you must say, 'It's a strange cowboy who sucks his thumb'". The analyst repeated these words. Louis said, "I'm the night time cowboy; I don't have any dreams", as if he was expecting his analyst to ask him if he had had any dreams. Then, changing his tune, "I dream that I'm training to shoot". According to his analyst, the virile identification could not be maintained without there being a regression to auto-eroticism. We may note, however an elaborative sequence thanks to the appropriation of his analyst's words. The formulation "strange bullet" came back in the form of a *"latent thought"* as "strange cowboy". In terms of the logics of the unconscious, these psychic movements are coherent with those of the sequence rib/belt/tie.

Four-and-a-half years after the beginning of his analysis, and after a session of paper-folding, Louis drew a man for the first time, no longer just in outline but with a certain density, dressed in a real pair of trousers, and not with a skirt on top of them. In a session that followed, he related a nightmare in which the skin of the characters was peeling off. Louis cried out: "I don't want to see them." In front of his analyst, he mimed with his hands how the skin was peeling off. The analyst thought about what the mother had said to her, namely, that the asthma mentioned earlier had disappeared. This confirms, once again, that the most horrible images remain in the order of the representable and are even a sign of elaboration. While many other things could be added concerning Louis' evolution, what has already been said suffices to show the importance of the "parameter" of paternal homosexuality in the "equation" of his psychic functioning. But this parameter cannot be treated in an isolated fashion since both the history of the parents and their psychic particularity have also contributed to giving it a singular character.

Notes

1 This section takes up the article, "De la consultation thérapeutique à la psychanalyse d'enfant. Deux experiences cliniques", initially published in *Psychiatrie de l'enfant*, 41(2): 443–473, 1998. Reproduced here with the kind permission of the Presses Universitaires de France.

2 Translator's note: another word for penis, normally spelt verge.

3 See the complex example which involves a visual-spatial dyspraxia (Villa and Danon-Boileau, 2008).

4 This section takes up again the article, "La place des 'états pré-psychotiques de l'enfant", initially published in the *Bulletin de la Société Psychanalytique de Paris*, 64: 200–205, 2002. Reproduced here with the kind permission of the Presses Universitaires de France.

5 Translator's note: in French, *connaitre/méconnaitre*. This could equally be translated by knowing/not knowing, but I found the former worked

better in the text. In any case, *méconnaitre* implies an "active" misunder-standing, misappreciation or not knowing on the part of the subject.

6 This section takes up again the article "Le temps du connaitre/méconnaitre dans l'espace de la consultation familiale", initially published in *Les Textes du Centre Alfred Binet*, 4: 101–110 (Ody, 1984).

7 This section takes up again the article "Troubles de la représentation chez un enfant de parent homosexual", initially published in the *Revue française de psychanalyse*, 1: 219–228 (Ody, 2003b). Reproduced here with the kind permission of the Presses Universitaires de France.

PART II
METHODOLOGY AND TECHNIQUE

CHAPTER THREE

Movements and settings of the therapeutic space

Between regression and withdrawal: concerning tensions between narcissism and drives in the child[1]

In the recent theoretical developments concerning the question of regression, I was interested by a problem in the recent history of psychoanalysis, namely, that of the infiltration into its field of application of the systemic, behaviouralist, and, more recently, neuroscientific disciplines, minimising and evacuating the concept of the drive and thus placing, correlatively, sexuality in the background. The intersubjectivist current of thought in psychoanalysis, which comes from the United States, shares in this orientation, with the risk of making the intrapsychic dimension disappear. However, we should recall that, for Freud, in this intrapsychic dimension, regression and sexual drive are indissociable.

I want to insist on the notion of sexual drive for, before the existence of the disciplines just mentioned, the Kleinian psychoanalytic movement had placed the accent on the drive of aggression, of destruction, as a decisive element in the dynamics of regression. The debates during the famous *Controversies* (1941–1945) which took place in England during the Second World War were on the scale of the issues at stake between Kleinians and those who asserted that, even after the introduction of the death drive in 1920, Freud had never changed his point of view on the necessity of linking regression and sexual drive.

In *Instincts and their Vicissitudes*, Freud (1915c) gave the following definition of the concept of the drive, one that is still relevant and each term of which has its importance:

> An 'instinct' appears to us as a concept on the frontier between the mental and the somatic, as the psychical representative of the stimuli originating from within the organism and reaching the mind, as a measure of the demand made upon the mind for work in consequence of its connection with the body. (p. 122)

This definition in no way contradicts the growing complexity of the theory, in particular after the introduction of the death drive in 1920 and of the second topography in 1923. As for the notion of regression, two citations from Freud come to mind: in his *Introductory Lectures on Psycho-Analysis* he notes that, "repression is a topographico-dynamic concept" while "regression is a purely descriptive one" (1916–1917, p. 342), which means that regression must be qualified.

This is the case when, in *The Interpretation of Dreams*, Freud (1900a) speaks of the three coordinates of metapsychology: *topographical* regression, as illustrated by the model of the dream which characterises its *retrogressive* character from the moment when "an idea is turned back into the sensory image from which it was originally derived" (p. 543). Authors such as Michel Fain, César and Sára Botella have given fresh thought to this notion of retrogression (*regrédience*) in the context of the dynamics of the analytic session. Formal regression and its "figurability" (i.e. visual representability) as well as temporal regression complete this Freudian trilogy containing indissociable elements. I will not go any further in recalling these Freudian notions, except to emphasise, where the drive is concerned, the question of masochism, which was developed particularly in, "A child is being beaten" (Freud 1919e), where the statement "I am being beaten by my father", once it has been formulated, "is not only the punishment for the forbidden genital relation, but also the *regressive* substitute for that relation" (p. 189). "The economic problem of masochism" (Freud, 1924c), which takes into consideration the introduction of the death drive four years earlier, also takes account of the role of *sexual co-excitation*.

These reminders seem to me indispensable in contemporary psychoanalysis which, for several decades now, has included within its scope of concern, so-called "difficult" cases. This term refers to "non-neurotic" patients (Green, 2006, p. 62) who undergo psychoanalytic treatment, ranging from the psychoanalytic therapeutic consultation to the institutional approach, including face-to-face treatments, whether it is children, adolescents or adults that are concerned, and irrespective of the number of weekly sessions. This evolution in the history of psychoanalysis does not imply in any way that the patients in Freud's time were "easy cases". It suffices to read the case of "Dora" (Freud, 1905e) or that of the "Wolf Man" (1918b[1914]), to be convinced of this. The evolution in question underlines above all the work of extending and going more deeply into the discipline, both in its theoretical and practical aspects, in association with cultural developments and the universals of the mind. It is not very surprising, therefore, that once the *corpus* that is necessary for all the neuroses had been established sufficiently, psychoanalysts, as the history of the discipline indicates, turned increasingly towards the so-called "difficult cases".

At the same time, the dynamics of the countertransference became more and more involved in these situations – countertransference, I should add, that could no longer be limited to the question of the analyst's desire, which had become classical since Lacan. And, to stay with this vocabulary, the whole question became: Where, in these cases, should the cursor be placed between what falls within the ambit of "desire" and what falls within that of "need"? Freud has been reproached for a certain *solipsism*. I have always thought that as there is a time for everything, he first had to be "solipsistic" in order to be able to develop a theory of the genesis, organisation and functioning of the psychical apparatus, including its different psychopathological manifestations. Furthermore, his work opened up enough paths for the most eminent analysts today to be able, when re-reading it, to still find elements of reflection that have contemporary resonances, including for what concerns the inter-cathexes between self and other. Melanie Klein, as we know, notwithstanding her contributions to psychoanalysis, difficult cases included, did not particularly place the accent on the environment of the subject or the pre-subject with regard to the form of the most archaic inner conflicts.

It is thus with Winnicott, who remains entirely relevant today, that openness to the other is operant, and particularly with regard to what is expressed in analysis in this connection in the dynamics of the transference/countertransference. Winnicott thus directed his attention towards what, in Freudian terms, we would call narcissistic failings (we know that he speaks essentially in terms of *self*) – failings that hamper the possibility of, I would say, an adequate or "good enough" expression of instinctual drive movements. These movements endanger the subject's narcissism. This was what, from the end of the 1940s, and thereafter in his work, led him gradually to identify, including in subjects in whom neurotic functioning seems to dominate, indications of factors under-lying neurosis that determine so-called interminable and/or repeated, or unsatisfying analyses. The identification of such factors can only be achieved through what emerges in the analyst's countertransference. It was in order to be able to reach the heart of the narcissistic dysfunction-ing of the subject that Winnicott (1954), in his article on regression in the analytic situation, was to link regression and dependence, in the sense in which the subject experiences in the transference a *regression to depen-dence*. Now, let us not forget that this state of dependence is precisely a state that the subject was not able to experience in a reliable way for all sorts of reasons concerning the family environment. Regression to dependence, in Winnicott's sense, is a regression that concerns first and foremost the *ego*, with reference to the Freudian topography, a regres-sion of the ego as a precondition, it could be said, of "reuniting" with the "true self", according to Winnicott's conceptualisation, so that the sub-ject feels "real". In reading this author's gradation, we realise that the more one advances towards absolute dependence, the less one should, if I may put it like this, touch the drives. Moreover, this was what led Winnicott (1971) to say in *Playing and Reality*: ". . . the instincts are the main threat to play as to the ego" (p. 52).

At this point in our considerations, we find ourselves faced with *two sorts of regression: instinctual regression and regression to dependence*. This implies rediscovering a certain dialectic between narcissism and eroti-cism, since the aggressive drives, including their destructive expression, are externalised or turn back against the self on a growing and histori-cising scale that is commensurate with the tensions between narcissism and eroticism. It is none the less true that Winnicott (1987), as he wrote to Enid Balint on 22 March 1956, avoided mixing regression to depen-dence and regression in terms of instinct stages. Still more precisely, he added that he wanted to "cut it loose from the phases of instinctual development and allow it to relate to ego-relatedness which precedes instinctual experience accepted as such" (p. 98). One cannot be clearer. I have put forward the idea (Ody, 1986) that Winnicott's point of view seemed to me to be too dichotomous because he was led to say "the instincts are the main threat to play as to the ego" (Winnicott, 1971, p. 52). Paradoxically, this did not prevent him at the same time from saying that a good spanking could put an end to overstimulation, which takes us back to Freud, if I may say so, and the possible role played by masochistic impulses in *reuniting the drives*. In other words, if the drives go out through the window, they will come back through the door, the door of the parental environment, whether directly countercathected, projected or denied. This is why the work of Denise Braunschweig and Michel Fain has struck me as being of particular interest, adding to the Winnicottian perspective the complexity of the inter-cathexes between parents and children and their *triangular modalities*.

The question of the use of the object in the transference/countertransference dynamics can also be examined from the angle of the dialectic between narcissism and the drives. Admittedly, the analyst has to be able to survive the attacks and testing of the patient, allowing the latter to experience long-term reliability for the first time, including the absence of any destructive retaliation on the part of the object/analyst. In such a context, work on the countertransference is vital. It is a matter not only of struggling against suffering and narcissistic wounds, by giving them meaning, but also of becoming aware of one's own sado-masochism, and consequently of one's own drive impulses. The narcissistic question is thus of special significance, so that, metapsychologically speaking, it is in no way surprising if the figures of the *double drive reversal* between patient and analyst play the role that Freud ascribed to them as one of the vicissitudes of the drives (i.e., "reversal into its opposite" and "turning round upon the subject's own self" (Freud, 1915c, p. 126)), a narcissistic vicissitude as he qualifies it. We are thus at the heart of the articulation between narcissism and the drives. It may even be added that analysis offers the possibility of transforming hate into sadism through sexualisation, which perhaps inevitably has an impact on the "vicissitudes" of *hate in the countertransference*, studied by Winnicott (1947).

Let us stay with Winnicott and his notion of *withdrawal*. Certain passages in his writings could suggest that this withdrawal concerns what

I described earlier as a regression to dependence. Since, in this area, Freud and Winnicott prove to be complementary, it seems more heuristic and coherent at the metapsychological level to speak of two forms of regression, *instinctual drive-based regression and narcissistic regression*, which do not necessarily function in a mutually exclusive manner. This does not mean, however, that in the session one must rush into a drive-based interpretation, even if it remains true that this is part of the representational work of the analyst, *the condition of all future interpretability*. "Notes on withdrawal and regression" (Winnicott, 1965) stresses the difference between these two situations: "Clinically," Winnicott writes, "the two states are practically the same. It will be seen, however, that there is an extreme difference between the two. In regression there is dependence and in withdrawal there is pathological independence" (p. 149).

In other words, to take an example, there are different ways of putting oneself under a blanket (Winnicott's "rug") during the session, while at the same time wedging one's head between the pillows; either this act is part of a movement of regression, the patient having acquired a sense of certainty concerning the reliability of the setting and of the person of the analyst, or this act is part of a movement of hostility or, at least, of great ambivalence. Of course, the two phases, helped by the compulsion to repeat, may alternate until gradually the work of the analytic treatment can begin. Last but not least, I want to address the question of "instinctual danger", in Winnicott's sense. I agree entirely that there is no point in interpreting an instinctual movement, *especially* in the transference, when the state of narcissistic functioning does not permit it. This links up with Winnicott's idea of a necessary phase devoted to *"holding"*, which requires us to be able to define the place of the cursor between what relates to *need* and what to *desire*, to use Winnicott's terms. However, both can result in a chiasmus at the point of anaclisis, since interpretation does not only pertain to unconscious contents. It pertains above all to a certain processuality supported by the preconscious – a preconscious with its intermediate elements (*Mittelglieder*), as Freud points out. This quality of the preconscious thus has a function of mediation between narcissism and instinctual drive functioning, not only between unconscious and conscious, the role of symbolisation at this level being complementary. If we take account of the conditions I have just mentioned, the result is that the cursor may shift more towards instinctual drive functioning.

A clinical illustration

When I met him, Jacky, of African origin, was seven-and-a-half years old and was in the second year of primary school. I learnt that he had benefitted from extensive pedagogical help from a special needs teacher from the French network RASED.[2] I also learnt that his parents had been informed that Jacky had the tendency to answer questions evasively, which they accepted was possible. The first interview with the mother took place with the social worker of my team at the Alfred Binet Centre. Jacky was the penultimate sibling of a family of six children, and apparently the only one to pose problems. He had apparently not presented any developmental difficulties, except that he he had only just begun to speak when he first attended nursery school at around the age of three. At school he was seen as a solitary child. As for his "evasiveness" in answering questions, it was difficult to obtain examples. He had a tendency, in class, to answer a question by talking about his life, without it being possible, however, to say that what he was saying was completely unrelated to the question from the point of view of primary processes.

Given his speech problems, it was suggested that he did some speech therapy at Saint Anne's Hospital, which the parents did not agree to because, as they said, their child "was not mad". Among the elements of the family history which may have had an impact, it is worth mentioning that the year before, after he had started primary school, the elder half-sister in the family (the child of the mother's first brief marriage), aged 17, had arrived in France, one year after the birth of Jacky's younger sister, the youngest child of the family. Furthermore, her mother had lost her own mother when Jacky was three years old. A first consultation, during a monthly work meeting with the child's school, enabled me, even before the consultation – which is unusual – to get a better picture of the situation. At the beginning of the year, during the inaugural drawing of the family, the teacher had noticed that he put the sister who was four years older than him in the mother's role, but the mother herself did not figure in the drawing.

Moreover, he had not wanted to draw his father. Jacky gave the impression at times of being echolalic; in the canteen he ate his food with his hands and led the adults to take a truly educative approach to him, which nourished the fantasies of a family that although deficient, was not abusive. He was a child who, generally speaking, gave the impression of being "in his own world". Likewise, with the school psychologist, during his assessment, he gave the impression at times of being present, while at others he seemed to be totally elsewhere. His WISC (Wechsler Intelligence Scale for Children) results were very mixed, even though he showed that he had obvious capabilties, which may explain why he was in a class of his age group. The teacher felt, moreover, that each time he returned after holiday periods, Jacky had always "regressed" somewhat.

After one weekend, he remarked that everyone had been present at home; but although the teacher was quick to emphasise the positive side of this, Jacky reacted by saying, "Yes, but no one saw me". This reaction led me to ask myself what was peculiar about this child. Similarly, with regard to his tendency to give answers to questions that were "beside the point", I had noted some that were unexpected and incomprehensible, for instance, the answer he gave to a maths question, when he replied, "They've killed him"; and while he was capable of answering the question, "What is a cow?" intelligibly, he produced a very emotionally-charged association to the nastiness of a bull . . . But given that some of his results in maths were brilliant, the teacher did not exclude the possibility of his moving up to the next class. His mother made a parapraxis in the first consultation. She got the time wrong, which meant that I saw Jacky alone. I noted that he told me that he did not write on the lines of a piece of paper and also, concerning his behaviour, that he talked in the corridors. I was a bit surprised. He added, "There are rules of life". I wondered about the possibility of a false-self personality, but I also thought about what I had heard about his father's severity.

One thing leading to another, I asked him if he dreamed. At first, he replied indirectly. Then, after he had replied affirmatively, he told me about a boy he knew who dreamed, but said nothing more. Jacky then associated to the fact that his friend had seen *Love Story*, but he had not. He added, "It's not good to watch that". Another "rule of life", as it were, related to the drives. I tried to draw him out again on the subject of his own dreams. This time he gave me an example. He was with a friend; they were on a cloud (there was no question about that!), but they fell into the water and sank, before being eaten by a shark. At that point he awoke from this nightmare. He associated by saying that when he was little he used to dream that his mother was a monster. He could not go any further after this confession.

The mother had come alone. Let me add right away that in spite of my attempts to include him, I never saw the father. Admittedly his profession – let's say, in transport – which was exacting from the point of view of his time schedule, made it difficult for him to come, but this certainly did not suffice to explain his absence which had become subject of humour between us. His wife assured me that she would let him know what had transpired in the interview, that in principle he would listen, but then never say anything about it. The mother confided to me, while remaining on a descriptive level, that she felt a bit lost when faced with her son and his behaviour. At the same time, I sensed there was basically a slightly depressive side to her, as well as an enigmatic aspect which went beyond cultural difference.

She came back to the question of "going off the rails", an expression that she accompanied with an upward movement of her hand. I intervened, saying to her son, "Hey, are you are flying away?", which produced a broad smile. This led me to think about his dream about being on a cloud. His mother emphasised above all her concern about the rude words that her son sometimes said to his schoolmistress, but without taking the context into account. Jacky simply said that this happened when he was irritated. Gradually, she noted a change in her son, in connection with his aggressiveness, which, she said, had in reality manifested itself the year before, which led her to think about the birth of his little sister. For the first time, she laughed briefly, telling me that when she had her daughter on her knees, her son sometimes tried to push her off. "So, you'd like to be mummy's baby instead of your sister?" I said to him. Jacky remain silent for a moment, looked at me, and then said in a rather firm tone, "Yes", which clearly moved his mother.

We separated with a new consultation planned for a month later. The consultation took place during the school summer holidays. Apart from during a number of very specific but significant moments, I had to encourage him frequently to get him to speak. With the help of this sort of holding and after doing a football drawing depicting the coloured flags of his own country and that of Brazil, he gradually moved on to the subject of his dreams. He sometimes had nice ones, he said, but could not give any examples. I asked him if he could remember anything else on this subject. "The nightmare," he said, thereby indicating retrospectively, thanks to this recollection, that the last consultation *had been therapeutic*. Jacky added that the nightmare was the one in which his mother had killed him . . . something, you will remember, that had not been said before. "I was little", he added, which made me ask him what might have led a little boy to have such a dream. He remained silent, adding a bit more colour to the Brazilian flag, and said, "I'm stopping". I commented on his reaction by saying that he had found my question a bit peculiar. He looked at me attentively and kept quiet. Later on, Mrs G. told me that she had noted a change since the last time, especially in her son's school work. Before, she said, "I had to push him the whole time; now, he wants to do it." Jacky intervened to say that he had had several marks of 10, which his mother confirmed, adding that he was going to move up into the third year of primary school. We came back to the question that had led to the consultation: his "evasive" answers to questions. I suggested linking them to his dreamy side, which he showed in class when he was asked a question. His mother's associations, though, had more to do with his behaviour in class.

He would play around, speak out of turn, or play on the floor. In short, she noticed that in the end it was the same behaviour as at home, that of a "baby", she added, which, of course, allowed me to link this up with the previous consultation concerning his little sister. Mrs G. recalled this and added, looking confused, that now it was the sister who rushed forward to separate Jacky from his mother when he wanted a hug. During this second consultation, I felt that the mother was more present, less enigmatic. At the same time, I think that her association to her son's behaviour, when he behaved "like a baby", established a libidinal circuit between her and him in the area of *regression*, where regression to dependence and instinctual regression can converge. The hypothesis that I had put forward, in the direction of *withdrawal*, had probably worried her more. She may have unconsciously changed this direction, because she had the means to do so in a libidinalised form.

However, in the past, faced with her incomprehension concerning certain attitudes or behaviours of her son, she had used the expression, *"il y a un truc"* (roughly, "there's something strange"), accompanying these words with a movement of her hand towards her head, the word *truc* signifying at that particular moment the inexpressible and unrepresentable. Experience shows that often, in these situations, it is madness that is being designated, the child having a sort of role assigned to him in the generational history, by being included in an *unconscious incestuous dimension*, even if Oedipus may have been "African", to recall the title of the book *Oedipe africain* by E. and M.-C. Ortigues (1966). This question came up again during a meeting in the first trimester of the following school year, the third year of primary school. In spite of the progress observed, Jacky's evolution had not been linear, for he sometimes lapsed again into his earlier forms of behaviour. At the same time, he could be brilliant in maths and science, or succeed in French, in spite of what were perceived as "moments of mental absence". Sometimes, during class, he would start singing or hitting the pupils next to him . . . but then, a short time after, he would go up to the teacher and say to her: "I think I have annoyed the others . . .". I had been led to refer to this "fooling about" (*"faire le fou"*) at the end of the last consultation, which linked up with the *association* of the child's new teacher who recalled having heard Jacky say, "I'm nuts, I'm mad".

You will recall that the teacher from the RASED, who had known the child in nursery school and who had considered the child to be "totally psychotic", had also said that, when she had asked to see the mother, the latter had replied, "My son is not mad!" The evolution, in spite of its non-linearity, followed its course, provoking contradictory, but sometimes complementary opinions in the protagonists concerned. But Jacky could also manifest new psychic movements; for example, within the framework of the RASED, which he continued to attend, on one occasion he said to his special needs teacher, who was a bit late, "I was worried". His class teacher then told us about a nightmare he had had, apparently quite often, in which he was crossing a bridge and was in danger of being crushed by two buses coming from either end of the bridge, at which point he would wake up. It was as if we were dealing with an opposition between the *verticality* of the "elsewhere on his cloud" and the violent *horizontality* of being "on earth". The following elaborative phase took place thanks to a circumstance that might initially be considered farcical. The school doctor had advised the parents to have a neurological assessment carried out, I would say, "just in case".

This assessment, rather foreseeably, proved negative. It was not necessarily a waste of time in the sense that the "*truc*", mentioned earlier, as designated by the mother, was therefore not organic. But, above all, this assessment attracted my attention by the mention, without any further details, of an injury, a fracture, during the third month of Mrs G.'s pregnancy, a fact we were unaware of. It was in such circumstances that the following consultation took place, which had been postponed until the second trimester of the school year. At this juncture, Jacky was eight and a half years old and in the third year of primary school (in

France, CE2). He was now able to differentiate his progress at school from the times when he "fooled around". He was able to speak about this spontaneously and even poetically. Then gradually, we came to his dreams. Once again, he had had a nightmare dating back to the time when he was a little boy. This time he was in hell, but with both his parents who had died in a flow of lava. His only association was to tell me that he had already told me about it, which was false, but it was still true that it retained its transference value. He continued by telling me a "good" dream: Jacky was in a lift and found himself in paradise. "Between hell and paradise," I said to him, which surprised him and quickly brought him down to earth, if I may say so, because after that he felt he had nothing more to say. He was happy for his mother to come. She clearly seemed satisfied with the way her son was evolving, especially at the level of his behaviour, at least quantitatively. Mrs G. even realised at one moment, feeling both astonished and touched, that her son, whom she had previously found incomprehensible, was able to tell the story of the *101 Dalmatians* in front of me.

But above all, she made my task easier by handing me a letter from the department that had carried out the neurological assessment. When I came to the fracture, I asked her if she could tell me about the context of it. It had happened in the third month of her pregnancy as she was crossing a road when the lights were red; all the cars were at a standstill, except one, which went through the red light, knocking her over. She had had a double fracture of the tibia, followed by fifteen days of hospitalisation in an orthopaedic ward, and three months in another service for physiotherapy. You will recall Jacky's recurrent nightmare about the two buses. No problem had been noticed as far as the child was concerned. The birth went well, which did not prevent the mother from continuing to worry, and from having something (*un "truc"*) on her mind. When I raised the question of the undisputable gap between material reality and psychic reality, Mrs G. gave me the following confirmation: "We both nearly died" and looked at her son with a tenderness that I had not seen in her before.

Things continued to evolve positively, with a complementary relationship between the therapeutic consultations and the work meetings at the school. I had no more accounts of nightmares from the time when he was a small child, nor indeed of more recent ones. Not everything was settled, if indeed that were possible. Although he no longer played the "fool", there was still something strange in Jacky's mode of contact with others which, at least on the surface, was linked in my opinion to certain pauses while he was speaking, when it was difficult to know whether they were of a reflective nature or whether they indicated that he had "switched off". In short, perhaps this boy will one day do an analysis of several sessions a week, involving a dialectic between regression and dependence, withdrawal, instinctual regression, and elaborative work. In any case, we may hope so.

Migration of a therapeutic project[3]

The observation of the evolution of what may or may not lead to the indications of an analytic treatment becomes even clearer (and mobilises the consultant a great deal) when he/she is dealing with a socially disadvantaged population in which there is a high proportion of migrants. Indeed, cultural facts may destabilise the consultant and confront him/her with zones of incompetence. But, at the same time, we must not forget that by over-emphasising the variations of cultural facts, we risk ascribing them with a *screen function* in relation to the universal referents of the unconscious. The therapeutic journey that will serve as an illustration for these introductory remarks took place over a period of six years, the project of a psychotherapy having acquired the position of the "Arlesienne"[4] throughout these years.

Georges, an African child, the second of four siblings, was referred to me at the age of four by a doctor from the maternal and child protection service (PMI in France) who had noted "a minor psycho-motor retardation". The social worker in our team began by seeing Mrs H., the mother, who was an intelligent and likeable woman but fell into moments of passive silence during the interview. She was a cleaning lady, 25 years old, and ten years younger than her husband who was a worker. Georges' father, who had been living in France for twelve years, had gone to fetch his wife in Africa, a situation that is quite common. She soon became pregnant with their eldest daughter, who subsequently had to have speech therapy. One year later, she gave birth to Georges, a birth that clearly followed on too closely for her in this context of recent relocation and material difficulties. Mrs H. mentioned her son's eating difficulties, which had appeared when he went to nursery school.

He was a precocious child who could not sit still, was able to walk at nine-and-a-half months, and was toilet-trained (day and night) by the age of twelve months. He could speak his maternal language at the age of two, French at two-and-a-half, was bottle-fed, due to a shortage of his mother's milk, until the age of seven months, which poses no problems in an African environment. This precocious development corresponded, it seems, to the mother's choice; it was the same for the other children, she said.

Mrs H. was the second of three children whom her father had with the last of his three wives. Her father died when she was only one year old and, in keeping with tradition, her mother then married one of the father's brothers, who subsequently had other wives. What is particular about Mrs H.'s history is that she apparently only learnt the truth about her line of descent once she had turned twelve. She continued to think about her father's death; it turned out that he was linked to the place Georges had in the mother's unconscious. There was a long gap between the first interview with the social worker and the following interview, all attempts at making contact by telephone in the meantime having failed. Georges was then five-and-a-half years old. His anxious state of inhibition and his agitation were striking. He said to me, "things are not going well", while showing me the place in his mouth where he had two missing incisors. When I asked him whether his disquiet sometimes appeared in his dreams, he replied that he sometimes saw lions in his dreams.

A dream narrative, which I actively encouraged, gradually took shape. The child mimed a lion jumping with its claws at a man, who in turn cut off the lion's claws. But the lion then ate the man's hand. I asked him: "Does it have teeth?" "No," Georges replied. "Like you?", I said. The child was surprised and smiled. I then got him to draw. He was still thinking about his dream. He drew a man, and took his time – "Wait", he said, – in introducing the lion, giving more and more detail to the character. Finally, the lion was portrayed, as well as the scissors for cutting its claws. This sequence takes us immediately to the heart of the problem of the therapeutic indication. The coherence and continuity of the expression of Georges' instinctual impulses, his reactions to my interventions, with their transference connotation, might suggest an indication of psychotherapy. The problem lay with the parents. I felt that they were not very receptive and open to a project of this kind. Mrs H. came alone on that day. Beyond the lengthy description that she gave of her son's difficulties, she became passive and silent, while none the less remaining present, when I shared with her my concerns. I showed her that Georges was obliged to hold back, to contain, what he could communicate, because powerful things welled up in his imagination and led him either to keep quiet or to be agitated. The psychological assessment that followed confirmed the child's mode of functioning and revealed an IQ without deficit. Following a school meeting, and given the uncertainty we felt about the participation of the parents, it was suggested that a play activity with the psycho-motor therapist from the RASED should be arranged and that the consultations should continue. I saw the child again shortly after. He was starting primary school (*cours préparatoires* – CP in France), at the age of five years and ten months. He described in detail a Zorro-like figure while drawing a hero with a laser weapon. When I asked Georges if he ever thought about things like that in class, he replied, in a sort of compromise, that he was going to write the word 'cowboy', a character that he immediately went on to draw. There was still an absence, even at a symbolic level, of any depiction of a woman. I found myself faced with the same problem that I had had a few months earlier. Mrs H., who had "forgotten" to inform her husband about the consultation, was tired, and even less available than on the previous occasions. A school meeting showed that the child was calmer in class, that he was expressing his aggressive impulses in the play activities with his psycho-motor therapist and was becoming less destructive. He was even able to take interest with a degree of continuity in the story of the wolf and the three little pigs. The third consultation took place during the same month. I moved on quickly, as usual, to the subject of drawing because Georges, during our verbal exchange, had reduced his responses to their most simple expression, by trivialising or staying silent among other things. On the other hand, when he was drawing, in spite of his retentive mode of functioning, the child was much more active. He drew a man with a knife. What was going to happen? "Wait," he said, and gradually he introduced cats into the drawing, but the man cut off their heads because they had scratched him.

After this emergence of violence that was reminiscent of the first consultation, in which claws had been a feature, Georges became inhibited again. So for the first time I decided to play with him. He took some men and male animals out of the box of toys, setting aside women and female animals. After a fight, which the child enacted between a cowboy and a soldier, I introduced the cowboy's wife and made her say: "You really defended us well, let's go and feed the horse". Georges agreed to come with me, but when I added: "My husband and I have got some lovely animals", it was clearly too much for the child who, with his cowboy, went to find the soldier, who had since regained his wits, to have another fight with him.

His father was still absent (this time he was ill) and Mrs H. was quite satisfied with her son's progress. She felt reassured because he was much calmer. But during a meeting that took place at the end of the school year, at a time when the family was not present at the consultation, it seemed that the child's progress had peaked and that he would have to repeat a year at school; his aggressive behaviour in class had also resumed to some extent. On the other hand, his psycho-motor therapist, who was now working with him in a little group rather than individually as before, had noticed that Georges was more sociable, that he was no longer acting like a "big shot" as before. The following consultation took place when the child was almost seven years old. Georges led me to understand that some things were worrying him, but that he could not tell me anything about it.

Subsequently he told me that he would prefer to be alone with his psycho-motor therapist than in a small group with her. He drew a multi-coloured boy who, with one hand, was holding a cat on a lead, and with the other, a balloon with its string and its tag. A degree of continuity had appeared in the material that he was bringing, except that on that day it was marked by a countercathexis. It was at that moment that I chose to bring in the mother (the father was still absent), while suggesting to the child that he continue his drawing. I was waiting for some aspect of the mother/son inter-cathexis to get the process going again; and indeed, it was not long before this occurred. While Georges was drawing, his mother told me that he was now more present in class, which was a way of telling me retrospectively that he had really been "elsewhere" before, that is to say, in his day-dreams, as the school had pointed out.

Georges proceeded there and then to portray this "elsewhere" in his drawing: a hole, a saw, a hammer, and a nail. When I asked him what the *link* was between these elements, he told me that the boy he had in mind had not used these tools but on the contrary had fallen into a hole, a trap set by another character that he did not draw. Once he had given this *very condensed* account of the drawing, Georges became inhibited again and was breathing heavily. Mrs H. was moved by this scene and said that her son was not blocked like that at home. I pointed out to her that the blockage was linked to his drawing, where powerful things were happening, and that that was what prevented him from going any further. Mrs H., who was still very moved, remained silent. I suggested that we should speak about this again at the next consultation. This fifth consultation took place a few months later and this time, as if by chance, the father was present. While the child continued to be less agitated, his attainments at school were not at the level that they should have been, given that he was repeating a year. Georges always became more active and alive when he was drawing. This time he introduced a field mouse (mentioned at school), which was lying on the ground because a man had killed it with a knife. I noted that he was quicker with his answers than usual and did not force me to wait. Georges introduced the man's father (*sic*), a father who was going to slap his son; and for the first time Georges took another piece of paper on which he drew a motorcyclist shooting at the driver of a car. The child confirmed that the son was taking revenge for the slap he had been given and introduced the police to have him arrested.

I had the parents come in. Mr H. spoke French with more difficulty than his wife, which did not prevent him, however, from sharing with me, albeit in a descriptive way, his concerns about Georges. His wife, on the other hand, emerged spontaneously from her state of passivity to speak about the strong impression that the last consultation had made on her. She added that, on leaving, she had gone to see the school teacher who confirmed that her son sometimes seemed to be "elsewhere" in class. I then suggested that we returned to the past, which led Mrs H. to tell me that her son had been "difficult" from the age of one (you will recall Georges' precocious development, a precociousness that was encouraged by his mother who had lost her father at the same age), which was in no way related to anything at the level of factual events; the youngest child, for example, was born two years and four months later. Both parents agreed that their son was *a particular case* among their four children. Clearly moved, Mrs H. returned of her own accord to the content of the previous consultation, without, however, wanting to take things further. The father spoke up to say that if his son continued like that, he would have more and more difficulties at school. A new dynamic occurred when the father began to compare his two sons, Georges and his younger brother. The latter, "had some respect", Mr H. said, as he himself had had when he was a child, whereas Georges was disobedient. In so doing, Mr H. was aligning Georges with his mother, while placing his brother in the paternal line of descent.

This leads me on to what I had been concerned about for some time in connection with Mrs H.'s history. In his mother's unconscious, Georges was the incestuous child of Mrs H. and her father (a condensation of her dead father and of her paternal uncle), a "night baby" as Braunschweig and Fain (1975) would say. The precociousness of the child's development, encouraged by his mother, can now be understood as a tendency to counter-cathect the child's instinctual forms of expression (the ego in relation to the instinctual drives) which, otherwise, would reveal their incestuous "identity". As both parents were present, I talked to them about the possibility of their son having psychotherapy and explained what that would involve. They listened to me attentively but made no comments. I suggested they should think about this project and asked them to let me know their decision before the next consultation. The sixth consultation took place without my having had any news from them in the meantime.

The last school meeting made me realise that Georges had not been making any significant progress since the end of the first trimester while, at the same time, he had become more aggressive again towards his schoolmates. His psycho-motor therapist felt, on the other hand, that he now accepted frustration more easily than the year before. He also took part in a little reading group in which he showed himself to be much more present than in class. The consultation kept me in a state of perplexity. Georges was pursuing his associations in the same direction. For example, he drew a character that went down to the bottom of a *hole* (he also drew a *saw* . . .). The police intervened. The first character, baptised "the villain" (this was probably what was said about him in class), explored a chest at the bottom of the hole and discovered a woman's handbag with a crown and a ring in it. It was the first time that Georges had introduced a maternal and feminine symbol. With Mrs H. (her husband was unable to attend), it was much more difficult to re-establish any continuity. She had lapsed back into her passive state, especially as there had been mention of orienting her son towards a special needs class so that he could benefit from the dynamics of a small group, and not because he had been functioning below par. Moreover, I learnt subsequently that Mrs H. had just suffered a significant bereavement, of which she said nothing on that day. I thus gradually re-established a sense of continuity by reminding her where we had left off the last time, which simply reinforced her sense of disquiet. If her son thought about so many violent things, what would happen later on? This was something she was unable to imagine. I then reoriented our work towards the past, which led Mrs H. to tell me that she recalled very well what we had talked about; then she fell silent again.

None the less, she gradually managed to speak about herself as a child, "nice . . . very nice . . . because I was ill . . . very ill", so she had received a lot of love and support from her family and was particularly "supported" by her mother, as I would learn later. She had suffered from repeated ear infections with secretions over a period of several years. She said that her biological father had also suffered from this problem. This was an opportunity for her to return to the "revelation" of her line of descent around the age of twelve and to describe the real "shock" that this had been for her. At the same time, she was very attached to her paternal uncle who, in spite of the other wives that he had had after Mrs H.'s mother, had always taken care of her. When it was time for us to separate, I told Mrs H. how perplexed I felt about what we had talked about together concerning the possibility of her son doing some psychotherapy, and also about how she felt when she spoke about herself and her past, elements that made her not want to continue. Mrs H. came to life and contradicted me. She was ready, she said, to continue. So I suggested that we meet again. In fact, I did not see the family again until one year later. This long absence was punctuated by the usual excuses linked to objective reasons or forgetfulness. But it was above all linked to a series of meetings with the social worker that were soon broken off. It was in the context of these meetings, moreover, that the mother had been able to talk about the death of a brother whose support had meant a lot to her. This brother had the same father as her and had died at the same age as him, at the age of 34.

This death had occurred one month before the previous consultation. Mrs H. had told me – something quite rare hitherto – about some quite personal elements to do with the traditions and rituals of her country of origin on the occasion of someone's death. The holiday break, and the occurrence of another death, this time in the paternal family, resulted in the consultations being broken off once again. Georges, who was now eight years and three months, was in a special needs class and continued to be followed by his psycho-motor therapist. He was working well, controlling his excitement better, and it was even said of him that he was a polite child. He told me that he was "better", without being able to say anything more than that. Re-establishing some continuity with the previous sessions was clearly a pleasure for him, judging by his smile, but did not result in any apparent recollections.

As usual, then, we moved on to drawing. He still made me wait a while before putting into words what he was portraying, but less than before. He organised quite a complex scenario of a robbery which involved climbing up the outside of a building with a rope until the inevitable arrival of a policeman.

"Someone will die," he concluded, without saying who. I noted that he had turned over his drawing of his own accord while I had gone out of the room to fetch his mother. He had explained to me beforehand that his mother would be less worried by his graphic productions. The father was in Africa for the "holidays". Mrs H. confirmed that her son was doing better from all points of view. The question of psychotherapy thus passed into the background. She said that the meetings she had had with the social worker, before the summer, were important. She wanted to make another appointment. The evolution, the rhythm of their meetings showed, in fact, that she was the one who made the decisions. I suggested we meet again to speak about Georges after the beginning of the next school year, unless a problem cropped up in the meantime, which turned out not to be the case.

I saw them again in October. Georges was almost nine. The father was absent again for reasons connected with work, a delay in the reception of his mail due to their recent move having prevented him from being able to organise himself. There is not a lot to say about this consultation. Georges spoke a bit more easily and told me that he was fine. Our exchange thus proved to be rather ordinary, his responses always being brief. He had grown up, seemed quite relaxed, and when I asked him if he thought his mother would also be happy, he smiled broadly with satisfaction. I did not get him to draw that day. Mrs H. was indeed happy with her son's progress, which made him smile again. We were thus quite a long way away from the project of psychotherapy that had been proposed. A certain ego-syntonisation had occurred, without any profound structural modification. The indication of psychotherapy seems to have provoked a crisis and allowed for a certain evolution, at the same time as the child saw himself being oriented towards a special needs class. It was in the context of this consultation that Mrs H. asked me if I could see her sister, who was 26 years old, the youngest child of the biological father. Her mother had been pregnant for several months when the latter died. Mrs H. absolutely wanted me to be her sister's consultant.

Shouting and resumption of the psychotherapeutic project

Not long after the consultation, Mrs H. failed to turn up for the planned appointment with the social worker. She had a bout of 'flu and said that she would make contact again later [which was at the end of November] via Georges' school teacher. In fact, Georges had since changed school because his parents had moved and, although he was still in a special needs class, this meant that he no longer saw his psycho-motor therapist, after having worked with her for three years, a relationship that certainly had had therapeutic value. Georges thus seemed to be quite well, except that he would sometimes start shouting in class when he felt vexed about something. Remarkably enough, however, it was he himself who had spoken about his psycho-motor therapist to his school teacher, saying that he missed her. This was what had led Mrs H. to make another appointment with the social worker. Once they were back in contact again, Mrs H. continued the same kind of meetings as before the summer. The ninth consultation took place in December of the same year. Georges was now nine. It was aimed above all at evaluating the "child's indirect demand" (the shouting in class), which he confirmed when I told him what had been communicated to me. As always, this confirmation was expressed in a minimum of words. I suggested that he did some drawing. The richness of the scenario he depicted maintained a process that we have already seen in the previous consultations.

What was interesting was that we could from thereon work at the level of the *processes of symbolisation*. Georges drew an ocean liner. No characters had been portrayed as yet, even though the anchor had just been dropped. He drew a car instead. When I drew his attention to this *displacement through contiguity*, he reinforced it by introducing a second car, then a lorry. I pointed out the *repetition*. He then drew a little green line on one of the cars. I said to him: "No people, but a little green line." Georges then drew his first man . . . in green, whom he then partly covered over . . . in black, with a "bit" in the same colour, along one of his arms. "It's because the garment is torn," he said, introducing a second person on the deck of the liner. The latter had, he said, fired with a "bow-gun", which explained why the first character's clothing was torn. I offered him the following *symbolic interpretation*: the man was shot at because he was looking at the anchor that he had thrown into the sea. Georges confirmed this but, above all, as if to index[5] the interpretation, he introduced a third character, using another felt pen, blue, for the sea. Finally, he drew the captain of the boat, who was going to tell the coast guard to arrest the bandit who had fired the gun.

Thus the evolution became clearer within the context of a mode of mental functioning that was now quite familiar. The quality of instinctual drive expression had been enriched thanks to its increase in small quantities, the activation of symbolisation, and the appearance of triangulation. Mrs H. seemed quite satisfied with Georges' progress, except, of course, for her son's shouting in class, which worried her, and which seemed to happen, she thought, mainly when he wanted to succeed. This brought us back again to the question of psychotherapy. She accepted the idea in principle, this time apparently without difficulty. She added that though her husband was not there due to his work, although it was a bit more complicated than that, he would have absolutely no objections to such a project. However, the child could not begin his psychotherapy immediately because there was no place available. I suggested that, in the meantime, we should continue the consultations. Two absences followed . . . In one case they had apparently not received a letter, and in the other they had forgotten. However, Mrs H. had made contact again with the social worker. The consultation followed not long after. She told her about her son's reaction to the fact that they had forgotten the second appointment. "It's a pity," he had said. The social worker had the impression that Mrs H. still took a certain pleasure in speaking with her, but clearly wanted to be the one who initiated these contacts with her.

The ordeal of fire

Georges was nine-and-a-half years old when I saw him again. I was struck by the effort he was making to recall the content of the last consultation. This effort of remembering, moreover, did not lead anywhere. He tried to master this helplessness by telling me that he had some thoughts, but that he did not want to communicate them to me. That was understandable. He did not know what would happen if he did. He accepted with relief the suggestion that he did some drawing, which helped to re-establish continuity. He drew *the sea*; the driver of a motor boat was pulling a water skier behind him. This peaceful scene changed rapidly as a helicopter appeared with a killer on board. The boat capsized . . . and Georges had more and more difficulty ending his sentences commenting on the action. I suggested that this blockage was a way of confirming his indirect "demand", and I spoke to him again about the indication of psychotherapy which we had already talked about together. He agreed with the idea.

His mother was still satisfied with the progress he was making, but as soon as I spoke about her son's "blockage", she said that she would like him to be in therapy here. She was clearly trying to liken this therapy to the one that her eldest daughter was having with a speech therapist of our team. I took up again my remarks about Georges, about his imagination and how powerful it was. Mrs H. was moved once again and reacted by saying that she agreed to resume our work again. When I asked her, in a register that referred to identifications, about Georges' "reserve", if he was more like his father or more like her, she replied: "Like *my* father", which was a real slip of the tongue on her part.

It was possible in principle for the psychotherapy to begin towards the end of the first trimester. The reality, however, became an ordeal of fire, for when the social worker met with Mrs H. to speak about this possibility, she noticed that she was not ready. Mrs H. said that the school psychologist to whom she had spoken about the psychotherapy had told her that Georges did not need psychoanalysis but rather pedagogical support. Mrs H. then went as far as to say to the social worker that if one let Georges say everything that crossed his mind, he would regress and all the progress that had been made would be lost. And especially as the school psychologist had apparently told her that Georges could now rejoin the normal school cycle. Mrs H. began to cry. So we suspended this project until the next consultation.

Psychotherapy as a risk of madness

It took place when Georges was ten years old. I went over the reasons for this consultation with him. After making me wait as usual, he replied that nothing had been said between his parents and him on the subject of his psychotherapy and confirmed with a firm "yes" that he was still ready to do it. It is interesting to note that, as in the consultation when Mrs H. had been confronted with her son's fantasies, the father was present this time. When we came to the crucial problem, Mrs H. soon expressed her concerns, the greatest of which was her fear that there was a *risk of madness* if her son began such a treatment, in the sense that all the progress made would be called into question again.

The father asked me what had led me to indicate such a treatment. He tried to remain on the level of "technical objectivity". He wanted to think things over before giving his answer. About two months later, Mrs H. telephoned the social worker to give her agreement. But as soon as she had done this, she added that they were not sure that they would be able to stay where they were currently living. They had changed their council housing accommodation by coming to an agreement directly with a neighbour who was leaving France, without following the necessary administrative procedures. After such a process lasting nearly six years, one is tempted to make an evaluation of it according to the principle of the half-empty bottle, as the psychotherapy had never been realised, or of the half-full bottle, since the child had undeniably made progress. What both includes and goes beyond these two readings is the understanding of the complex destiny that resulted from introducing into our exchanges the *particular object* represented by psychoanalytic psychotherapy, a destiny that reached its culminating point when the mother began to imagine that a risk of madness could disorganise all the progress made hitherto.

This process had been punctuated by a number of dynamic moments involving both the child and his parents. The first high point was the mother/son encounter around the latter's fantasy productions in the presence of the third party that I represented. It was what had led Mrs H. to go and speak to her son's teacher; it had also resulted in the father coming to the next consultation.

This development was confirmation for me of Georges' function as an incestuous child, in association with the mother's unconscious. Following this development, Georges portrayed the first maternal symbolisations in his drawings, and Mrs H. expressed her concerns about the "instinctual" prognosis of her son. The indication of psychotherapy, which had been discussed with the parents, was gradually put on hold owing to the child's progress at school. The second phase, which called this equilibrium into question, even though it was planned that Georges would reintegrate with the traditional school curriculum, was determined by the child's shouting in class. It was a real alarm signal for the mother which could not fail to mobilise her.

Now this shouting was clearly linked, in Georges, to the loss of his psycho-motor therapist, who had worked with him for three years. During this time, noticeable progress occurred in the sense that the expressions of his mental functioning became more refined with, in particular, the appearance of capacities for symbolisation and triangulation that were more adapted to the period of latency in which he found himself. The indication of psychotherapy was therefore reconsidered, and apparently accepted by the parents. Having to wait for a place to become available played a part in the discontinuity that followed. We were led to redefine the principle of the treatment, which in turn led to the reappearance of the mother's anxiety once a place had become available for her son. The father then came, as had already happened once before when Mrs H. had expressed her concerns about one of Georges' drawings, which strengthened her belief that psychoanalysis risked making Georges mad.

The latest announcement of the 'Arlesienne' was that this time the psychotherapy could begin, but there was a possible and serious risk of a house move. Such a trajectory is not linked to the African identity of this family, for it can be found in families from the Norman bocage, among others. In this sense, Georges' function as the "night baby" (Braunschweig and Fain, 1975), and its unconscious incestuous connotation, is a universal referent of the unconscious. It is its translation, its secondary elaboration, based on cultural facts, that finds its African expression here. On the side of the paternal image, there was the dead father, the paternal uncle, thus the father's brother. On the side of the maternal image, there was the mother, who, according to Mrs H., had loved her, (moreover her brothers and sisters definitely made her feel this), especially as she had been "ill" and "very sweet". This was a mother she had thought about "every minute" on arriving in France, when she was pregnant, not to mention what remained unsaid about the other wives of paternal referents.

At another level there is the problem of communicating factual information that may throw light on certain forms of behaviour, information that is bound up with traditional rites. Thus, the absence of the father at a consultation on account of holidays in the middle of the school year could only be understood over the course of time. This father was supposed to go alone to Africa but had delayed his trip because one of his brothers had decided to do the same thing. Now, traditionally, we were told, two brothers cannot be welcomed together in their family when they are coming from abroad. As Mr H. was not the priority, he had to put off his trip. The death in the family of a significant person, owing to the importance of the accompanying rituals, was often revealed to us rather late in the day. This means that a parent who is going through a process of bereavement but says nothing about it to avoid revealing certain rituals in front of a foreigner, pushes the consultant towards zones of incompetence, while he/she tries to manage his/her sense of being at a loss or in the dark by means of various rationalisations. It is thus through work that is very demanding in terms of time, often marked by periods of discontinuity, that the *universal determinants of the unconscious* and their *secondary elaboration by culture* can gradually be linked up, while neither of these two registers should have a function that excludes the other. It is the hiatuses between these two registers which, far from needing to be interpreted negatively, should be a sign that the work remains open.

A tentacular heart: on repetition in therapeutic consultations[6]

We know that Freud's essential text on the compulsion to repeat is *Beyond the Pleasure Principle* (Freud, 1920g). "Remembering, Repeating, and Working-Through" (Freud 1914g) ascribes the compulsion to repeat to the repressed unconscious. In the first text, Freud points out that this compulsion to repeat reproduces experiences from the past which include *no* possibility of pleasure. He adds that these experiences, "can never, even long ago, have brought satisfaction, even to instinctual impulses which have since been repressed" (p. 20). This means that these impulses did not suffice at all to transform the situation.

We are thus faced with two forms of repetition: that of the article of 1914, where the repressed is acted out and where the pleasure principle still functions, including in the sense that what is unpleasure for one psychical agency is pleasure for another; and that of 1920, present in traumatic neurosis and in the wooden-reel game, which leads Freud to say that what characterises this form as "more primitive, more elementary, more instinctual than the pleasure principle which it over-rides" (ibid., p. 23), has the function of *dominating excitation*, including sexual co-excitation. This domination of excitation is achieved by psychic binding in the sense that the stimulus barrier has been breached, either by the force of a traumatic experience or by its premature nature in relation to a protective barrier that has not yet had time to establish itself sufficiently.

Freud's approach, which he himself describes as speculative in *Beyond the Pleasure Principle* (p. 36), poses the question of the nature of the relationship between instinctual drive activity and the compulsion to repeat. He initially puts forward the idea that repetition is a general characteristic of the drives (the "instinct of the instinct" according to Francis Pasche (1965, p. 87)), then emphasises what forms part of the definition of the instinctual drive, namely, that it seems to be "an urge inherent in organic life to restore an earlier state of things which the living entity has been obliged to abandon under the pressure of external disturbing forces" (ibid., p. 36). We are familiar with what followed. The introduction of the death drive gave rise to a second reorganisation of the theory of the drives, after the first relating to the introduction of narcissism (Freud, 1914c). Though Freud notes that it is the characteristic of the compulsion to repeat that first put us "on the track" of the death instinct, it is still true that his hypotheses, according to which the aim of the instincts consists in restoring an earlier state, concerns all the instincts, and consequently also the sexual instincts.

Freud then goes on to speculate on the opposition between body cells, linked to the ego-instincts and germ-cells, linked to the sexual instincts. With regard to the latter, he refers to the myth of the Banquet, where it is indicated that the earlier state to be restored is that which is known as "androgenous", where the two halves of man are reunited after being separated by sexuation. It is worth noting that an author such as Robert Barande (cited by Hollande and Soule, 1970, p. 90) confirms to some extent this point of view by considering that the compulsion to repeat can only, starting from the lost unity, be related to incest. This is an example, among others in the psychoanalytic community, of those, who, when confronted with clinical experience, do not resort at all, or at least as late as possible, to the death drive in order to theorise what unfolds in this clinical context. Michel Neyraut, for example, insists that it is necessary to reject the idea that the death instinct can have an immediate interpretive value. Whatever the essential interest of this notion may be in the speculative and deductive approach of Freud, this "logical tour de force", as Frank Sulloway (1979, p. 390) rightly defined it, remains in the background of what is mobilised between a psychoanalyst and his adult or child patient in the dialectic between repetition and change.

From this point of view, and once again in *Beyond the Pleasure Principle*, having said that the existence of an *instinct of development* does not exist, Freud emphasises that all progress, all development comes from the *outside*, an outside we have already referred to in connection with the genesis of the instinctual drive. Such a position is coherent with contemporary science which is interested in unstable and *open* systems with complex organisations, where randomness plays a great role. As far as we are concerned, the "outside", for a patient, is represented by the psychoanalyst with his/her particular mode of functioning. Authors as different as Herman Nunberg, René Diatkine, and Serge Vidermann place the accent on what is *new* in an analytic treatment, as a precondition of change, compared with what is repeated from the past. But what is *new*, a potential source of the unknown, will itself be the seat of processes of repetition in the sense that the two forms of repetition to which I have referred meet and link up with each other, even though their relations had appeared to be mutually exclusive. In other words, the encounter with the analyst, with his/her interventions and interpretations, creates the conditions of a relationship of elaboration, this time between repetition of the repressed and repetition of the traumatic, or alternatively between repetition of the same and repetition of the identical, to take up the formulation of Michel de M'Uzan (1969).

This elaboration will also be subject to repetition due to the transference, and more particularly to the repetitive part of the transference as a "safeguard for the subject", as René Diatkine puts it, a safeguard against an opening towards the unknown that is too abrupt or too traumatic. It is through this repeated dialectalisation that repetition enters into the effect of meaning, into the effect of linking that Neyraut (1988) draws attention to when he notes that repetition is not only a standing-still of meaning. What would we be without it, he adds, given that it is not just a repetition of *negativity*. When we think about a clinical experience which demonstrates repetition, it is as if we are led irresistibly to evoke patients who repeat untiringly the identical of the negative, thereby putting their analyst to the test.

I will now look at a different situation concerning a boy whom I saw in three stages, a child who, in a certain way, repeated the "positive". Olivier repeated with absolutely anyone, known or known, a behaviour of proximity including kissing, a behaviour of familiarity that can be found in certain children who are particularly hypomanic, but probably closer to the allergic object-relationship described by the psychosomaticians, with the difference that this child had not, to the best of my knowledge, had any somatic disorder of this kind. In any case, Olivier, a charming and likeable child, exuded a particular power of seduction, except that those who were faced with it quite quickly experienced it as being "too much".

Olivier had just turned six when I met him for the first time. He was the only child of a couple who ran a small business in the provinces, and his early childhood had unfolded in a rather agitated atmosphere. The difficulties of the business had played a part in the tension in the household. His mother, who was rather inexperienced, had provoked bouts of serious vomiting by giving him poorly dosed bottle feeds, which led to an intervention by the social services as a result of which the child was placed in a nursery. The father, who was quite likeable but also violent during alcoholic episodes, went to fetch his son from the nursery on Christmas Day because "they" did not want to let him take care of his son, even on that day. He burst in, making threats with a gun, in reality an alarm gun, and took his son away with him.

He had to spend some time in a psychiatric hospital as a result, while the care of the child was entrusted to a paternal aunt and her husband. The evolution of this situation was such that Olivier was able to return to his parents' home, this time in Paris, just a few months before I met the family. Until then, Olivier had seen his parents regularly during holiday periods. Beyond the immediate contact that I had with the child, it turned out that Olivier had speech disorders, a speech delay, but also an obvious pleasure in communicating, even if it was in a particular way, as we shall see. He told me right away about the letters of the alphabet he was learning to write at school; spontaneously, he wrote a few down and spoke about his teacher using her name. She was the first person he had mentioned in front of me, and immediately after Olivier switched to the logic of the primary process. "There is no school any more", he said to me.

In fact, as the logic of the secondary process gained the upper hand, Olivier showed me that he had "wanted" to tell me that there was no longer a school for him in the town of his uncle and aunt with whom had been living only a short time ago. We can appreciate the effect on his mental functioning of this family bi-partition. I then asked him if he would like to draw. He began by drawing a building and then coloured in four different ways the closed curtains of one of the windows of the building. To the idea of "inside", which I suggested to him in the form of a question, Olivier replied by saying "outside". In effect, the child drew two characters *outside* the building, whom he described as a man and a woman holding hands. These characters were in fact symmetrical in their feminine appearance. Olivier then moved closer to me to show me the Mickey Mouse that was printed on his tee shirt. This movement was complex due to the transference connotation that it implied, though it promoted it at the same time. Olivier "prohibited himself" from portraying male/female closeness, transforming it instead into a symmetrical female/female closeness; then, he turned towards me in a seductive manner signifying that we were "among men". This bi-partition was itself split in two. I said to him: "When you drew the man and the woman holding hands, I think you said to yourself, 'It's not possible!' So now we have two women holding hands!" Olivier laughed and picked up his felt pen again to draw, using a "verticalised symbolism", in contrast to the earlier symmetries, a sun, and then, at the bottom of the sheet of paper, a car which he immediately made me the owner of.

This brief sequence already illustrates the essential aspects of the theoretical points I was making earlier. Olivier's compulsion for contact without any appropriate distance shows us that it is underpinned by the negation of difference, beginning with the difference between the sexes represented in the drawing; and further that this difference is all the more difficult to mentalise in that it is infiltrated by the difference between the parents, and between the uncle and the aunt. We find ourselves faced with the seat of the traumatic factor. The conflictual instinctual potentiality that is expressed in difference can only be denied; the child has no choice but to remain repeatedly a nice boy with restricted psychic space, while distance and difference have no right of place. The boy then met an analyst who gave him quite an ordinary interpretation, reflecting the logic that he had deployed, which, from the child's point of view, was a rather new form of language.

This was enough to transform the situation for a moment symbolically. Olivier drew a sun, and then a car, which he said was mine. We had thus rediscovered a situation of proximity, but at the same time a symbolic level of expression which showed that triangulation was working. This was confirmed, moreover, before we separated. Symbolic continuity was maintained, and Olivier drew a pneumatic drill lying on the ground in the street. But he could not think of the name of this tool. Faced with what did not work at the level of the *code*, the child returned to the *body*. Indeed, he said: "It's lost." He was thus condensing both the situation of the drill and his inner state of searching for the name of this tool: he was just as "lost" as the pneumatic drill. Then, putting his hand on his nose, he mimed a big nose to express what he wanted to say to me. With the mother, who was alone that day, my work consisted in making her more aware of this aspect of her son's *functioning*, which was an expression of a certain obligation he felt to be very nice with everyone. She listened to me attentively, somewhat perplexed, then she had a thought which had a rather spectacular associative value.

She said that she felt that her husband was attached to her more as a mother than as a woman. Olivier's psychological and speech therapy assessments confirmed, independently of the "instrumental"[7] problems, the particularity of his mental functioning. It is worth noting, for example, apart from his desire for immediate contact that we are already familiar with, the fact that on one occasion he spontaneously went up to the psychologist and said to her: "It was good with the other man." On another occasion, when faced with an image implying the difference between the sexes, he said: "A little boy or a little girl . . . *I don't have any*." You will recall his words, "There is no school any more" in connection with the problem of being and having. When I saw Olivier again, following his assessments, after giving a kiss to each person present, he came towards me to speak about the the fact that his father was in hospital. He was undergoing an addiction treatment, and was also being followed regularly in psychotherapeutically-oriented sessions. There is not much to say about this consultation except that, after giving me this information, he made a portrait of me with a concern for detail that I had noticed before.

This direct involvement of my person, which was repeated and amplified, left no space for any story that the child might have imagined. With regard to the interview with his mother, two things are worth noting. First, when I reminded her of what we had spoken about the last time, she told me that her son's behaviour had deteriorated again after this consultation and since his father's hospitalisation, whereas she had thought that her son's behaviour was going to improve. But at the same time she was able to express the contradiction that she was experiencing. By saying to me, "You are going to think that what I'm about to say is not very nice for you", she was telling me that she had noticed that Olivier had been actively helping his mother with the housework (if she "needed" to tell me this, in a movement of projection, it was because she thought I was probably thinking that she was "feminising her son"). She understood that it had something to do with the father's absence.

I stayed with her at this level, for there was no question for the moment of showing her the personal satisfaction that she derived from this. After this consultation, it was decided that Olivier should see a speech therapist, as the mediation implied by this work seemed more adequate, given the functioning of the parents, than psychotherapy or analysis. Let me sum up how things had evolved prior to the consultation I am going to talk about. Olivier was clearly making progress at the level of speech, but his speech therapist was increasingly concerned by the poor quality of his imagination during the sessions. At the same time, his reading ability had reached its limit at the level of linking together the syllables making up words and phrases so that they make sense. When I saw him, he clearly remembered my office and immediately mentioned the drawing of my portrait that he had done a few months before. He gave quite a detailed description of it from the memory he still had of it. I was thus "at the heart" of the subject. For Olivier, there was no question of speaking about anything else but me. He came back to it again when I suggested he did another drawing. In short, I was surrounded by this overwhelming "love", another term that came to my mind retrospectively, like that of the heart already mentioned.

However, in the few spaces that opened up briefly between him and me, the child told me that he had nightmares, though he was unable to say anything about them. Then, after he had told me a detail about his daily life, he was caught up in an expiratory movement of exhaustion and came back to me by asking a question, either implicating me directly or indirectly through his drawing of my portrait. "Choosing" a middle road, I asked him to imagine what had become of this drawing. Olivier replied that it was behind the drawing board; then, having seen that this was not the case, he imagined that I had it at home, along with the drawings of other children, of which my house must be filled. I intervened countertransferentially, for I needed as it were to "free myself", by saying to Olivier that he could not help thinking about me when imagining something, and I added this somewhat special formulation: "Try to imagine something *of your own* now", an intervention made in a tone of voice that accompanied this suggestion. A transformation now took place that was commensurate with that of the first consultation, but which went *even further*. Olivier drew the moon, then a house, and finally a male character, which he said was himself. He corrected himself immediately, saying that it was the man to whom this house belonged. I pointed out to him in a light-hearted tone that it was a repetition. He continued with the drawing. This character had big feet. He then made a further enlargement involving the little heart portrayed as a figurative element on the door of the house. It had now become an enormous heart covering the entire façade of the house.

Oliver's imagination had become particularly productive, for this heart became anthropomorphic with the features of a face, legs and arms which surrounded the house in a *tentacular* manner. This heart was "nasty", the child said, when I asked him what was going on. And for the first time a fight took place, in this case between the heart and the character with the big feet. Olivier drew a pair of boxing gloves for him and, as with the pneumatic drill in the first consultation, he could not find the word, which suggested that this process was not unrelated to the limit reached in his language development, especially where writing was concerned. "I can't remember it", the child said to me. I told him the word and added that I was now better able to understand why he could not let himself go when imagining things; if he did so, it would only be about fights which were at once a source of pleasure and fear. When I brought the parents in, Olivier, who was hiding behind the door, emerged suddenly pretending to shoot with a revolver in his hand, like his father's alarm pistol. On that day, the day of the consultation, Olivier took part in a group that included two people invited by his therapist, who created books for children, and he had found this very interesting. Was it the conjunction of these two types of encounter?

In any case, it was from that moment on that the child *began reading without difficulty*. To conclude, I will make just a few more remarks. I wanted to illustrate certain problems raised concerning the factors of repetition and change in a situation that is sufficiently illustrative to show that even at the level of the therapeutic consultations, during the time before an eventual psychotherapy or analysis, these modes of functioning can *already* be mobilised. We have seen that, to bring about change, it was necessary to "enter into" repetition. I mean that it was necessary during the process of the consultations for me to let myself be increasingly confined by Olivier's negation of any distance in relation to me, with everything that this implied at different levels, including the countertransference level. This served as a springboard for the transformation that followed, whose path had already been indicated in the first consultation.

Olivier portrayed very precisely what was at stake, and more exactly what *could become play*, as can be seen from his emergence from behind the door with a revolver in his hand following his drawing. It was thanks to the various transferences and games that the repetition became plural. From thereon, the path was opened up towards symbolisation, the repetition of the identical being replaced by the compulsion to symbolise, as de M'Uzan (1969, p. 10, citing Groddeck, 1969, p. 274) calls it. When Olivier gained access to symbolisation at the figurative level, *he lacked words*, those of phallic symbolism (the pneumatic drill, the boxing gloves), which meant that he also lacked the process of hypercathexis by word-presentations specific to the preconscious, which would have brought the movement of symbolisation that was underway to its conclusion. However, the system remained open to the "outside", to take up again the words used at the beginning of this paper. Triangular replication took place, since Olivier, by noticing his helplessness in connection with the words "pneumatic drill" or "boxing gloves", had considered me as *the holder of the code*. As long as the word had not been given to him, attraction by the body, as a last resort in his relationship with me, manifested itself, as, for example, when he mimed the pneumatic drill with his nose.

If the Greeks place at the origins of life a series of solitary begettings such as a Chaos begetting Night, who, by himself, in turn begets Hypnos and his brother Thanatos, Repetition does not have such a status in Greek mythology. However, if we turn towards Sisyphus, a great grandson of Deucalion, the Greek Noah, everyone will agree that we find ourselves faced with a model of the repetition of the identical. Sisyphus is condemned to pushing his boulder for eternity up a hill, only to see it rolling back down again from the top each time, so that the hero has to begin his task all over again.

What "crime" had brought about such a punishment? According to one version of the myth, it was because he had betrayed Zeus by revealing the whereabouts of Aegina, the daughter of the river god Asopos, whom Zeus had seduced. Who was it that Zeus sent as a first punishment? Thanatos, precisely, who is less abstract here because he was tied up by the crafty Sisyphus (one version of the myth makes Sisyphus the father of Ulysses, a cunning hero par excellence). In this way Sisyphus managed to postpone the punishment of rolling the boulder eternally. It was into this rapprochement between Death and Repetition that Cunning or Craft inserted itself, thereby creating a detour (*Umweg*), as the Freud of the life drives notes. It is this detour that we psychoanalysts, who come from the "outside", try to enrich with our *technè* in order to transform repetition in such a way as to increase the gap between Thanatos and the most automatic features of repetition.

Concerning the notion of reparation[8]

The model and the limit of the standard analytic treatment can be represented, to paraphrase Braunschweig and Fain (1975), by the situation in which the patient only needs the analytic protocol in order to associate. In short, ideally, the patient would need nothing other than such a setting, which would not even need to be protected, unless an external breach were to call it into question. The only requirement made of the psychoanalyst would thus be not to break the thread of the analytic discourse. And yet, even in these conditions, close to the model, an excess of benevolence with regard to the famous notion of benevolent neutrality, an excess of presence, cannot fail to work in opposition to the perception of lack which stimulates associations and representations. But it is this excess of presence that threatens each one of us in difficult situations. From the excess of benevolence to the notion of *reparation* there is then only a small step to be taken.

Freud did not particularly use this notion, which is no doubt not unrelated to the fact that he did not dwell on the question of the inter-cathexes between parents and children, even if the role of the external object is clearly present at different moments in his work. It was above all with Melanie Klein that this notion flourished. It is interesting to note, moreover, that one of the first terms that she employed is one that may be translated into French as *restauration or rétablissement* (*Wiederherstellung*), a term that Freud himself used in 1920 in *Beyond the Pleasure Principle*. He used it in connection with the drive, which *restores* or *re-establishes* an earlier state. But here it was a question of the death drive, which should make us a bit suspicious about what can lead to the notion of reparation. Be that as it may, Klein was to link this notion to the consequences of early infantile sadism, when the child reaches the depressive position between the ages of 3 and 6 months. The defence against depression, linked to destructive impulses towards the object, which, for Klein are present in the mind from the outset, involves a desire for reparation, with the help of manic defences, such as *magic reparation*. The excessive nature of the latter can obstruct "true" reparation which is linked to the emerging sense of guilt and participates in the possession of a good object, which strengthens and structures the ego.

Thus, in Klein's work, love and reparation, which are henceforth linked, stand in an antagonistic relation to the destructive impulses. For her, even *sublimation* and *symbolisation* have their role in this work of reparation. For Klein, the utilisation of symbols serves to express the conflicts between love and hate, between destruction and reparation. Sublimation, which makes the object beautiful, participates in reparation of destruction. We can refer here to Lacan, for whom *the beautiful* and *the good* make a sign to destruction. The central role that Klein attributes to reparation is univocal in relation to the destructive impulses. This is the reason, moreover, why she identifies this dynamic, not only in all work of mourning, but also in obsessional mechanisms and their compulsive nature, as well as in reaction formations.

With Winnicott, the notion opens out on to the active involvement of the other, and principally the mother. If, for example, what he calls the period of making use of the object is not unrelated to Klein's depressive position, what is specific to Winnicott is that he drew attention to the importance of the baby being able to see that its mother mentally survives its (pre)fantasised and/or enacted attacks. This is what Bion would formulate as the mother's capacity for reverie in her containing function and in the dialectic between beta and alpha elements. But what Winnicott identifies as reparation is what the patient formulates as guilt, which results from an identification with the mother's unconscious guilt. This stems from the mother's organised defence against her own depression.

In this connection, it is important to recall Freud's famous footnote in the last chapter of *The Ego and the Id* (1923b) concerning the sense of guilt that is "borrowed" through "identification with some other person who was once the object of an erotic cathexis" (p. 50). In analogy with the model of the child "full of liveliness and colour" responding in this way to the mother's defence against depression, Winnicott suggests the possibility that a comparable process occurs in analysis itself. He was referring to those patients who produce *what the analyst likes to receive*, and in whom the process is all the more true in that his or her expectation is unconscious. In short, the patient repairs the analyst, protects his/her person, while the latter loses his/her function as guardian of the setting, etc. This field was extended by other authors to everything that is mobilised in the transference/counter-transference dynamic.

The analyst thus finds him/herself the bearer of "the effort to drive the other person crazy" (Searles, 1959), or assigned to an excessive position of "violence of interpretation" (Aulagnier, 1975). If I have wanted to place emphasis on the question of the notion of reparation, it is because it is needed in the situations with which we are confronted, and particularly those where traumatic aspects dominate. The more these are in the foreground, the more those with the task of intervening may be led to take steps to separate the child from his or her parents as a "measure of reparation". Now we know that one measure, more specifically, "placement", can *in certain cases* be indicated, but that it will only have any meaning if the parents are involved; and particularly as there is a gap between the way in which a child protects his or her psychic activity and the traumatic experiences he or she suffers.

This gap is increased by the responses of the parents or therapists, due to the counter-attitudes they may have towards the traumatic experience. When I speak of protecting the psychic activity of the child, I mean his or her represented drive activity, even if only proto-represented. To add greater complexity to our subject, we can see that after envisaging the protection of the analyst's functioning, we are now considering the protection of the child's functioning by the child himself. In this sense, beyond the question of reparation – the child repairing the adult at a deeply unconscious dynamic level – it should be recalled that, whatever a child has suffered from a traumatic point of view, he or she has nonetheless been able, with support, to reach us. The problems begin for the consultant once this encounter has taken place because he/she is "caught" up in the repetition of the wounds and post-traumatic narcissistic weaknesses. This repetition tends to impede the emergence of any form of instinctual drive expression.

The issue for the therapist is nonetheless to preserve/protect his/her capacity to be open to the instinctual emergence of the child, *otherwise the reparative "good intentions" will be very much in danger of "paving the way for the hell" that will follow.* The situation can, moreover, be subtly reversed, as in Winnicott's apparently paradisiacal example, *contrary* to the hell to which I have just referred, where the lively and animated child responds to the unconscious expectation of the analyst. It is time to note that both Klein and Winnicott put the accent on the destructive impulses, which skips over or leaves in the shadows the evolution of the erotic impulses, whereas Freud, concerning the "borrowed" sense of guilt, clearly notes the necessity of a prior erotic cathexis of the object of identification. Paraphrasing Winnicott, we could say that the vicissitudes of erotic life do not need to be taken into consideration as long as the narcissistic foundations (the Self) have not been sufficiently constituted, for such vicissitudes can only serve to stir up excitation.

Owing to the existence of the unconscious, of infantile sexuality, and of child/adult asymmetry, the child/adult inter-cathexes necessarily mobilise, in the adult at least, erotic instinctual impulses. It is certainly to be hoped that these impulses will be counter-cathected but not denied. The necessity of these counter-cathexes in no way impedes dynamic functioning. They are inseparable, moreover, from all triangulation. The counter-cathecting activity of the adult, both towards the child's impulses and towards his or her own, can help the child to pass over from discharge to the activity of representation and symbolisation, an activity that is sustained by erotic life. In this sense, we could say that *if there is something that "repairs" the mind, it is the elaboration of the instinctual drives.* It is narcissising, in the sense given by Green (1983) to positive narcissism. It is not necessary to be a psychoanalyst to evoke counter-cathecting activity in the relationship with the child.

Therapists who are not psychoanalysts, those who practise mediation therapies (speech therapists, psycho-motor therapists), know this well. On the other hand, failures of this activity, when they are repeated, call for reflection, and this must be supported by psychoanalysts. Recalling the fundamental role of the erotic impulses does not consist in putting oneself in a symmetrical position to that of Klein or Winnicott who, for their part, give priority to the destructive impulses. As the two major groups of the drives are both fundamental and asymmetrical, linking, the activity of binding, occurs through the erotic impulses, including its psychic expression of narcissistic libido. Thus Winnicott's perspective, placing the self first, suggests a genetic point of view. When the discharge of excitation mobilises the destructive drives, even in their form of "fundamental violence" (Bergeret, 1993), both drive qualities require the sexual co-excitation that participates in the work of drive elaboration. In short, every therapist can find himself enacting a form of behaviour which tends to place him in the position of an ideally good mother repairing the initial damage. The therapist puts himself in the position of an *"ego-psychologist"* who considers (unconsciously as well) that everything refers to him.

It is worth noting in passing that that certain Kleinian interpretations do not escape this risk, being more psychotherapeutic than psychoanalytic. M'Uzan (1994) makes a distinction between Kleinian tactics and Freudian strategy, a ternary strategy of interpretation. Likewise, Winnicott, in a polemical context with the Kleinians, asserted that the phantasies underlying Kleinian interpretations existed more in the psychoanalyst's head than in the child's. In any case, for "ego-psychologists", a position that may threaten every analyst at the level of his/her countertransference, there is no lack, there is no thirdness (Green, 1990). Apart from on the symbolic level, this dimension is somewhat absent in Klein and Winnicott's work. In such a configuration, the analyst is in danger of repairing his own narcissism by repeating the problems of the parents. He may find himself in the situation of being an actor of "the demon of the good and of the misfortunes of virtue" (Braunschweig and Fain, 1974).

These authors note that, faced with situations where there is a failure of primary counter-cathexes, the only means of reinforcing them consists in "interpreting the hysterical identifications corresponding to unconscious desire of the other for the missing third" (ibid., p. 173). Admittedly, here we are in an analytic situation. But such a model is operative in every clinical situation as long as its potentiality is preserved in the functioning of the therapist. As a model, it protects the totalising function of the ego. Braunschweig and Fain write: ". . . the restriction of the limits of the analyzability of a given subject will depend on the scope of the mental transgressions of his/her mother in the domain of her homosexual relationship with her own mother . . ." (ibid., p. 170). They are speaking here, naturally, about unconscious homosexuality. They add that, at worst, *"the child of a mother whose latent homosexuality exceeds the usual limits is in danger of psychosis"* (ibid., my italics) Now, working with difficult cases exposes us particularly to this type of situation. These mothers preserve their homosexuality unconsciously, whether through idealisation of their own mother or, on the contrary, through disappointment that is preserved *masochistically*. The extremely ambivalent cathexes that are mobilised push into the background those concerning the father of these mothers, who often confirms in reality that he has distanced himself psychically and abandoned his role as father. These problems, which every analyst is familiar with in the case of certain analyses, are particularly accentuated when one is dealing with difficult cases. In effect, in such situations, where many different professional workers have a role to play, there is a lot of "noise". This aspect of *quantity* is represented by the accumulation of the phenomenal, of factuality, of acting out, including in our own reports. All this noise, in Henri Atlan's (1972) sense (Atlan emphasises the constructive side of noise, but he points out clearly that if there is "too much", the negative side prevails, and this is the sense I am referring to here), results in maintaining the mother's underlying homosexuality and of impeding any emergence of thirdness, of reducing to silence the function of the oedipal attractor, of making a mutative emergence disappear from memory. It is the longitudinal approach of the present study, and reflection that is often taken up again retrospectively, that make it possible, in the best cases, for the signifiers of thirdness, beginning with the paternal signifiers, to be gradually identified, remembered, approximated, deployed and thus preserved. Paraphrasing Prigogine and Stengers (1979) and Francisco Varela (1989) we can say that everything begins with the organisation of the initial conditions of this emergence.

Notes

1 This section takes up again the paper, "Régression, repli", presented in the context of the "Thursday Lectures of the Paris Psychoanalytic Society", 13 October 2004 (Ody, 2004).
2 Reseau d'aides spécialisées aux élèves en difficulté (Provision of special needs for pupils in difficulty).
3 This section takes up the article "Migration d'un projet thérapeutique", initially published in *Les Textes du Centre Alfred Binet*, 16/17, Paris, ASM 13, 1990, pp. 29–42. Reproduced here with the kind permission of the Alfred Binet Centre.
4 Translator's note: term derived from Alphonse Daudet's (1869) short story, "L'Arlesienne", referring to an invisible or ghostlike character who, in fact, never appears; or more generally, to a project that can never be realised.

5 Translator's note: "indexing" here refers to the mode of associativity which follows an analyst's intervention or interpretation. For further detail see, "L'indexation de l'interprétation" (Danon-Boileau and Tamet, 2016, pp. 180–183).

6 This section takes up the article "Un coeur tentaculaire ou d'une repetition dans les consultations thérapeutiques", initially published in *Les Textes du Centre Alfred Binet,* 12, Paris, ASM13, 1988, pp. 19–28. Reproduced here with the kind permission of the Alfred Binet Centre.

7 Translator's note: "instrumental" refers here particularly to speech therapy and its technical rules for speaking, reading and writing.

8 This section takes up the article "A propos de la notion de réparation", initially published in *Les Textes du Centre Alfred Binet*, 24, Paris, ASM13, 1996, pp. 7–14. Reproduced here with the kind permission of the Alfred Binet Centre.

CHAPTER FOUR

Work of interpretation

Concerning interpretations in child psychoanalysis[1]

Associativity and interpretation

I t is useful to recall (Ody, 1987, Ody et al., 2011a, 2012) that all interpretation in psychoanalytic work with the child is based on the
child's *associativity* during the session. Speaking about associativity
in the child consists, as I have said, in marking what differentiates it from
free association inasmuch as it approximates to the model of the standard
treatment in the adult. The patient who is lying down expresses him/
herself essentially through words, which are accompanied by affects
and sometimes acts. We know that the situation is different with the
child, for whom the lying position cannot be envisaged before adolescence; and even then, this depends on his/her development as well as
on what could evoke with too much "reality" the unconscious phantasy
of seduction of the child by the adult. Furthermore, the child engages
in diverse forms of expression, and in varied proportions depending
on his/her age: verbalisations (in the best cases), play activities with
more or less figurative objects, graphic activities involving drawing or
writing, and finally bodily acts which range from somatic expression to

symbolised acts. The sequence of these different manifestations must be followed by the analyst, particularly when the child, owing to his/her inner tensions, switches rapidly from one register of expression to another. These sequences, this concatenation, thus have nothing linear about them. This is because the associativity is constantly underpinned by a process of binding/unbinding/rebinding. A graphic manifestation, for example, that is too close to a sexual content, directly or sexualised, may undergo various vicissitudes depending on the particular nature of the child's mode of functioning. The child may either distance himself by shifting his/her graphic productions towards others that are desexualised and symbolised or scribble a drawing and then be taken by a need to go to the toilet, or alternatively get agitated to the point of acting aggressively towards the analyst. The list is not exhaustive. These moments in which there is a *change of register* are, however, favourable for the interventions of the analyst, for this activity not only has the function of supporting the child's activity of representation, but also of permitting the child to enrich what he/she is trying to express at this level, something the child could not do before.

The conditions of associativity

What I have just been saying about the subject of associativity assumes the existence of the conditions that allow it to be exercised. These conditions concern both the child and his/her parents. All this will determine the therapeutic setting that is to be proposed. Therapeutic consultations conducted at more or less frequent intervals, with or without mediation therapy (speech therapy, psycho-motor therapy, pedagogical help, therapeutic expression group, etc.), can have a role either in institutional work, psychotherapy, psychodrama or psychoanalysis. As far as the child is concerned, there is a threshold beneath which it is illusory to propose an analysis. In this situation his/her associative capacities are extremely limited and essentially oriented towards behavioural discharge or massive inhibition. Between these extremes and their opposite, that is, a "well-tempered" neurotic state, there is a whole range of situations that can lead to other forms of therapy.

But a child depends, from all points of view, on his/her parents. This is merely pointing out the obvious, which can nonetheless lead to an apparent paradox whereby the consultant envisages an analysis for the child, after meeting him/her once, but then has to suspend the proposition after meeting the parents. We are generally faced with this type of situation when at least one of the parents, the other presenting him/ herself as complementary, cathects the child in a way that is primarily *narcissistic*. The parent exhibits denial and projective activity as soon as the consultant tries to make him/her aware of the instinctual life of their son or daughter, that is, of what makes the child a potential subject. It is a matter, then, of appreciating the degree and quality of the *associative complementarity* of the parents. We can be helped in this respect by what the parents have communicated on the subject of their child's symptomatology, and also by what we have been able to clarify in terms of understanding the child's mental functioning.

Thus we can communicate to the parents the fact that their child cannot participate in a play or graphic activity either due to inhibition or because he/she shifts too readily from one register to another (choice of other object, agitation, etc) or alternatively because he/she exhibits separation anxiety, fears, sleep disorders, and many other things as well. The essential point is that when we communicate such modes of *functioning* and/or such *contents* to the parents, we encourage them to speak about it; one of them may then have an association along the lines of, "that makes me think of . . .". The association may have a bearing on some aspect of the child's behaviour in daily life (games, school work, relationships), thereby confirming what the consultant had proposed, or evoke the child's infantile past for one of the parents through a movement of identification or counter-identification with their child. Though we cannot immediately expect the parents to be sensitive to the existence of the unconscious and infantile sexuality, this type of process can nonetheless lead to it.

The question of indication

The conditions of complementarity between the child and the parents, which I have just been discussing, are the basis of all psychoanalytic work concerning them. Everything begins with the first or rather the first two meetings, favouring the possibility of meaning emerging retroactively (*après-coup*). It is these meetings that will orient the indication in two main directions: either towards spaced therapeutic consultations, eventually combined with a mediation therapy, or towards psychotherapy or analytic treatment. It is necessary to distinguish child analysis from what differs from it for a quite simple reason connected with the history of child analysis and psychiatry: analyses represent a small minority of the therapeutic indications concerning the child. Once the period of discovery was over, as well as the time needed to have sufficient distance to learn from experience, it turned out that the limits of what could be expected from a setting involving several sessions a week had been reached, limits that were determined by the psychopathological spectrum and by technical advances at the level, for example, of the transference/countertransference dynamics. As a result, psychoanalysts, and in particular those who were faced with a general clientele in sectorised public centres, had to find solutions that did not mobilise a family several times a week when this was impractical. More attention was paid henceforth to the initial conditions of encounter.

It was Winnicott (1971) who opened up this path for us. His practice as a paediatrician, facing him with many varied situations, was certainly not unconnected with this opening. It is necessary, however, to return to what is to be understood, especially at the technical level, by a therapeutic consultation from the psychoanalytic point of view, before discussing psychoanalysis proper. This is especially true in that it will then be easier to specify the psychoanalytic process as such, knowing that a large part of what will be advanced will be found in the analytic work itself.

The therapeutic consultation

The therapeutic consultation has two main fields of application. These are situations where we find ourselves at a distance from the conditions of complementarity evoked above. This does not mean, however (and this is also the vocation of a public healthcare centre), that we have to leave it at that. Like anyone else, the consultant proposes, but the family disposes. Even if the outcome of the first meeting is apparently negative, it is always possible, with everyday words and a suitable tone of voice, to show what one thinks, to back up with concrete examples the feelings of the parents and children during the consultation. It is not a matter of convincing, but of proposing. This avoids making use of openly seductive manoeuvres, given that, at the unconscious level, this seduction will take effect as a result of lack. This stems from the fact that it is only a matter of a proposition and not of persuasion. If it is accepted, there is some chance of it being renewed allowing a process to get underway and gradually acquire a therapeutic function. If the latter is accepted, we can then embark on a process that will gradually have a therapeutic function. In certain cases, an individual treatment can be envisaged with the child, which will often involve mediation rather than being strictly psychotherapeutic, simply because the parents accept the first scenario more easily, especially as it is very likely that their child will present difficulties at school and/or "instrumental" difficulties, that is, difficulties related to the techniques necessary for reading, writing, drawing, etc.

But this type of relationship implies a relationship with an adult just as much as an analytic situation. The mere fact that the adult replies in a different way to what the child experiences repeatedly in his/her family can have therapeutic effects. Non-analytically trained therapists know this well, both through the play activities that they offer the child to breathe life into those aspects that are too instrumental, and through the way the child speaks to and confides in them. Their own functioning, and particularly their creativity, often leads them to make symbolic interventions that are positive for the child. This kind of approach can also have therapeutic effects, in the broad sense of the term. This was what led Diatkine and Van Waeyenberghe (1990) to say that the distinction between psychotherapy and re-education is not pertinent. It is often more useful to proceed in the way just mentioned rather than "forcing" the indication of psychotherapy, even though it may "at last" seem feasible. It is worth reflecting here on the case of Georges' family who, faced repeatedly with their son's problems, fitted in, apparently, with the unavoidable necessity of a psychotherapy. You will recall that, as soon as this became possible, the mother panicked and cancelled everything, telling us that she was afraid that her son would go mad. The complex resonance with the mother's history was insurmountable.

The second field of application of the therapeutic consultation is where there is an alternative between consultations at irregular intervals and psychoanalytic psychotherapy or psychoanalysis, it being understood that there are transitional stages between these two fields. Even if the situation is less accentuated than in the case of Georges and the conditions of associative complementarity are present, the indication of analytic treatment may seem either far from obvious or obvious, but the parents still prefer to wait, and this can go on for quite a long time. I am thinking here of Alexandre who evolved favourably in the context of consultations at irregular intervals in spite of a slight tendency towards pre-obsessional functioning. Two years later, in the course of the oedipal period, he manifested quite a virulent and rich organisation of his infantile neurosis, which raised the question of the indication of psychotherapy. It was necessary to wait almost a further two years until it was really accepted under good conditions. This had not prevented the child from continuing along a positive path, which was of crucial importance, while leaving his parents with the possibility of waiting further.

The consultation is not equivalent to a neutral observation. The comparative metaphor between classical mechanics and quantum mechanics has, as we have seen, often been advanced. In the work of psychoanalytic methodology, the observing subject modifies the object observed, and vice versa. This problem becomes all the more pertinent as soon as the consultant analyst wants to evaluate a process in order not to remain at the level of a sort of recording chamber. He intervenes, or interprets, which may trigger new psychic processes. Thus, it may very well be, in relation to what happened in the first meeting, that when the consultant meets the parents and child again, he or she finds that their difficulties have improved notably. Apart from certain typical situations, it is better for the consultant not to turn the analytic indication into a purposive idea.

To put things simply, a series of consultations may prove sufficient to get the child's development going again, and it then becomes clear that such a situation does not concern children whose psychic functioning is progressively and sufficiently organised from a psychopathological point of view. In such a scenario, generally speaking, we are dealing with events that have had, to a greater or lesser degree, a traumatic function (bereavement, actual trauma, birth of a younger sibling, important change in the life of the parents and/or the child, etc.) and which have not been added to a fundamental underlying psychopathological problem. The child's psychic functioning presents a certain temporary and more or less repetitive disequilibrium in the relationship between primary and secondary processes, along the lines of the notion put forward by René Diatkine (1969) of a pre-psychotic state. These two processes, as well as the relationship between them, are intrinsic to psychic functioning. The primary process refers to unconscious desire, which is countercathected by the secondary process at the preconscious level, the seat of word-presentations, and there is a permanent dialectic between the two.

The problem is to assess whether, during the associative processes, the first does not invade the second too repeatedly. There is a difference between a slip of the tongue or its equivalent, and a regular disorganisation of a child's drawing in which all visual representation serves as a basis for a more or less "archaic", "pregenital" sexualisation with a destructive colouring which is a sign of drive defusion. The unconscious, or the id in its crudest form, with its discharges of excitation, finds a way out which breaks the continuity of secondary thinking, that of narrative put together with the help of language, in such a way that all the transitions are possible between these two extremes. Within this field, we can find neurotic states, intermediate states between the two extremes. We may take as an example a child with a phobic/obsessional tendency, who will "apply himself" to making sure that figurative images do not come into contact, but who, owing to the pressure of the primary processes will "succeed" in spite of everything in depicting such a contact, before erasing it immediately. The pre-psychotic child, for his part, will produce, for example, a series of graphic productions that are barely recognisable, or abstract, out of which will emerge a man who is more and more equipped and armed, in the style of a superhero. But as excitation is at its height, it overwhelms and breaks up the narrative, transforming everything into an explosive and incendiary scribbling, while the felt pen becomes a blunt instrument that goes through the sheet of drawing paper. The child, inhibited and depressed after so much effort, will produce a sad, immobile and shrunken drawing at the bottom of the page.

The issue is not to present an exhaustive catalogue of illustrations of psychopathology, but rather to indicate by such concise examples, that from the very first consultation we find ourselves at the heart of the question of interpretation. In fact, the consultant is free to intervene in all these situations in order to point out to the child that when he/she has finally succeeded in expressing the "first" psychic content (contact between images, depiction of a very strong man), he/she has not been able to prevent him/herself from producing the "second" psychic event (the contact did not take place because the child moved on to something else, or the man, in spite of his protective armour, was destroyed). This type of intervention goes beyond a mere paraphrase, in the sense that it re-establishes links between the elements that are objects of unbinding.

It is not the kind of thing a child hears in his/her daily life. Afterwards, he/she can introduce new elements that will have their own destiny in his/her psychic functioning, except that the fact of having heard these rather special words from the adult can trigger in the child more or less symbolic representations in connection with the consultant, which already suggests a movement in the transference.

An example of interpretive work in therapeutic consultations[2]

The example given here is quite a simple one, centred on a single consultation. This example will bring us closer to the situation of analysis, because this single consultation confirms an indication of psychotherapy. It concerns Aurélien, a boy whose little sister was in treatment with one of my colleagues. The family situation was quite complex, but it is not necessary to describe it in order to make my point. In any case, at a certain moment the question of the indication of psychotherapy was raised for Aurélien, due to a tendency to isolate himself, to a concealed state of depression, and difficulties in relating to his peers. He was approaching the age of ten and was in Year 5 (in France, *cours moyen*, CM1).

I was asked to see him to confirm the indication, it being understood that the child knew why he was coming and had agreed to do so. When I met him, I found myself in front of a boy who was both likeable, attentive and reserved, with a discreet femininity that was striking. He formulated the reason for his presence in a somewhat surprising way: "*It's because I am not there.*" Rather than asking him why, I took him literally and said to him that he might be "elsewhere", which he confirmed, just as he also confirmed that he could be in his dreams, except that he found it difficult to speak to me about them. So we came back to his feeling of not being there. Aurélien eventually mentioned a context in which his problem emerged, for example, when his school teacher "was not there", because she had just gone out of the room for a moment. So I said to him: "As the teacher's not there, nor am I!" He was surprised, smiled, and compared what happened in class, where he was supposedly more present, with what happened in the school yard: "Things are going better in class, I am taking *advantage* of this, so that I can "not be there" when I'm in the yard. I repeated the word he had used, which unsettled him a little. He then described a situation to me during which he had a certain pleasure in being alone in a corner of the yard, as long as no one came to disturb him, he added. I imagined that he was provoking the sadism of certain pupils. As my new attempts to learn something about his phantasies were unsuccessful, I enquired about his dreams. He replied by saying that he did not dream. My attempts to put things into perspective led Aurélien to tell me about a past dream. He was picking up a golden key off the ground and "someone" (he couldn't remember anything about the person in question) came and snatched it from him, even though he was in the middle of a group of people. In a sort of secondarised movement, Aurélien said that it was a game. The symbolism of the snatched golden key had brought us to the heart of the subject. And yet the issue here was not to interpret the symbol, *but to keep us on the symbolic level.* So I asked him what the purpose of this key might be? Aurélien replied trivially, saying that it was just for getting into a yard which had nothing special about it. I said that given that it was a golden key, the story seemed to end in a very trivial fashion. He smiled but said nothing.

I then thought about a *change of register*, which would favour a formal regression, and said that he could draw whatever he wanted. I hoped that what had just happened would permit a latent thought to emerge while he was elaborating on his drawing. Fortunately, this was the case. I noticed he was drawing in quite an alert way in comparison with everything that had gone before. He drew a castle with a large door that was well protected and closed. I made a symbolic (and/or analogical, according to Rolland (1997)) intervention (or interpretation): "Once again we have the golden key for opening such a door; it was well worth a castle!" Aurélien, who had just drawn some guards, stopped drawing, smiled and told me that one of these guards was not happy to find himself *there* during the night. The symbolic interpretation was met with a symbolic response. Aurélien enriched the content of his symptom, "not being there". *The unconscious phantasy of the primal scene* became increasingly prominent, following the earlier appearance of the phantasy of *castration* (someone snatching the golden key). The child continued, moreover, in this direction, even if he had to negotiate a series of internal conflicts, which confirmed in passing the indication of psychotherapy. This castle was for the king, who was alone in his room. "There is no queen?" I asked him. "Yes, but she's not there," he replied. I drew his attention to this expression, which led Aurélien to smile again and to colour two separate and illuminated rooms in the castle. The king was in one of them and the queen in the other, sleeping with her cat, which threw some light on a possible determination of his inverted Oedipus, with reference to his "feminine" tendencies mentioned above, not to mention his identification with women who are "not there".

I then tried to introduce the question of marital separation, mentioning the possibility of a dispute. Aurélien began by reacting with a denial but then introduced a third character, another king. He then took up the word dispute that I had used and told me that this had been triggered by the second king who wanted to give cats to the queen. I psychodramatised the situation by saying that the first king "must find it intolerable that the other king wants to give children . . . no, cats to his wife". My deliberate slip of the tongue surprised Aurélien somewhat, who then set about deconflictualising things by giving five cats to each of the kings. In so doing, he reversed his identification with the second king by putting himself in the place of the queen giving five children to each of the two men, like the number of fingers on each of his hands.

The evolving process of this consultation confirmed the indication of psychotherapy. The way it unfolded made it possible, by means of interventions and interpretations, to resolve a conflict expressed through the relations between primary and secondary processes and their relations with unconscious phantasies. This process seemed to underlie the symptomatology of "absentation" to which a meaning was given. The consultation with the parents, which took place thereafter in the presence of the child, and with the help of their own associations, confirmed this indication.

On technique: what consultations and analysis have in common

The type of technique that I have just illustrated can be used both in child analysis and in therapeutic consultations insofar as it is a matter of taking into account preconscious and symbolic movements. In 1987, I proposed the term "symbolic interpretation", on the condition that the word "symbolic" be understood according to the first definition given by the 1970 edition of the *Robert* dictionary, namely, "what constitutes a symbol . . . what is based on a symbol" and not what interprets a symbol. Concerning what constitutes a symbol, we may take the example of an uncertain depiction in a child's drawing, which he/she cannot express in words, but for which a certain meaning can be suggested when put into words by the analyst. If there is a sufficient gap between the child's preconscious (in the process of organising itself) and that of the analyst, the proposal of meaning will give rise to a new psychic production in the child, which acquires greater certainty. Without concerning oneself as to whether the content was latent or not, or even potential, one can at least say that the analagon of a *symbolon* (union of two parts into a whole) has emerged or been constituted, so that the concatenation can continue its course until the next obstacle. This *symbolic constitution* stands in a structural and analogical relationship to Winnicott's squiggle, except that its dynamism is not part of an inaugural proposition of play made by the analyst. On the contrary, it will be part of the process, depending on what has or has not emerged in the child, thereby participating in a sort of "construction of the analytic space", to use Viderman's (1970) formulation.

As for what is *based on* a symbol, this involves a situation where one shows a child, by whatever means, that if "A" is brought closer by him/her or by the analyst to "B" (the elements of a drawing or a game), it can give rise to a psychic event "C". With this discovery, the child will have a greater tendency to give fresh impetus and scope to the process of symbolisation, as a psychic event "D", than its contrary, which risks resulting in a process of de-symbolisation due to excitation which may be disorganising. Formal, topographical and temporal regressions may, however, occur, which, even if they are not necessarily de-symbolising, are nonetheless the sign of a conflict, of a transference/countertransference dynamic. It is worth noting in passing that this "abc" of symbolic interpretation has a triangular function which, as we have seen, is coherent with the notion of symbolisation, of thirdness, of the attracting function of the Oedipus, as well as with the Freudian strategy of interpretation, a so-celled ternary strategy (M'Uzan, 1994).

It is in the context of such dynamics with symbolic and metaphorising power that interpretations can be offered to the child, referring to the latent thoughts that he/she does not readily communicate (any more than his conscious thoughts). These latent preconscious thoughts may concern a moment of fantasy activity in the session, just as they may concern a significant and conflictual thought in the child's current or past life. He/she can directly confirm the existence of such a thought (or react with a denial), but it is the associative process that will determine whether what has been deduced and proposed is pertinent or not. All this is part of the task of working-through, *Durcharbeitung*, in Freud's (1914g) sense. Aurélien illustrated the opportunity for symbolic interpretation from the moment he was able to tell me about his dream of the "golden key".

The first phase of the process consisted in my drawing attention to the contradiction that he had introduced by giving an ordinary destiny "B" to such a key "A". The psychic event "C" was, at the manifest level, a smile, the expression of an affect combined with the probability of the construction of a latent thought. It was this chain of events that led me at that precise moment to suggest that he did a drawing, a change of register which, by encouraging *formal regression*, made it possible to open up again what had closed defensively. Thus, once Aurélien had reached, through graphic but "alert" means, the large door of the castle, which was protected and closed, there were grounds for a second phase of symbolic interpretation, consisting in bringing the key of the first phase "A", closer to the door of the second phase "B". The psychic event "C" occurred soon after and even introduced the issue of the symptom "not being there", as the guard was not happy to be "there" that night. It was an indexation of the interpretation resulting from these micro-processes as Green once called them. These processes, however, did not stop there. The associative sequel "D" occurred, based on the reference to the king, and a new psychic adventure began that would confirm the indication of psychotherapy. The concentration of the material in a single session, with the process that unfolded in it and which led to the indication of psychotherapy, can, as we have seen, develop over a longer period.

The technical problems, however, remain the same. In particular, what has already been said concerning symbolic interpretation can concern elements of different therapeutic consultations (or sessions). Finally, two further remarks. *Symbolic and/or symbolising interpretation does not consist in interpreting the symbol.* Such an interpretation would be going in exactly the opposite direction to everything that I have just been saying. We would then be dealing with a real short-circuiting of the preconscious, which would be giving priority to the analysis of *contents* rather than *processes*. The interpretation of a symbol might have its place, at the appropriate time, during an analysis. Its meaning can be deduced, logically, and proposed to the child in order to give meaning to the chain of events that have just unfolded. But what about the age of the child? The processual point of view that I have just been developing does not seem to be linked to this question. In the case of a young child, the order of graphic representation (from its initial stages to more accomplished figurative images) and language will be less formally structured; on the other hand, his/her anxiety linked to separation will mean that he/she will have to be seen with his/her parents (it is only around the age of three a child can follow you alone into your office). This will not impede the associativity expressed through the prolegomena of graphic representation, the series of movements involving the grasping and rejection of play objects, including the most elementary ones. In such a context, the phases of child/parent inter-cathexes will be part of the associative dynamics and, in a general way, represent a specificity of the work of conducting a therapeutic consultation.

Psychotherapy or psychoanalysis

We have seen that the number of sessions per week, however frequent they may be, does not in itself guarantee the existence of an analytic process, but it is also clear that when an analytic process is present, it will be helped by the existence of frequent sessions. Once this is accepted, everything is a matter of degree and not simply "instrumental". It is a question of evaluating with the family whether what will be proposed "ideally" as the most adequate solution is achievable in practice. It may seem illusory to mobilise a family three or four times a week, when it is faced with material limits and a problem of geographical distance. It is better, therefore, to provide a preparatory work of therapeutic consultation which makes it possible, if things finally move in the direction of an analytic indication, to propose two sessions a week. Equally a higher frequency of sessions should not be ruled out when it is feasible.

In my following remarks, I will be adopting the point of view of the analytic process and not one which consists in regarding analysis as work based on three or more sessions a week and psychotherapy on two. The only question that is raised where the latter is concerned, for its name does not indicate it a priori, is whether it is psychoanalytic; which means that both in what is called "analysis" or "psychotherapy" the child works with a psychoanalyst. It is a matter, therefore, of evaluating whether, in these settings, a process, as well as psycho-analytic work, exists or not.

The psychoanalytic process

From the moment the conditions of indication are met, what the frequency of sessions offers, through their repetition, through the lever of the transference, and through access to regression, is the possibility that opportunities will be created for interpreting *unconscious phantasies* in connection with infantile sexuality. What matters is that the child has the possibility of gaining access to the constitution of his/her history, and that he/she can gradually identify him/herself with the interpreting function of his/he analyst both along the trajectory of insight as well as of self-evaluation. Finally, it is also important to be able to bring the analytic work to a close, while bearing in mind that it is not possible to analyse "everything" in the child.

Elements of history

It is a long time since Freud (1909d) presented us with the analysis of "Little Hans", conducted by his father under the supervision of Freud who, in addition, had the child's mother in analysis. Whatever the conditions of the "setting" of this treatment of a "child neurosis" may have been, this document remains, from all points of view, an inexhaustible source of learning for psychoanalysts, particularly in connection with transference/countertransference issues. The numerous texts written on this analysis are evidence of this. The essential question that has divided psychoanalysts is that of the child's analysability, not only in terms of his psychopathology, but in terms of the very fact that he was a child. In other words, is a child analysable? This is illustrated best by the famous controversy between Anna Freud and Melanie Klein.

Anna Freud, who was interested in the developmental point of view, ego-formation, the defence mechanisms and environmental conditions, among other things, where hospitalised children were concerned, was doubtful about the possibility of analysing children. She considered that a prior "educative" period was necessary, for the age of the child meant that the distance between his imagos and his real parents was too limited. This called the very notion of transference into question. Melanie Klein, for her part, who was concerned by the early aspects of psychic life, developed her conceptualisation by focusing on the emergence of the life and death drives. She held that these have an influence from the outset on the evolution of the object, which is first a part-object before becoming a whole object, on the evolution of projective identification which is first pathological in nature before becoming "normal", and on the transition from the paranoid-schizoid position to the depressive position. This conceptual framework as well as her analytic practice with children led her to consider that the transference was possible and analysable, including the negative transference. The oppositions between Anna Freud and Melanie Klein gradually diminished, even if it is still possible to distinguish an "Anna Freudian" analyst from a "Kleinian" analyst.

The debate that took place subsequently between René Diatkine, Anna Freud and Hanna Segal (Diatkine, Freud and Segal, 1971) resulted in an important clarification because, insofar as it is true that the participation of a psychoanalyst in a child's play has psychotherapeutic effects, only the work of interpretation allows for a mutation on the psychoanalytic level. It is clear, however, that these mutations do not arise from the effect of an interpretation alone, even if it is "brilliant". The interpretation in question is always preceded by a series of others, which concern both the session of analysis and the therapeutic consultation. In other words, it depends on the existence of a prior process, which supposes that the thread of the transference/countertransference movements have been closely followed, as an essential support for the emergence of the interpretation.

The transference

Generally speaking, following the transference movements, both positive and negative, with their counterpoint in the analyst, enables the latter to limit the element of *méconnaissance*,[3] that is always possible, however much knowledge has been acquired in the course of the history of psychoanalysis. This does not mean that it is necessary to "interpret the transference" as it presents itself. More specifically, the question of whether the negative transference should be interpreted swiftly or not is one that is still relevant today. Thus, as with other questions, there is the problem of whether significant elements of the family history should be utilised with the child or not. But everything is a matter of opportunity; it is not possible to have a pre-established programme.

As for the negative transference, the example given by René Diatkine and Janine Simone (1972) is exemplary. In their book *La psychanalyse précoce*, they present an analytic process that was established during an analytic treatment of one session per week, which is not "exportable" as easily as that. It is true that the two protagonists had a lot of talent. The little girl, Carine, aged three and a half, was unable to be separated from her mother during the first sessions, which consequently took place in the latter's presence. Carine took some of her mother's belongings, "went visiting" (no doubt through identification with her mother), and threw into the dustbin the only toy, a doll, that she had taken from among those put at her disposal by the analyst. Janine Simon interpreted her fear of being treated like that by her mother when she wanted to take her place. The child also carried off some of her analyst's belongings, and then went to look for her "husband" in the office because he "often forgets meal times". The analyst then linked the reversal of the attack she feared by the mother into the aggressive attitude towards the doll to the father, an object of desire, which put her in a situation of rivalry with the mother. Carine "showed" that she was not interested in the father by clinging to her mother during the session.

But, in the following session, she told her analyst she wanted to tell her a dream: *a wolf was attacking her with its claws and teeth*. Shortly after this symbolic introduction of the father, Carine played the wolf, while Janine Simone put herself in the child's place. Thus the initial interpretation of the negative transference was swiftly surpassed by one of a processual nature permitting access to triangulation. This transference, moreover, did need to be interpreted "manifestly", for it served as a pivot for the first interpretation. It would lead to the introduction of the "husband", after the child had carried off the analyst's belongings. The interpretive work was based on the words of the little girl, introduced others that linked up with them, and made it possible to make a connection between the words of the interpretation and the preconscious representatives of the unconscious phantasies. Furthermore, as the authors note, the oedipal context was quickly demarcated in spite of what one may think theoretically about the immaturity of the Oedipal complex at this age. The fact that the analyst was immediately sensitive to the triangulation meant that it was possible to avoid the confinement of a mother/daughter duality in which the "archaic" and pregenital dimensions would have been given priority. At the same time, the authors note, it is not a matter of drawing the child towards a more developed direction, that of the Oedipal conflict, while underestimating the pregenital elements. Interpretation serves to re-establish the *link* between different preconscious elements separated by the attraction of primary repression. The pertinence of these new links is shown by the material that the child brings associatively thereafter, either directly in the session (Carine carried off some of her analyst's belongings, and then went to look for her "husband") or in the following session (she wants to tell a dream). This is the indexation to which I referred earlier.

Generalised triangulation as the basis for interpretation

In keeping with what has just been said, Simon (1991) cites a humorous remark by James Gammill (1986). A seven-year-old boy, who was beginning his analysis with him, stood there immobile and rubbed his knees compulsively in silence. His analyst, following good Kleinian technique, told him he was checking that his knees were there, as if he wanted to check that his mother's breast were there. The child replied: "Yes, my parents are in London for the weekend, and I am wondering if they will have an accident" (p. 472). The child's reply certainly "indexed" his analyst's interpretation, but not necessarily at the level of the link breasts/knees as a pre-existing link; but, at the same time, once this link has been made, it is a constituted link, like a quantum metaphor, which can form a trace. The indexation depends on the mother's absence, contained in the interpretation, which in turn involves the mother's breasts. The boy broadens the question by establishing a link with the *unconscious* phantasy of the primal scene, since this time it is the parents who are involved; the ambivalence that stems from it plays a part in the preconscious/conscious fantasy of an accident. I agree with Michel Fain (1982) when he notes that the psychoanalyst's words link words and things better when he/she emphasises the effects of lack, *the lack of being located "at the centre of the interpretive field"* (p. 712).

In short, a "Kleinian" interpretation, by virtue of the symbolic aspects that it may also contain, can lead to psychic events of processual value.

In the present example, the interpretation went beyond the content of the pregenital impulses (the breasts) alone; otherwise the interpretation might have been as partial as the instinctual drive impulse itself (Fain, ibid.). In a certain way, this is what Gammill confirmed when he told us, three years after this interpretation, that the analysis of this child *took place*. With the humour that precedes this comment, he notes what the child said to him, after these three years, recalling (reconstructing?) this first session: "You see Dr Gammill, the first time I came to see you, I couldn't move because I was very afraid. I saw you as a big wolf that was ready to jump on me" (Gammill, 1986, p. 472). There is no guarantee that an interpretation bearing on the castrating father, a hypothesis Gammill put forward, would have been more effective.

Once again, it is less a matter of content than of process; to be more exact, it is a matter of the *quality of the relationship between process and content*. De M'Uzan (1994) does not seem to say anything different when he suggests that if the distance separating the different analytic practices, including Freudian and Kleinian approaches, can be reduced, it is more in relation to the *montage* of eventual common values than in terms of their *content*.

This brief example takes us back to what I was saying on the subject of thirdness, the attracting Oedipus and the Freudian strategy of interpretation. The issue is not one of interpreting any material whatsoever in terms of the oedipal complex, any more than in terms of paranoid-schizoid or depressive positions. It is more a matter, against the background of a lack of being, correlative to all triangulation due to the difference between the sexes and generations, of being attentive to the missing third element. This is what we find in the examples given above. With Aurélien, the trivialised golden key of the first phase implied this missing third element, if only through the symbolism that was inherent in it.

But it was in the second phase, after an interpretation containing the first phase, that the third element emerged. The guard was not happy to be there, because a derivative of the primal scene was active in Aurélien. This led to the complex scene with the queen and the two kings. With Carine, it was also an interpretation by the analyst that made the missing third element of the first phase appear. The "husband" first, the wolf in the dream next. A comparable process occurred in Gammill's young patient, because the analyst's interpretation bearing on the link between breasts and knees, but also on the relationship between presence and absence, led the child to refer to the absence of his parents, not to mention his reference to Gammill of the big wolf three years later. *In all these situations, the representatives of the missing third element emerged by themselves, and retrospectively, as a result of interpretations.* This is a good moment to note that, from the processual point of view, there is an *intrinsic relationship between thirdness and the phenomenon of après-coup.* As these representatives were not named and contained in the analyst's interpretation, they risked having the function of a purposive aim, of a pre-established programme. They were catalysed, in connection with the personal *emergence* of each child, by the formulation of an interpretation that contained the *principle* of thirdness. This begins at a very early stage, and it was undoubtedly not without reason that Klein founded the Oedipus on the depressive position, before it is possible to speak of the Oedipal complex. More recently, without even mentioning Lacan, Braunschweig and Fain (1975) confirmed this precocity with their notions of primary hysteria and censorship of the woman-as-lover (*censure de l'amante*), reintroducing sexuality, however, which had been somewhat pushed into the background in Klein's work given the importance she attributed to the destructive impulses.

In other words, if the notion of triangulation can be generalised in this way, it is easy to imagine that we will be able to find it in any analytic process, if only because children who are in analysis already have their place, positively and negatively, in this triangulation. The analyst is part of it even more so, and moreover it is the gap of functioning between the analyst and the child patient which makes him/her the missing third element and that will make it possible for an analytic process to begin. This gap must, however, be *vectorised* by preconscious functioning, and this was what was involved with the question of symbolic interpretation. The considerations that have been formulated so far relativise the question of the "right" interpretation, in the sense of being the only one possible. We are familiar with the propensity of each analyst, when listening to material presented by a colleague, to want to offer "another" interpretation, which naturally is thought to be "the best". This may be the case, even though the mechanisms of displacement and condensation of the primary process, polysemy and overdetermination, can give rise to several types of interpretation which may have associative consequences before we can speak of a "mutative" interpretation (Strachey, 1934). This obviously does not mean that an analyst can say anything whatsoever, and that is why we give priority to the process before the content, the preconscious, thirdness, the phenomenon of *après-coup*, and symbolic interpretation.

In such conditions, it is not possible for there to be either only one correct interpretation or any interpretation whatsoever. In the case of non-neurotic patients, who seem to express themselves primarily at the level of what is "primary", "archaic", etc., and provided that the possibilities of associativity exist, attention to the missing third element is just as necessary. It is here that the formalisation – with its pregenital air of omnipotence and helplessness – of the third element in relation to a child whose neurotic organisation is in process will change. Analysts who have been involved in treatments of autistic children are well placed to know that the third element is missing all the more when negativity is at its peak. The analyst's psychic functioning is threatened because the gap between his/her own and the child's has either become immense or abolished. Maintaining distance, in all senses of the word, means being able to retain a capacity for play with such children, having the patience to wait until the elements introduced by the analyst, in relation to the slightest psychic movement of the child, finally lead to an emergent associativity that will perhaps not always be destroyed subsequently.

An extract of analysis

This is a situation that illustrates what can be obtained from regular sessions (three times a week). The session in question took place at the end of the first month of analysis, after a period of therapeutic consultations with a colleague. Lea was a little girl aged five years and three months with a strong assertive character featuring in particular a need to dominate which, while having repercussions for her relationships with others, did not prevent her from suffering from frequent nightmares. As my aim is to illustrate what goes on in a session, I will confine myself to the essential points. During the session, after looking around my office a bit, she asked me about the drawing board: "Which session is that for?" I pointed out to her that she knew. I had already referred to the difference between this type of drawing board, which she had used with the consultant, and the 21 x 27 cm sheets of paper that she had at her disposal for the sessions with me. Lea smiled, but insisted. I told her that it was perhaps a way of asking me what had made her consultant refer her to me, a problem that had already been discussed in connection with her difficulty in separating from her.

Lea: "Was it because you had more animals than her?"
Me: "Is that a way of saying that men have something more than women?"

A silence followed. Léa then took hold of a floor-standing ashtray, the particular feature of which was that its bowl opened in two. She opened it, closed it again, evoked "the mouth of a fish", and was taken for the first time by a need to "have a pee and do a poo".

Faced with this manifestation of sexual co-excitation, I made her understand that what she was perhaps trying to tell me was that the difference between men and women, between boys and girls, is that the first have something "extra" (like the animals she had just spoken about) and the second something that opens and then closes again. I added that "thinking" about all that made her want to go out to have a pee and do a poo. "Yes, that's right, boys, they have a tap," Léa replied, reasserting herself again. She exaggerated, moreover, by standing upright on the radiator in my office and by testing the third party that I represented by asking me if she could go out on to the terrace. During the following session, which contained certain elements of the one before, both on the preconscious and unconscious level, she arrived with a cuddly toy and sat down as if on a throne with the cuddly toy on her head.

I said: "A crowned queen".
Léa replied: "It's doing a poo on her head", transforming and displacing on to the cuddly toy the sexual co-excitation of the previous session.
Me: "It's so happy to be so high up that it makes it want to do a pooh like a baby."

She then put the cuddly toy under her dress and pretended to give birth; the baby got bigger and she taught him to walk and jump, then she slept with him.

I asked her: "What does the daddy say?"

Léa was surprised by the introduction of the third party and said that he was in another room.

But after this definition of the nocturnal separation of the parental couple, she moved closer to me to ask me to *write*, which had a certain symbolic value for thirdness.

This example illustrates the application of the points I have presented hitherto, both on the theoretical and technical level, while accepting that there can be other interpretations. The essential point is that the interpretations formulated were followed by new psychic movements that were coherent with those that preceded them, but according to a logical coherence of *après-coup* while being unpredictable at the same time. In other words, the difference in all psychoanalytic work is less to do with the interpretive structures than with the conditions of analysis. The more these conditions refer to the couple regression/ (topographical, formal, and temporal) transference-countertransference that is deployed there (the process), the more the interpretive structures will be capable of linking the elements (the contents) that would otherwise have been unreachable. At a certain point in the treatment, it becomes possible to give interpretations relating to unconscious phantasies which, as we have seen, relate to the primal phantasies (Freud) of seduction, castration, and the primal scene. These phantasies have never been conscious; their content is introduced into the interpretation as a deducible content that has the potential to give meaning to the material that unfolds at a precise moment. Some analysts will only use the word interpretation to refer to that which relates to unconscious phantasy, which seems to me very restrictive. All the work that has just been illustrated in relation to the preconscious is interpretive. The term intervention may be reserved for the connections made by the analyst between certain separated terms or elements in the material, which implies a work of interpretation by the analyst.

Another example of interpretation in therapeutic consultations with children

Five consultations took place over almost two years. As the consultations seemed sufficient and the work was focused on family "interactions", there was no transition to analytic treatment. Julian was ten-and-a-half years old. His parents, Mr and Mrs I., brought him before the summer due to his sleeping difficulties, his fear of the dark, and his mediocre school results in the 5th year of primary school (in France, *cours moyen*, CM2). He was a likeable and attentive boy but at the same time not very talkative, which meant that I had to encourage him frequently to avoid getting into a negative silence. He finally told me that his sleeping difficulties had diminished and that they featured, among other things, a fear of wolves. Thus, the reference to the infantile persisted in him. He told me that as soon as his mother sensed that he was not sleeping, she came to reassure him while his father continued to sleep deeply. I intervened by pointing out to him that by doing this he was separating his parents during the night, which was why the wolf came back to bite him. Julien allowed himself to show some emotion, which turned into a smile once his parents were present. At a certain point the subject of the father's irritation with his son came up, irritation that was expressed repeatedly whenever he tried to help his son with his school work. I said to him: "The wolf comes back to bite you", which made him laugh, as well as his parents who were familiar with this theme in their son's dreams. I also learnt during this consultation that the mother was a bit agora-phobic and made use of counterphobic mechanisms. She had become more balanced after convincing her husband to restrict the range of his business trips. I suggested that we met again once Julien was in Year 6 in order to evaluate the eventual degree of his mobilisation and the qual-ity of the work of differentiation between what was internalised and organised and what pertained to a "catalysing" effect of the parents.

During this second meeting, Julien told me that he was no longer having nightmares. His school results on the other hand were some-what variable, which could be attributed to his entry into secondary school. Gradually, however, he showed that at the level of his thought processes, when he had to express an idea in class, after a while he no longer knew what it was and tended to "get lost" (see his mother's ago-raphobia). Now, when I drew him out with regard to his imaginative activity in connection with this problem, Julien was able, without any difficulty, and even sometimes with a certain prolixity, to talk about a story he had been reading such as a criminal mystery investigation. I pointed out to him the contrast between the two situations: the situ-ation at school and the "criminal" situation. He smiled and was both interested and surprised. Julien thus seemed to differentiate quite well between what referred to something inside him and what origi-nated in his parents (a certain overprotectiveness on his mother's part and an excess of authority on his father's part), his complaint that he could never receive friends at home, etc.), which meant that it was also necessary to make progress with them. He agreed. However, while his mother, in particular, confirmed the change that had taken place with regard to her son's sleeping difficulties, she complained at the same time about another change: she said that Julien often opposed her. It was quite easy to show her that this was to do with a pre-adolescent desire for greater autonomy. She was then able, through an association of ideas, to recognise herself in him when she was his age.

This evocation of the past enabled me to take things a bit further. Indeed, at a given moment, once she had told me about certain elements from her past family history, she made a gesture of bringing her hands together, indicating her need to keep her husband and children (Julien had a younger sister) close to her. Thanks to my intervention concerning her gesture, which she repeated, as if in counterpoint, she understood what she had experienced *centrifugally* for herself: bringing together her parents who subsequently separated, bringing together the couples of her remarried parents. Her son's quest for greater autonomy could not fail to reproduce these centrifugal forces from the past. The emotional effect of my intervention was immediate. Mrs I., moreover, did not forget this moment in the consultation. Both the father and the son were clearly interested in what had just happened. The question of how the father exerted his authority still had to be broached. With time it became apparent that there was a difficulty there in the sense that the father had the impression that he was going round in circles. He agreed to come back to this issue next time. For his part, his son wanted nothing more than to continue working along these lines.

A few months later, Julien told me that he had an average mark at school of almost 14. He now had friends too, whereas previously he had been rather isolated. This openness to *social relationships* had led to a conflict with a special friend who practised karate and often took Julien as a target. They then had it out with each other, which put the matter to rest. Julien then expressed a wish to learn judo, something his mother was opposed to. There was not much else he had to complain about, he said, and it was because I asked him about his former sleeping difficulties that he introduced a new element. While he no longer suffered from nightmares, when the rest of the family had gone out for the evening and returned home late, it took him one hour to get to sleep, time which he spent thinking about the *violent* image of a film he had recently seen on television. After an initial moment of inhibition, he communicated to me aggressively the content of a child kidnapping scenario with its *happy end*. This contradiction enabled me to make a link between this type of fantasy and his interest in crime riddles and to note a certain blockage that he had in relating violent events. I put the idea to him that this might be related to his judo, a subject of conflict between him and his mother. He smiled and was moved. Once his parents were present, it was the mother who quickly took centre stage and stayed there, leading me to put off the project planned with the father at the last consultation, even though this project might have been linked with the mother's behaviour hindering what had been planned with the father.

Once the father had talked about his son's inhibitions during exams, during which several classes are assembled together, his wife intervened with expressions such as: "He's no longer in his little world" or in his "close-knit world", which led me to raise the issue of his sensibility, a subject we had already talked about. She reacted immediately, saying, "I remember very well," once again making the gesture of bringing her hands together. This woman's reaction was subsequently quite spectacular. She told me about a conflict that had taken place between Julien and three big lads who wanted to take his ball away from him. Mrs I., against the advice of everyone around, was ready to go and settle the score with them. I pointed out to her that this seemed to me to be in contradiction with the fact that she was opposed to her son practising judo. She understood perfectly what I wanted to say, speaking of the first thing that she had seen in the judo hall, a poster displaying a stretcher. She rationalised again and again until she finally told me that friends had pointed out to her that if she continued to act like that with her son, she would turn him into a homosexual. I did not mention at that point the fact that my suggestion that she should think about the idea of consultations leading eventually to a psychotherapy had not been followed up. We separated on the same understanding as usual.

In the course of the first term of the next school year, it was the father who was in the foreground. Julien was in Year 8 (*cinquième* in France) and "only" average in his class. Initially, there seemed to be no explanation for this, except for the fact that the process of entering Year 7 (*sixième*) was repeating itself. Finally, Julien said that he often thought about other things than his work. But what he was communicating was no longer coloured by the previous line of fantasies. In reality, he expressed the desires of anyone of his age: of having, like his friends, a pair of Nike trainers and a games console to replace the one he had which was getting a bit old-fashioned. As for sleeping, he said he had "no" problems. So we spoke about adolescence, about peer groups, about his sense of being excluded, which he confirmed, and eventually about his father, whom Julien described as the main source of opposition to his desires. This conflict with his father was an opportunity for me, once the parents were present, to inquire about the father's past life, once the father's criticisms had been put aside. Mr I. told me that he had humble origins, and that the four members of his family, including his brother, had slept in the same bedroom. It was therefore not possible to have a friend at home (we have seen that this was one of Julien's complaints). Subsequently other matters were talked about. After a moment of irritation concerning the material conditions that his son enjoyed in comparison with what he himself had experienced as a child, Mr I. seemed sensitive to what I was suggesting to him: his concern that the conditions his son enjoyed should not "exceed" too much those that he himself had experienced could produce the *opposite* result from the one he wanted, even if one could understand the paternal educational principle of not satisfying a child's every slightest wish. In this way, I was offering him a symbolic counter-oedipal version. Mr I. was moved.

This practical and economic compromise, followed by a date, involving father and son, was agreed upon as far as the problem of the objects the child wanted was concerned. The next time, one month after Christmas, Julien told me that he had received the two objects he had wanted and that he had participated in their purchase with his personal savings. He added that he had had 20/20 in class. This enabled him to talk to me about his father in quite subtle terms, about his father's family, about the aspects of his father's attitudes that were too authoritarian for him, and about the awkwardness he felt when his father helped him with his school work. Now, after confirming what his son had said, Mr I. complained in turn about the conflicts that he had with him whenever he tried to help him. Gradually, Mr I. went beyond the register of his own involvement with his son and admitted that he tended to react too strongly to what he perceived as his son's passiveness. It was at this moment, after an associative mimic on Mrs I.'s part, which I acknowledged, that she said that her husband felt that he had a son who was a bit like a girl and a daughter like a boy. Surprised, Mr I. reproached his wife for what she had just said, because he had never spoken about this personally to his son. I intervened, saying that it would be surprising if this was a totally new discovery for Julien, which he duly confirmed. I then recalled the episode in which Mrs I. had wanted to go and settle accounts with the three strapping lads that had behaved aggressively towards her son.

"She was Zorro", Mr I. commented, observing in so doing that the problems of sexual identification were rather complex. After thinking a bit, he told us that, basically, his son had taken him a bit for a wolf. He was quite moved by his own observation, and he understood that it might be difficult to give an answer to a question at school when one had the impression that one could be eaten like a lamb. We separated, having the same view of the situation, except that the psychic movements, even unconscious, belonging to each of them, were now better differentiated. Julien seemed to understand, in spite of the evolution that remained positive, that if he found he was faced repeatedly with inhibitions that were peculiar to him, that he might benefit from doing psychotherapy. The few consultations that took place subsequently did not change this perspective, and there has been no particular demand since then. Faced with such an "intermediate" situation, another consultant might have suggested indicating psychotherapy for the child. It would certainly have required a particularly active mode of functioning on the part of the therapist, to offset Julien's passiveness. Furthermore, the continuity of the treatment would not have been guaranteed, on account of the mother's counterphobic tendencies. As far as I was concerned, I preferred, therefore, given the weight of the elements relating to the character of each of the parents and of the parent/child relationships, to give myself time to evaluate what could be mobilised within the setting of the consultation itself. Such a choice involves "accepting" that the eventual resolution of symptoms that might occur would have the effect of postponing the possibility of organising an individual psychotherapy, even though the structural quality remains present.

This was what happened with Julien with respect to his sleeping difficulties and school results. He continued to have difficulties at the level of his thought processes, which questioned the links between the three registers of passiveness-masochism-femininity in the child. Moreover, it was towards this theme that everything converged at the end of this sequence of consultations, both in respect of what, in spite of everything, was active in the child and of what found an echo in each of the parents, including at the level of sexual identifications. But for Julien all this could probably only have its place within the context of an adult analysis. In this respect, experience shows that when analytic work took place during the patient's childhood or even adolescence, and if the work of repression, especially for the child, was possible, clear traces of it emerge in the associative functioning of the patient once he/she has become an adult.

On technique

If the therapeutic consultation has a certain specificity, it lies in the period during which the work is carried out with the child and with the parents who are present. I have described its broad outlines. The critical points are when the consultant communicates to the parents what he/she has identified concerning those elements of the child's functioning that underlie the difficulties for which he/she is seeking help. The reactions of the parents can be very varied: avoidance, apparent indifference, "as if" acceptance, different forms of negation (including denial), or, on the contrary, associative resonance which may include the personal past. At this level of the parent/child inter-cathexes, becoming aware of direct or inverted repetitions – repetitions that are fixed in the past of each of the parents – is the only thing that will help to mobilise each of the protagonists. These repetitions concern, of course, the vicissitudes of their oedipal organisation. An initial phase of this work will consist in giving the child's instinctual drive impulses an opportunity to express themselves, which is in the nature of the "subject", of subjectivation. What can be communicated to the parents may lead to reactions of a banal anticathexis-value unless, in the fortunate cases, there is a reaction of immediate associative resonance.

In the most worrying situations, the reaction mobilises above all the prevailing narcissism of one of the parents who tends to deny or control any instinctual expression of their child, in which case it will take them a long time to become aware of the repetitions mentioned above. Achieving such awareness implies that, during the ongoing process, the parent is able eventually to orient his/her cathexes towards "another" child, that is, *his/her own inner child*. A space that is necessary for the child's instinctual life is thus re-established. A triangular movement occurs, and we will not be surprised to find a correlation between this space and the potential of the oedipal situation. What is mobilised in a parent, beginning with what he/she expresses in an *anti-instinctual* mode vis-à-vis his/her child, including the encounter with his/her own past, concerns above all his/her ego, and more particularly his/her identifications and counter-identifications.

The portion of energy that is enclaved in the ego, and which is thus unavailable, can just as much play a part in establishing a new homeostasis as it can in creating an opening towards personal work for one of the parents. The therapeutic consultation has, in effect, its limits and is not to be seen as a panacea. It has a dual function of avoiding untimely indications of child analysis and/or of preparing for them better. The confrontation of a subject who is sufficiently mentally developed with the realm of his/her instinctual drive functioning, his/her sexuality, can only take place within the setting of a personal analysis. Before that (I am thinking of those children who have taken contact again with the centre in adulthood), the therapeutic consultation can sometimes take place at cruising speed, based on appointments at more or less frequent intervals. Development and progress always involve conflicts, and even occasional crises when change is the order of the day, the new cathexes giving fresh impetus to the evolving dynamic. In short, the consultant has become the family "shrink", like the family doctor.

Interventions and interpretations in psychoanalytic work with children[4]

In their article "Quelques réflexions sur l'interprétation en psychanalyse des enfants", Diatkine and Simon (1975) considered that forty years after Strachey's (1934) article, "The nature of the therapeutic action of psychoanalysis", the metapsychological understanding of the effects of interpretation had not progressed decisively. And yet today, we can say that there has been a general progression, and that Diatkine was one of the figures that helped psychoanalysis to progress. He did so without having any revolutionary aims and, moreover, was scarcely concerned with aims and purposes. But he had a sufficiently critical mind not to be taken in by what was supposedly new, however "well dressed up", and Freud remained for him, in terms of dialectical questioning, an inescapable referent. His practice as an analyst of adults as well as his practice as a psychiatrist/psychoanalyst thus always nourished his thinking about child analysis. In the article cited above, an article that may be considered as a "metapsychological complement" to the book written with Janine Simon, already mentioned, Diatkine emphasises from the outset the distinction that needs to be made between psychotherapeutic effects that can be brought about by varied techniques and those that relate to the specificity of psychoanalysis.

At the same time, this distinction did not result, as one might expect, in his thinking being infiltrated by a sort of idealisation of psychoanalysis. Evoking at the metapsychological level the conditions that must be met for a therapeutic process to be considered as psychoanalytic, he writes: "A certain number of economic and dynamic modifications must occur, translating a new transformation of the instinctual drive energy at the level of the ego, diminishing the negative effects of the repetition automatism" (Diatkine and Simon, 1975, p. 220). He adds, however, that such modifications can occur spontaneously or as a result of psychotherapeutic action. He thus introduces the supplementary condition of a "certain increased awareness of unconscious psychic activity", which specifies in its turn the "contrast between insight and the development of resistances" (ibid., p. 221). But it has been pointed out that what we know about the question of insight in the child before he/ she reaches adolescence places serious limits on this specificity. It will therefore come as no surprise that this context of reflection was marked by a certain pessimism evoked with reference to Strachey's (1934) article. Diatkine then changed direction, so to speak. He returned to the first sessions of the analysis of Carine with Janine Simon, putting the accent on the rather specific quality of the process that took place in connection with the analyst's interventions which may be described, for the time being, as having an interpretive value. In short, Janine Simon intervened swiftly at the level of the child's behaviour, at the level of – and in connection with – word-presentations, thereby deploying triangulation in several spirals, including a spontaneous account of a dream about a wolf.

The commentary of 1975 notes that "an important mutation occurred in five sessions" (p. 228), the psychoanalytic specificity of which was defined retrospectively. Diatkine was careful to point out in passing that such an interpretive strategy does not give priority to the Kleinian emphasis on the necessity of giving a swift interpretation of the negative transference, any more than it does to Anna Freud's "therapeutic alliance", which would imply a treatment aim which the child is not yet capable of. The Oedipus continues, therefore, to play its referential role, not only in the sense of the complex. The attention paid to the child's words, including those clearly referring to parental criticisms that the child reproduces through identification and which function as equivalents of day residues, takes account of the organisation of the child's unconscious. The interpretive interventions elaborated on the basis of the patient's language create new links, which gives rise, as Diatkine notes, "to a new possibility of pleasure for the ego" (p. 233), in relation to the anxiety provoked by the contradiction between oedipal wishes and pregenital instinctual drive derivatives. The analyst's interventions are, in short, a "story", which it is possible to repudiate. It should be added, however, that the negation that follows something the analyst has said may be a sign of its "validation", *provided that* a broadening of the associative field follows from it. Diatkine concludes that "the text of an interpretation must be studied not only in terms of unconscious phantasies and of the aspect of the transference to which it refers", but also in terms "of its links with the word-presentations that are part of the preconscious organisation of the young patient" (ibid.).

Concerning the metapsychological reflections taken from the article of 1975, and in favour of the echoes that they met with, it may be added that the metapsychology Diatkine makes use of falls within the Freudian trajectory; it is attentive "to the logics" underlying it, as described by Neyraut (1978). The exercise of these logics has its field of application in the space/time of the session, and in the transference/countertransference orientation, in such a way – and this seems to me to be coherent with what I shall call the author's position as a "general" analyst, that we are dealing with a methodological unity of technique, irrespective of the age of the "subject". In other words, it is a priority during the session – irrespective of the age and the psychic functioning of the child – to evaluate the singularity of his/her associativity, as well as his/her difficulties. The references to age, stages, positions, the different organising phases which unfold up until adolescence should only serve as a "safeguard", in conjunction with the priority concerning the associative singularity. If I have dwelt at some length on the article of 1975, it is because it seems to me to be a fine example of what was to appear in the subsequent contributions of the author.

In his paper, "Propos d'un psychanalyste sur la psychothérapie d'enfant", Diatkine (1982) returns to the question of the difference between analysis and psychotherapy, a question that had been left unanswered owing to a "change of direction". The essential object of his considerations pertains to the difference between what is psychotherapeutic and what is psychoanalytic in the practice of psychoanalysts, as well as to their respective effects. It is true mankind did not have to wait for psychoanalysis to exist to notice such effects. Words, nourished with symbolism, as well as by the unconscious of the "interpreter", have interpretive value. Let me add that in an article written with Madeleine Van Waeyenberghe (Diatkine and Van Waeyenberghe, 1990), Diatkine, bearing in mind the historical development of "psychoanalytically-inspired psychotherapies", considered that the distinction between psychotherapy and re-education was *not pertinent* concerning their effects. But this question did not concern him for very long, as the psychotherapies in question were oriented more towards the ego than the drive. Consequently, it is the problem of working-through (*Durcharbeitung*) that is at stake, for it cannot be defined solely in terms of symbolic expression or play.

Once the field of the non-psychoanalytic psychotherapies of psychoanalytic inspiration had been opened up, Diatkine introduced, within the analytic space itself, the distinction between interventions and interpretations. He notes that the first concern both psychotherapies and psychoanalyses, whereas the second concern only psychoanalyses and their working-through. Interventions, which are a feature of psychotherapies, only refer to the preconscious even if an indirect reference to the unconscious is not excluded, whereas interpretations convey directly the contents of the unconscious. Interventions involve making links, directly or through contrast, between elements of the material. As the author indicates, these elements are obviously in and of themselves already known to the child, *"only the link between the two terms is new"*. This approach can eventually lead, associatively, to the latent thoughts of the child, who we know does not easily express his/her thoughts before adolescence. Diatkine restricted the category of interpretation to unconscious phantasy and to desire, which is no less unconscious, thus adopting a contrary position to the previous category of the preconscious – a restriction that concerned this time of "what has *never* been thought by the subject".

In fact, in this text of 1982, he shows us that there is inevitably a moment when the two registers are articulated, thereby avoiding the impression that the dichotomy between intervention/psychotherapy/preconscious and interpretation/psychoanalysis/unconscious is too pronounced. It was probably this type of problem that led me in 1987 to propose the term *symbolic interpretation*. Diatkine would no doubt have included this type of interpretation within the register of interventions, except that in both cases it is an analyst that is at work. Furthermore, while this type of intervention or interpretation certainly involves the preconscious, it also involves the whole of the first topography of each of the protagonists.

To return to the articulation mentioned above, the author tells us that in the context of a psychotherapy, the psychoanalyst's capacity to give an associative response plays a part in re-establishing in the child an element of *continuity* which enables him/her to free him/herself from the repetitive processes that resulted in the difficulties that had led to the treatment and to discover a new coherence. Sometimes the treatment will end without it having been necessary or desirable to interpret at the level of the unconscious, leaving aside over-hasty interpretations of the *contents* of the unconscious. In other circumstances, the repetitive component of the transference can constitute, as Diatkine notes, a sufficiently important resistance to induce the analyst to change strategy by taking a more direct approach to the unconscious.

This type of work can occur at an early stage, as I mentioned in the case of Carine, by using both interventions and interpretations, as defined by the author. In one and the same analyst, or in a *psychotherapeutic* situation with a child, there can be overlappings, *a zone*, but only one, *of intersection* with non-analytic therapies. Beyond this, the analyst's work is specifically psychoanalytic insofar as it is concerned with the preconscious understood as the dynamic unconscious (Freud). The task of psychoanalytic working-through has the same function as interpretation in relation to unconscious phantasies, which have "never" been conscious (by revealing the processes of binding/unbinding underlying them them). It is worth noting in passing that an author like Rolland (2007) insisted on the presence of this word "never" in Freud's work. The context is emblematic, since it is Freud's text "A child is being beaten" (1919e), and concerns the second stage ("I am being beaten by my father") of the organisation of mental functioning. Freud writes that this second stage "has *never* had a real existence" (p. 185, my emphasis), which is added to the idea that *psychic masochism* (before it becomes *moral masochism*) cannot find its deep field of interpretation in the child.

During the same year of 1982, Diatkine introduced the Deauville Colloquium, whose theme was *interpretation*. He extended the considerations mentioned above and, concerning the work conducted by a psychoanalyst, proposed two meanings for the notion of interpretation: the first is the one to which I have just referred, while the second refers to the interpretation that the psychoanalyst makes *for him/herself* about the patient's psychic situation. The implication of this is that *interventions will necessarily be psychoanalytic* because they are based on the *internal* interpretive level of the analyst. Here is an illustration reported by Diatkine at the Deauville Colloquium. A six-year-old girl experienced a certain inhibition when he invited her to imagine the inhabitants of the house that she had just drawn. She then drew *outside* the house a little girl in a multi-coloured dress and with shining, golden yellow hair. Then she drew the sun above the little girl. Diatkine *intervened* (or *interpreted symbolically*, as I suggest) and said to the child: "The little girl has hair that is the same colour as the sun." The child emerged from the somewhat sad state in which she had been since the beginning and began associating in a much more sthenic mode. It might be claimed that anyone could have said that, but that is by no means certain. For the consultant's intervention was part of his interpretive space at an internal level. Moreover, when it is a matter of creating links between elements that are removed from each other in time (by months or years), there can be no doubt that it is necessary to be a psychoanalyst, even though we are still at the level of the preconscious. In connection with the dialectic preconscious/unconscious, Diatkine recalled a remark made by Fain (1982, p. 709) who noted that *interpretation was the anti-work of the dream*, and that the analyst's interpretations remained, insofar as they are latent thoughts, in the patient's preconscious. He added that these utterances had an effect of *attraction* for the cathexes arising from the unconscious.

Be that as it may, the psychoanalyst's various forms of response, including silence, can only exacerbate the ambivalence of the cathexis, thereby mobilising, as Diatkine (1989) points out, the "psychotic side" of mental functioning. This implies dealing with the contradictory relationship between pregenitality, which refers to the "total possession and intolerable annihilation of the other person", and genitality, which "must deal with the constancy of desire for, and preservation of, the object" (p. 725). On the other hand, there are also situations where the psychoanalyst is too passive, which leads to well-known situations in which "the desexualisation of the child analysis leads to a rupture" (ibid.). In the development of this strategy of intervention/interpretation, the opportunity, one that does not arise frequently, of interpreting at the unconscious level, while at the same time being prompted by an approaching "zone of incomprehensible repetitive contradiction", provides the "missing piece of the puzzle" (ibid., p. 727) as well as a new coherence. Age, moreover, is not a matter of indifference, and Melanie Klein was not mistaken on this point. Contrary to the case of Carine, we can take another example presented by Diatkine, that of an adult. The patient, a woman, behaved for several years like an anti-analysand, but at the same time engaged in a seductive and cultivated discourse (films, novels, music, etc.). The analyst gave her no interpretations, and in particular avoided any interpretation at the level of the mechanism of projective identification. The analyst remained at the level of interventions, which allowed his patient to feel her analyst was always listening.

A few years later, she sometimes wondered what it was that drove her never to miss a session, a position that enabled her to give meaning to her childhood memories. This evolution led her analyst to give her an oedipal transference interpretation, which in turn helped the patient to analyse the over-erotisation of the first years of treatment. This example is consistent with the conclusion of Diatkine who notes that "the 'ideal' interpretation" is probably one that can be formulated when the unconscious processes have *lost* their imperious necessity. Thus, in "Destins du transfert", Diatkine (1988) points out that interpretation is an *evolving ensemble*. He also notes that the elaborative value of an interpretation implies that it is *refutable* in Popper's sense of the word, and transformable in accordance with the discoveries of the other person. Likewise, he adds that when one is dealing with *preconscious* functioning, the question of the transference must not become taboo on the pretext that it is a first consultation. Thus, as a consultant, Diatkine, suggested to a girl aged eleven, who had lost her mother at the age of two, that she did a piece of free writing, after noticing, at the beginning of the consultation, that she presented herself with a sort of mask whenever she was in the presence of her father. She then wrote the story of a little girl who lived on a mountain with her grandfather. Diatkine intervened by telling her that here, too, she was with a grandfather. She smiled and became much more talkative.

In his text "Interprétations et processus psychanalytique", Diatkine (1989) introduced a distinction between the effects of interpretation on the analytic process and the effects which take root directly in the field of representations. As for the question of the process, he refers to the schizophrenic patient in analysis with Hanna Segal who would change the subject immediately after an interpretation, while showing that the analyst's interventions within the field of representations had a direct impact on the *unconscious* discourse of the patient. The interest of this text lies chiefly in the reflections of the author inspired by a paper by Jacqueline Schaeffer on the subject of two contrasting female patients, which led her to ask herself whether recourse to the Kleinian or post-Kleinian technique was necessary or not, depending on the difficulties encountered with certain patients. The discourse of the difficult patient, Milena, was one of a single voice, while the evolving situation showed that this monody was only apparent. Referring to something that was familiar for Freud, Diatkine returned to the subject of the other voice that is present in the psychotic, like that of the classical reciter. On the other hand, the discourse of Virginie, the neurotic patient, quickly occupied the place of the Proustian "narrator" as well as that of the protagonist. With time the divide between the two patients became less radical. The author draws attention to the fact that interpreting the negative transference and projective identification immediately has an impact on a certain approach and on a certain metapsychology: "From the moment one decides to interpret the projective identification immediately", he writes, "an entire strategy is put in place as well as an approach to metapsychology stemming from this strategy" (ibid., p. 809). Admittedly, the charge of anxiety must be named if the patient is to be able to introject and elaborate it. But the analyst's words do not necessarily avoid a certain degree of abstraction in spite of being rooted in the body (breast, good and bad, penis, babies, faeces, etc.), not to mention their explicative charge, which Strachey considered had very little therapeutic effect. Yet "it is the analyst's words and not the patient's that are taken up again", Diatkine notes (1989, p. 810).

On the occasion of the Deauville Colloquium on the question of remembering, Diatkine (1990) wrote a text which had direct implications for another question, namely, the end of analysis and of "analysing everything". Freud's articles, "Constructions in analysis" (1937d) and "Analysis terminable and interminable" (1937c) were at the basis of his considerations. At the time, Freud was dwelling on the fact that very often the patient could not recall repressed material, while noting that a work of construction could have the same effect as a recovered memory. He reiterated this in another form when he maintained that, by the end of the analysis, the patient should be expected to have refound or reconstructed the memories of infantile traumatic events. As Diatkine points out, Freud seemed more concerned with the question of truth (or of error) than with the question: "Is an interpretation correct when it is right or when it is given at the right time?" (Diatkine, 1990, p. 913). Such a question has, of course, its roots in the turning-point of 1920. It is connected with the idea of traumatic experience breaching the protective shield, and with the idea of the repetition automatism, including elaborations on the notion of the unrepresentable and the quality of the transference/countertransference dynamics in such contexts. Diatkine thus transforms the question: "Should interpretation convince the patient of a selective historic truth that has left behind it a pathogenic unconscious mnemic trace, or should it give a form to the psychic contradictions of the patient that allows for less restricted preconscious work?" (ibid., p. 915).

We can compare this methodology with the fact of recollecting a traumatic experience, even though we know that new resistances can appear, with, moreover, as the author points out, the possibility that the patient may create out of a recollection a "legend" feeding his/her resistances. Thus it seems even more heuristic to index the analyst's interventions to the novelty of the representations coming to the patient's mind than to the patient's approach to what his/her analyst has understood. The end of analysis depends then, much more on the internalisation of the dialogue between the patient and the analyst, which, let it be said in passing, will enable the two protagonists to separate from each other without maintaining the impossible ideal of "analysing everything". The permanence of the activity of the drives and of the unconscious will, in any case, have the effect of lowering this ideal. We can imagine the nature of these problems – becoming aware of unconscious phantasies, remembering forgotten past experiences – with children and their specific mode of organisation before the fundamental reorganisation of adolescence. Accordingly, Diatkine already considered the analytic experience of the child as a second phase during which both the child's earliest and more recent experiences are reinscribed. One of Diatkine's adolescent patients, whom he had treated in a context of therapeutic consultations at irregular intervals, came back to see him when she was an adult, having acquired the freedom to ask him to refer her to someone else. She said to him: "I haven't understood much about what went on with you but, since our meetings, I have a different understanding of what others think, and that is very useful to me" (ibid., p. 920). Diatkine's humour here may be a form of provisional conclusion, provisional because the dialogue, through others, is far from over.

Notes

1 This section takes up the article "A propos des interprétations en psych-analyse d'enfant", initially published in *Monographies de la Revue Fran-çaise de Psychanalyse*, Paris, Presses Universitaires de France, 1999, pp. 137–158. Reproduced here with the kind permission of the Presses Uni-versitaires de France.

2 This clinical case was first described in a paper "Interprétation symbol-ique, symbolisante" (Ody, 2012) read at the Paris Psychoanalytic Society Colloquium (19 November 2011) on *L'interprétation, Monographies et débats de psychanalyse de la Revue Française de Psychanalyse*, pp. 33–42, Paris: Presses Universitaires de France, 2012.

3 Translator's note: *méconnaissance*, an "active" misappreciation, whether on the patient's or analyst's part, ranging from negation to disavowal.

4 This section takes up the article "Interventions, interprétations dans le travail psychanalytique avec l'enfant", initially published in the *Revue Psychanalyse et Enfance du Centre Alfred Binet*, 30: 39–51 (Ody, 2001). Reproduced here with the kind permission of the Alfred Binet Centre.

CHAPTER FIVE

Concerning insight, the limits of "analysing everything", and the end of the analysis

*The limits of "analysing everything" in the child,
and the end of the analysis*[1]

Limits

Adult analysis confronts us less with the impossibility of "analysing everything" than with its pointlessness, the "utility" of it having more to do with the acquisition of a self-analytic functioning faced with the permanence of unconscious activity. Child analysis, on the other hand, confronts us with an additional limit, that of the elaboration of unconscious phantasies, given that this can only occur within the framework of an adult analysis, after the *ananké* of the second phase represented by adolescence. This is not because unconscious phantasies, relating to primal phantasies, cannot be interpreted, more or less symbolically, here or there, in the course of an analysis. The problem lies elsewhere. The child has a psychical apparatus whose organisation is evolving. It's "time arrow" (Eddington, 1928, p. 34, taken up subsequently by Prigogine) orients this organisation towards the constitution of *symbolisation*, *sublimations*, and *social relationships*. The thrust of the drive impulses of this ensemble leads the child to move away from the sexual contents most directly linked to the unconscious phantasies, precisely on account of the sublimated symbolic elaborations.

The vicissitudes of such elaborations orient the analyst's interpretations, and eventually even those that concern primal phantasies. In general, in the child, the associative contents that follow these interpretations are swiftly symbolised; they distance themselves from the sexual contents. If, on the other hand, a child dwells on what has just been interpreted, his/her associations will lead him (or her) to his infantile sexual theories. It remains the case that it is the quality of the symbolisation thus provoked that indicates whether the interpretation has been integrated or not. Such functioning is complementary to the physical and sexual immaturity of the child; being confronted with certain interpretive contents cannot fail to face him with his immaturity in the form of a gap between his analyst's body and his own. The risk, then, is that the analyst, by means of certain interpretations, will act out the primal phantasy of the seduction of the child by the adult. But here the analyst is with a real child, so that a limit is imposed on the possibility of "analysing everything" in the child. The aim of a child analysis, especially when it is conducted up until adolescence – as is the case in the example below – is not so much to analyse everything as to help the child to acquire a certain type of functioning. The traces of his (or her) experience will permit him, if ever he does further analytic work as an adult, to engage in the process differently, elaborating contents that were out of his reach before.

I will illustrate these remarks with the analysis of Daniel, a boy I worked with for seven years, from the age of nine to the age of sixteen, on a twice-a-week basis, and then once a week during the last years. The situation could be considered as a theoretical model, since sublimatory activities play a considerable role here. On the other hand, and as a limit, sadistic (and masochistic) incestuous phantasies and unconscious homosexuality (beginning with that induced in the transference) have been kept in reserve for an eventual resumption of analytic work "later on and elsewhere".

Movements of the treatment

A secondary enuresis had been the starting-point for the work undertaken. This symptom ceased permanently about two years later. Certain elements in this process played a part in the cure of this symptom.

For example, the fact that this boy, who did not draw, talked to me regularly about the use of his computer and the way it functioned, put me in a position where I lacked the "intermediate links" while, at the same time, being in danger of getting bored. Until the day, that is, when, fantasising about children's drawings, I asked him what kind of image might emerge from this computer. In the style of "whatever", he replied, "Oh . . . well, for example, a dandelion." The child was surprised when I picked up on this word. This first and powerful irruption of a *double meaning*[2] was what made him sensitive to the existence of the unconscious. This was the starting-point for the elaboration of a wide range of symbols and an activity of remembering with urethral connotations: eating problems at home, the number of litres of ink necessary for this or that comic strip, a feeding-bottle that he had kept during his early childhood as a toy, and which, one day, he used to sprinkle "joyfully" the walls of his bedroom, the fluidity of his writing, a "crazy" dream" evoking the disappearance of his younger siblings down the toilet hole. Then, last but not least, I noticed repeatedly that no sooner had he indicated to me that his enuretic symptoms had improved, or even disappeared, than they quickly reappeared. So my role in the transference was gradually taken into account by the child. It was this process of working-through that led to the permanent cessation of the symptom. Moreover, Daniel, who was an excellent pupil at school, had the particularity of having practically no memories or any activity of remembering concerning sexuality. On the other hand, his epistemophilic curiosity and sublimatory activity were quite intense.

Other than his collection of prizes for excellence, he manifested a sustained scientific interest which oriented him gradually towards the domain of electronics, one of his father's areas of interest. I couldn't help thinking of what Freud (1910c) wrote in connection with Leonardo da Vinci: "a component instinct of sexual desire . . . evades the fate of repression by being sublimated from the very beginning [*Anfang*][3] into curiosity" (p. 80). Anyway, Daniel seemed interested by the *logical contrast* that I noted between his epistemophilia and his apparent absence of any sexual curiosity. He was attentive, therefore to the deductions that I put to him on the basis of his own associations, deductions that implied sexual contents. Things didn't go much further than that, though Daniel was able to say to me at the beginning of a session: "I have been thinking about what you said to me and it's true that I have no memories about sexuality." This did not prevent him from continuing to elaborate his dream life. Just as his enuresis was abating, he had a dream to do with the symbolic exploration of the maternal body, while describing in a very detailed way the inside of a house.

Although the activity of exploration in the dream did not seem to have an ending, Daniel was able to make the link with the cessation of his symptom. On the other hand, he was unable to realise that such a dream was a retroactive sign of the incestuous connotation of the symptom while, at the same time, the "royal road" of the dream indicated a process that was underway. Approximately one year after his enuresis had stopped, he had another dream in which he put his finger into the lens of his mother's camera, only to get it bitten. Daniel was "interested" by the sexual content of his dream, but his associations once again took him in a different direction. Moreover, it was this type of example, owing to the incestuous sado-masocistic sexual content, that led me think about what had seemed to me difficult to approach other than through an adult analysis. About two months later a new dream allowed us to go further. The camera had become a video recorder, a thief wanted to get hold of it, he was fourteen years old. Daniel fought with him, but as he could not get the better of him, some "big tough guys" arrived to help him. This triangular dream indicated the mental trajectory that Daniel was taking towards adolescence, even though at that moment he was only eleven and a half years old. In a context of lateral logic and symbolisation, the unconscious phantasy of sadistic penetration was expressed once again. Daniel presented, in fact, a sort of new symptom in the form of a fear of destroying the program of his computer by making a false manoeuvre. The work we did on this symptom led him to say, at a given moment, thanks to the work of linking I was doing with him: "I see now, the computer is like my mother's camera." The manifestations of the symptom clearly diminished and disappeared totally at the onset of puberty, that is to say, following a summer vacation. Daniel had now reached the age of thirteen and his physique had changed. He said nothing of this, continuing practically straight on from the last session before the holidays when he had been talking about his computer. I pointed out this contrast to him. He seemed surprised, while agreeing with what I had said. I then linked this movement up with the dream of the video recorder, announcing the onset of adolescence. His reaction was immediate and full of humour: "Ah, adolescence, crime, delinquency!"

The session after, he told me that he wasn't afraid any more about his computer. I am not going to dwell on the signs of improvement in Daniel, for instance, a new ability to make friends, greater autonomy, a broadening of his leisure activities, etc. As for girls, Daniel always claimed that he was interested . . . naturally. But in fact, he said, "that will be for later". His evolution continued without any new symptoms, and it was just before the summer holidays (he was approaching the age of fourteen) that he wondered for the first time about ending his treatment. He said he would think about it during the holidays. But it was still a bit more than two years before it actually ended. It is this period that I want to discuss now, focusing on the meeting-point between the limit to "analysing everything" and the dynamics of the end of treatment in a child who has become an adolescent.

Limits and the end of the treatment

The first time that Daniel reflected on the end of his treatment had been the result of a brief symptomatic reactivation on the occasion of a movement of autonomy in his relationship to me. In the month of May, just before the summer holidays in question, he had preferred not to replace two sessions that fell on public holidays. But the following session he was gripped again, "just in my mind", he said, by the fear related to his computer. The link that I then suggested to him between this thought-symptom and what I translated as a wish for autonomy regarding his unreplaced sessions prompted him to say: "I didn't think about it; it must be unconscious." I should add that just before the holidays, he had a dream of separation in which he was merrily firing away at a series of teachers with a pistol of good quality. He decided "all the same" that he would turn himself in ('Ah, adolescence, crime . . .'). It was now that his first thoughts about the end of his treatment emerged.

On returning from his holidays, he mentioned nothing leading in this direction. But following a certain number of considerations linked to change, he came back to the famous computer. He said he wasn't afraid any longer and wondered why. I said to him that this perhaps suggested that he needed to continue his sessions a bit longer, even though he was thinking of stopping. He said nothing on this subject but evoked it in connection with what had happened in May concerning his unreplaced sessions, telling me that after the holidays he had planned to mention, before the beginning of each session, his wish to stop, but that curiously, during the session, it didn't cross his mind. And this latent thought was followed by another. If he stopped, would his fear concerning his computer not come back again? He realised then that this process was not unsimilar to that relating to the end of his enuresis. Taking account of these types of latent thoughts kept out of the sessions allowed others to be formulated, this time in relation to his past treatment, which had hitherto also remained outside the sessions. These concerned fantasies in which he was building empires, cities, under the sea, in particular. This had nothing to do with Alexander the Great; they were empires just for him, for his tranquillity, the pleasure being to build and invent mechanisms. For example, he had "invented" what, much later on, he would call "reverse osmosis", a procedure of hydrostatic pressure consisting in increasing the passage of seawater, with a view to its desalination, through a membrane that could retain salt.

As he grew older, his fantasies became less grandiose. Thus, when he was imagining himself as a single-handed sailor, it was primarily a question of improving the features required by such a boat, even the most sophisticated, in order to perform at its best, and for comfort and safety. Electronics was, of course, king. From what could have become a thought-activity, with a particular orientation, Daniel none the less managed to identify the function that it had in connection with the relations from which he was trying to protect himself. As is often the case, it was an emergence of polysemy that enabled us to move forward. Daniel was fourteen and a half at the time of a session in which he found he had no associations, being very occupied with his work. He talked about the natural sciences and, as if by chance, the anatomy of the heart, about which, of course, he knew everything in advance. I pointed out that we had already talked about the heart, albeit from a different angle, in the past. He immediately understood the meaning of what I had said: "Love!", he said, immediately engaging in "well thought-out" considerations on the subject of "passionate love" (*amour-passion*) in Racine and "reasonable love" (*amour-raison*) in Corneille. He then recalled, however, the amused reproach a friend had made about him: "A heart of stone, everything in the brain!" After defending himself a bit, and after I had reminded him of his isolation and suffering in the past, I asked him if having a "heart of stone" and "everything in the head" was not a way of ensuring that he could protect himself against *feelings*.

Daniel then spoke "plainly", telling me that if he were to give free expression to his feelings, he would undoubtedly be afraid of not being able to control them. But, as was his wont, he went no further; just as when he touched on the sexual impulses of his now adolescent body. Daniel contented himself with saying that "that" didn't bother him; his interests were elsewhere. If I insisted too much, I would be in danger of putting myself in a position of seducer and of stirring up deeply unconscious homosexual feelings, undoubtedly of decisive significance but completely unapproachable. There was a *limit* here, too, to "analysing everything". From thereon our exchanges became more desexualised. We had reached a sort of cruising speed, with Daniel talking to me about his interests, his discoveries and his inventions. He told me all these stories and even took me in with them. Admittedly, the potential seducer was seduced; indeed, I was never bored. It was a sort of tale of the Arabian Nights. The "cruise" was such that I "woke up" *in extremis* during the last two sessions before the summer. He would soon be sixteen, and that was the time when he had begun to think about ending his treatment. But he had not spoken any further about this. My remark on this apparent forgetfulness led him gradually to express some significant latent thoughts. He then told me about the thoughts he had recently been having outside his sessions. Since everything had gone well that year, he thought he could stop. But, in addition, after this sort of verification, of preconscious testing, as if to convince me, he told me that sometimes, while he was walking along, he had a "Dr Ody in his head", whom he talked to, like during a session. Finally, he had even thought that the moment of stopping shouldn't necessarily correspond to the holidays, and that he could still benefit from a few more sessions. Later, he decided he would stop when the Christmas holidays came.

After the summer, Daniel, who had enjoyed his holidays, continued to talk to me about his interests until one day he told me could not find the name of a well-known game he had programmed. Then, *Fiat lux!* "*le morpion*",[4] he said. Faced with this polysemic emergence, I experienced a certain amount of hesitation; some analogous but distant examples came back to my mind. I shared my thoughts with him. Daniel admitted that he did not know the sexual meaning of this word. It was an opportunity for him to return to the theme of sexuality, as if to take stock of the situation. It was still not a problem for him; he would deal with it later. He had noticed, moreover, that some friends of his who, two years earlier, had tended to be quite agitated on that level, now spoke about this subject much more calmly. However, everything that had just been said came up again in the following sessions, when he noticed that he was thinking about two things at the same time: the computer and sexuality. I said to him that it was perhaps a way of establishing a link between them. He associated to the fact that he had noticed that his friends avoided using the computer too much because "it stops you from working". This masturbatory equivalent was not valid as far as he was concerned. The thought suddenly came to him: "The computer is a replacement for sexuality!" Astonished by this "vicissitude of the drive", he added: "It would definitely be a problem if it replaced it."

A few days later, he forgot a session. He was surprised that he had only realised this the day before the next session. He realised that this parapraxis was part of the process of ending the treatment. It was a "successful attempt", he even said. He spontaneously compared this situation with that of two and a half years earlier when he had appre- hended the return of a symptom following sessions that he had inten- tionally not replaced. It was at that moment that he imagined that our work would end when the Christmas holiday period came. He sup- posed that these holidays, which he likes a lot, would attenuate the effect of the separation. This was an opportunity for me to return to the expression of his feelings (the "heart of stone"). He was moved, while going on to speak about his friendships, by how he was dealing with those he had created during the summer, during the period of separation.

The two last sessions

I will now say a few words on the last two sessions. In the first, he talked about a conflict with his younger brother, whom he described as the "antithesis" of himself, on the subject of their grandmother. Daniel defended her in a very lively manner. I pointed out to him that he was not a "heart of stone". He was surprised, and acknowledged this with a smile, while evoking his tendency to control his feelings. A silence fol- lowed. Somewhat "heated" by the limited time remaining, I intervened and reminded him of how he had protected himself before with fanta- sies to do with building empires and cities. Daniel relaxed. He said he was more "realistic" now, also about sailing single-handed. We gradu- ally came to see that in everything that he built, imagined and invented, there was no risk of an unduly prolonged encounter developing. Daniel replied that this was precisely what irritated his mother with regard to the television whose system of reception he was perfecting. His mother was unable to watch her favourite programme as a result. I found myself, therefore, *in extremis*, in a situation similar to that of the "*morpion*". I shared with him what came to my mind, the dream of his mother's camera, as well as the dream of the videorecorder. Daniel was intrigued, for he had completely *repressed* these memories. He justified himself by saying that we had not mentioned these dreams recently, which was why he didn't recall them.

Now that these links had been (re-)established, I showed him that his technical improvements perhaps had the function of preventing him from finding himself in a similar situation to that of the dream of the camera, a comparison which, through the intermediary of his mother, suggested the difference of the sexes, and sexuality. "Ah, now that's too much!", Daniel said, surprised, amused, and worried. This brings us to the last session. It took place after the holidays because a metro failure had meant that Daniel arrived too late for his session. I proposed to replace it when he returned from his holidays. The holidays "went very well", he said. A new conflict had broken out, though, between him and his brother. Their mother had taken his brother's side. "It was too much," Daniel added. "So that was too much, then", I said. He didn't remember. I pointed out, then, that this session was the last. Daniel returned to his problems with his brother, adding that he persecuted their sister. "Because she's a girl?" I asked him? "Perhaps," Daniel replied. I reminded him in connection with the subject of "that's a lot" that the dream of the camera was also about the difference of the sexes. "I got my finger bitten by the diaphragm," he said! "Perhaps it's a situation that symbolises sexuality," I replied. He confirmed this intellectually and, irresistably, returned to the subject of his brother.

"Last session," I said to myself. I waited. The minutes went by. I thought about my "last card". I said to myself, "too bad, it's going to be a lot". I said to Daniel that as it was the last session perhaps he didn't really want to "leave" on the subject of sexuality, and that he would prefer to speak to me about his brother. He acknowledged this.

I then added that the sexuality I was talking about in connection with his dream was like that which a child (for whom the first woman is his mother) may apprehend . . . as a risky form of sexuality. "Ah, *la femme piège*!" [lit. the woman trap] Daniel replied, laughing. Finally, something was emerging here as we were coming to the end of the session. Daniel knew that his work would continue and that if he wanted to see me again one day, even if just to take stock, it was of course possible.

Oh well! we cannot analyse everything . . .

Insight in the child[5]

Among the different points of view that could refer to the child/adult dialectic in analysis, there is one that is necessarily in question, namely, insight, and more particularly insight in the child.[6] The first difficulty is that of its definition as an English term, since no French equivalent has been found. Insight is related to the idea of perspicacity, of penetration, of sharp perception (in-sight = *vue dedans*). This denotation exists before any directional connotation, which, as far as psychoanalysis is concerned, concerns the subject himself. It is worth noting that this term, or its German equivalent (*Einsicht*), was not particularly developed by Freud, even though he used it. Its translation into French can sometimes lead to an element of abuse, such as that which can be found in the French translation (*Psychanalyse d'un enfant*, 1973) of Melanie Klein's (1961) book, *Narrative of a Child Analysis*, where the term insight is translated by *prise de conscience*. Strictly speaking, the latter implies the first topography constituted by the *Unc./Pcs./Cs.*

Correlatively, one is led to wonder about the links between this idea of *prise de conscience* and the Freudian term *Bewußtwerden* ("becoming conscious", and in French, *le devenir-conscient*). In Freud's work, becoming conscious is linked to the thought processes that have their roots in the unconscious starting with links between thing-presentations. It will depend, as we know, on their linkage with the "verbal residues" which lead to word-presentations. In "The unconscious", Freud (1915e) writes: ". . . the existence of the censorship between the *Pcs.* and the *Cs.* teaches us that becoming conscious is no mere act of perception, but is probably also a *hypercathexis*, a further advance in the psychical organisation" (p. 194, Freud's emphasis). We know that this hypercathexis is one of thing-presentations by word-presentations, psychic work that is situated topographically at the level of the *Pcs.* It is worth noting in passing that contemporary psychoanalysis has placed the accent on the fate of affect and its vicissitudes. As hermeneutics is situated exclusively at the level of the *signifying effect (signifiance) of représentance*, it was no longer relevant for "difficult cases". Finally, as far as the affect representative of *représentance* is concerned, it is no longer considered purely as a means of accompanying the formal, for example, visual representability (*figurabilité*), but as a witness "in itself" to psychic life at an even more fundamental level than the *Unc.*, that is to say, in the most opaque aspects of the Id itself.

This led psychoanalysts to turn towards the unrepresented, or towards the unrepresentable. Although being receptive to affect in the dynamics of the transference/countertransference is of crucial importance in analysis, at a given moment affect will have to deal with the transformation that will link it to signifying *représentance*, for example language in the human being. These remarks can only serve to reinforce the fact that becoming conscious, far from being a fact in itself, enters into the processual movement of every analysis, and that this concept goes beyond the notion of *insight*, which is too limited to perception. This coincides, moreover, with another consideration of Freud in the same text of 1915: "The more we seek to win our way to a metapsychological view of mental life, the more we must learn to emancipate ourselves from the importance of the symptom of 'being conscious'" (Freud, 1915e, p. 193). In this sense, if the process of becoming conscious is a first metapsychological linkage with the notion of insight, there is a second which is the notion of elaboration (or working-through, *Durcharbeitung*).

The notion of working-through was, moreover, the subject of divergences concerning the appraisal of its very definition, of its status, at the 8th Conference of the European Psychoanalytic Federation in 1989. Some tended to extend its meaning to the therapeutic process itself, and even to the process of development impeded by the subject's psychopathological functioning. Others tended to limit its definition to what was supposed to overcome resistances. As foreshadowed by the evolution of the concept (or notion?) of repetition compulsion between 1914 and 1920, many insisted on the fact that the extension of analysis to nonneurotic patients meant that the narcissistic dynamics of these patients had to be taken into account in the process of working-through. Green noted that there was a dialectic between resistance to working-through and the working-through of resistances. In addition, the difficulties met with in these patients required elaboration on the part of both the patient and the analyst through the transference/countertransference dynamics.

The notion of co-elaboration was thus put forward, referring to the outcome of work in process on this particular tenacious resistance to elaboration as the expression of a negative narcissism (Green, 2001) and an attack on activities of linking (Bion, 1959).

Beyond these questions which concern general psychoanalysis, it is also worth noting the relationship between working-through and the work of mourning, in the sense that the subject must renounce or abandon something in order to acquire something else. Resistance is, of course, included in this movement. Remember that adolescence is a second stage of psycho-sexual development separated by latency, whose uncertainties are well-known in clinical work with children. Thus, all the problems of working-through, of the process of becoming conscious, of insight in the child, are dependent, in their expression, on the quality of the constitution of this period prior to the second stage. This last remark indicates that with children things are made more complicated by the fact that the psychical apparatus is still evolving.

Regardless of the sometimes surprising capacities (that are often subsequently repressed) which certain children show during sessions, they are situated more on the *trajectory of insight* than on that of "accomplished" insight, if we understand that to be the sign of an identification with the analyst's interpreting function. But not all *self-observation* amounts to insight, something Anna Freud had clearly noted. In this connection it is remarkable, moreover, that in *The Technique of Psychoanalysis: Discussions with Anna Freud* (Sandler et al., 1980), in which a chapter is devoted to this notion, the clinical examples presented involve either self-observation or, which tends to confirm what I am saying, the characteristics of insight. An example is given of an 18-year-old adolescent who is capable of making an interpretation but who begins by saying to the analyst: "I know what you are going to say" (p. 72) as an "intermediate stage" in the development of insight. The latter, moreover, is defined as "becoming aware of what has previously been unconscious" (p. 69).

For Hanna Segal (1981) things are not very different, for what she defines as insight from a psychoanalytic point of view concerns the "acquisition of knowledge of one's own unconscious" (p. 124, translated from the French). Thus, both authors, even though they insist on the necessity of the process of working-through, bypass the concept of becoming conscious. I was insisting earlier on the fact that, in the child, the psychical apparatus is still evolving. This evolution is marked by organising stages which provide anchorage for this evolving "pressure" (primary triangulation, the Oedipus complex, puberty), anchorage both for erotic cathexes inhibited in their aims and for identifications. The trajectory leading to insight and its limit – the second of which depends on the identification with the analyst's interpreting function – will, however, depend on the quality of secondary, in other words, post-oedipal identifications. Moreover, all identifications play a part in the subject's sense of identity. In the child, their trajectory, from the most primary to the most secondary identifications, has a certain dynamic lability owing to development.

This is why identifying with the strange discourse of his psychoanalyst, behind closed doors, is for the child both an object of interest and a source of danger. Admittedly, the danger of seduction illustrates the primal phantasy of being seduced by an adult, but the analyst's strange discourse also mobilises a sense of uncanniness and sexual co-excitation in response to the "intellectual strain" (Freud, 1905d, p. 204) that can seize hold of the child when faced with any interpretive situation or with any change that he/she introduces into his/her discourse. All this disturbs the child's sense of identity, even if he/she presents rapid capacities for regression and recovery in comparison with the adult. Thus any movement of insight can resonate with the omnipotence of thought, since animistic thinking can be activated regressively. This dynamic plays a part in moments of insight in the child which emerge like a flash and then disappear for a long time because they have been repressed. Could we thus be faced with an aporia concerning the question of insight in the child? If every progressive trajectory mobilises the dangers that I have just mentioned by considering that the potential adult in the child, represented here by the trajectory towards insight, can only have a function of purposive aim for the analyst, this can only reinforce the analyst's attention to the dimension of working-through and to the processual aspects of analysis.

During this process, manifestations of this process of becoming conscious emerge, most of the time in unpredictable ways, which count among the felicitous moments in analysis. This brings us back, then, to the problem of *associativity* in the child, with the particular feature that it has before puberty of being subject to sudden changes of expression. Remember we are talking about the swift transition from a verbalisation to a figurative (drawing, play) or behavioural action, even though the child does not necessarily communicate his/her latent and even conscious thoughts. The analyst's interpretive activity is thus frequently situated at the symbolic level. Spontaneously or deductively, it can lead him/her to the child's latent thoughts concerning his/her daily life and past, and ultimately to the interpretation of unconscious phantasies, which hark back to the primal phantasies and their derivatives. All these conditions play a part in the process of becoming conscious and in the trajectory towards insight. The aforementioned strangeness of this stranger that the psychoanalyst is for the child gradually becomes more familiar. The very fact that an analysis may last several years serves as a support for the formation of secondary identifications in which the investments that the child makes in his/her analyst, in association with his/her function and position as a real person, play a part. Indeed, as with the adult, every intervention or interpretation, the tone and the music with which it is formulated, will have a particular effect as an immediate association, whether it is in the form of words, play or graphic expression, containing the interpretation directly or symbolically. The content may emerge after a period of latency. There is also the possibility of a destructive and/or disorganised reaction, or alternatively an absence of any reaction.

What may take the form of insight will intervene in such moments. However, progressive access to the familiar that I was speaking about will not suffice for the child to be able to speak about his/her process of "becoming conscious". He/she may very well, just as is the case with his/her preconscious and conscious thoughts, keep them for him/herself, especially as it is a new situation in the analysis. Sometimes he/she will speak about it much later on when evoking the past. This temporal distance will play its part in the potential adult that is taking shape in the child and can manifest itself in various ways. Thus Jean-Éric sometimes referred, directly and verbally, to what I was communicating to him, the indexation referring to his associations in his play or graphic activities. He would sometimes say after one of my interpretations: "I know how you think, Dr Ody." I should add that given his narcissistic difficulties and, correlatively, the great rapidity of his manifestations of excitation and sexual co-excitation in the face of any progressive emergence, he feared intensely what he experienced as my strangeness and its consequences. A good way for him to ward off "overwhelming" excitation was to attack my analytic function, whereas during more relaxed periods, he could speak to me with humour. This was the case, you will remember, during a moment of sexual co-excitation, when he left a session to go to the toilet, but he was able to take this up again in new and different context saying: "I know what you are thinking: you're thinking that I'm going to go to the WC! Well, no, I'm not!" Another example is Daniel, about whom I have spoken at length and whose treatment was at moments punctuated by movements of insight, especially during the process, as he was entering adolescence, that led him to sexualise "devices" (camera, computer, cassette recorder).

The theoretical and clinical ideas developed above indicate that during a child analysis the trajectory towards insight raises the essential problem of what becomes of the analyst's interpretations in connection with the identification that the child forms, via his/her cathexes, with the function of the interpreting analyst. We have considered the fact that there is a limit to this function, a limit that is related to the "incompletion" of the psychical apparatus of childhood and adolescence. Nevertheless, the process of analysis can also open up the path towards adult potentiality, as the "royal road" of dreams shows. The child is necessarily faced both with regressive tendencies and with potentiality. This is what leads me to speak of the "trajectory towards insight" rather than simply of insight, given that certain psychic contents can only be elaborated within the setting of an adult analysis. It is also worth bearing in mind two remarks of Freud which lead in the same direction. One, where he points out in his paper "The unconscious" (1915e) that the separation between the *Ucs.* and *Pcs./Cs.* systems only takes place in puberty; and the other, in a text that appeared one year earlier, "On narcissism: an introduction" (1914c), where he links the dream censorship with the ego ideal, an "ego ideal" that he considers as a separating principle between consciousness on the one hand and self-consciousness on the other.

Notes

1 This section was first published as an article titled, "Limites du 'tout analyser' chez l'enfant, et fin de la cure" in *Revue française de psychanalyse*, 4, 1107–1115 (Ody, 1994a). Reproduced here with the kind permission of the Presses Universitaires de France.

2 Translator's note: *Pissenlit* may be understood also as "pissing in bed".

3 A question that was explored in depth by J.-L. Baldacci (2005) in his report: "Dès le début" . . . la sublimation?".

4 Translator's note: *morpion* has various meanings in English: it may refer to the game "noughts and crosses", or to the crab (pubic) louse, or perjoratively to a child in the sense of a "little brat".
5 This section was first published as an article titled, "L'adulte dans l'enfant et *l'insight*" in the *Revue française de psychanalyse*, 3, pp. 681–689, (Ody, 1994b). Reproduced here with the kind permission of the Presses Universitaires de France.
6 A question I returned to in relation to reflexivity (Ody, 2012).

Conclusion[1]

B
y way of conclusion, I would like to stress the importance of two concepts, present throughout this book, for understanding analytic work with the child and the adolescent: the first is the preconscious and the second is Oedipus as an attractor.

The Freudian concept of the preconscious has certainly helped me in my psychoanalytic work with the child, concerning what can be shared with him/her, ever since my report to the Congress for French-speaking psychoanalysts on the theme "Le langage dans la rencontre entre l'enfant et le psychanalyste" (Ody, 1987). The question of the pre-conscious has served me as a compass, enabling me to keep my bearings as a general analyst of children and adults.

What is commonly described as "contemporary analysis", start-ing particularly from the vertex of the contributions of André Green concerning non-neurotic situations, raises seriously the question of the preconscious, especially as, like the whole of the first topography, it is undermined in the context of such clinical situations. The numerous contributions by Green over the last decade, in which he has explored in depth the question of the second topography as well as that of the death drive, attest to this. A number of his formulations have great merit, such as the one, concerning the period after 1923, where he speaks of the irrevocable character of Freud's abandonment of the concept 'unconscious' which is no more than a psychic quality; or when, in the *Voies nouvelles de la thérapeutique psychanalytique* (Green, 2006) he speaks of "the instinctual drive impulses which constitute the id and which henceforth replace the concept 'unconscious'" (p. 17).

If we follow the current evolution of psychoanalysis, we continue to find confirmation of the existence of a complementarity between reflections on "non-neurotic" situations with adults and those relating to psychoanalytic work with the child. A personal example is that of a child/parent(s) psychoanalytic therapeutic consultation which makes it possible, at least in situations that go beyond the indications of psychoanalytic psychotherapy (or analysis), to carry out work that is nonetheless psychoanalytic within situations marked by a dysfunctioning of *représentance*. At the other end of the chain, still concerning the child and, more specifically, cases of autism and psychosis, the evolution of the work by Geneviève Haag and more recently by Laurent Danon-Boileau emphasise their compatibility with the evolution of the general metapsychology based on Freud's work. In other words, the extension of psychoanalytic work over the decades has nourished its complexity, which, in turn, has enriched the open coherence of the discipline as a whole.

One aspect of the question was in a certain way foreshadowed by Freud himself. Indeed, as early as the *Project* (Freud, 1950[1895d]), Freud had referred to preconscious thought, and he then named the preconscious as such in the following year in his letter to Fliess dated 6 December 1896 (Masson, 1985, p. 208). While the concept is present in a large part of his work ("The Unconscious", 1915e; *The Ego and the Id*, 1923b), Freud nonetheless declared in *An Outline of Psychoanalysis* (1940a[1938]) that he would "attempt presently to attack the problem of the true nature of the preconscious" (pp. 162–163), while asking himself a bit further on: "What . . . is the true nature of the state which is revealed in the id by the quality of being unconscious and in the ego by that of being preconscious, and in what does the difference between them consist?" (p. 163). And his answer was, "But of that we know nothing. And the profound obscurity of the background of our ignorance is scarcely illuminated by a few glimmers of insight" (ibid.). An impressive confession when we consider that it was written in 1938! In order to differentiate between the unconscious state and the preconscious state, Freud then returns to the notions of freely mobile energy and bound energy, of cathexis and hypercathexis, of primary process and secondary process, though it is noteworthy that the term representation, and even less the term word-presentation, does not appear on this last page of Chapter 4 of the *Outline* . . . on "Psychical Qualities".

A leap of 45 years leads us to the Report by Andrée Bauduin (1987) titled "Du préconscient", a huge work on the subject that deserves to be re-read. For my present purpose, I will simply extract two ideas from it. The author resolutely links the preconscious and repression, with its consequences at different levels, and illustrates the question of the status of the preconscious in difficult cases. As far as the first is concerned, she is led to conceive of the preconscious as the "result of the work of repression", to define repression as an "organiser of the *Pcs*." or, in relation to the second topography, to define the *Pcs.* as "the part of the ego where repression is operative" (p. 480). What follows from this with regard to the dialectic between repression and the return of the repressed will concern as much the anti-cathexes, and their function of protecting against stimuli, as the intermediate formations where the linguistic operator is engaged with its symbolising function, and ultimately also constructions, such as those based on infantile sexual theories.

This rapid overview of Andrée Bauduin's Report resonates essentially with the first topography. The author does not stop there, and moves on to the second point mentioned, relating to difficult cases, those which continue to be a feature of what is called contemporary clinical practice. She goes on to reflect on the question of the alteration of the preconscious and, given her experience in the domain of psychosomatics, and more particularly with asthmatic adults and children, it is not surprising that the analyses and illustrations she offers us come from that domain.

This served as a starting-point for fresh theoretical elaborations by authors such as Pierre Marty, Michel de M'Uzan – the latter in connection with paradoxical phenomena in analysis – Denise Braunschweig and Michel Fain, along with authors such as André Green and Francis Pasche, César and Sára Botella, concerning the question of limits, the problem of the double, and of the unrepresentable. Finally, however much importance is ascribed to the archaic, Andrée Bauduin points out that it can serve as a screen against sexual drive activity and secret sexual theories and/or masturbatory erotic fantasies, which leads her to say that the preconscious, even though it does not reveal itself immediately, is our only therapeutic lever. At the opposite pole from the "archaic as a screen" is the "danger of non-representation".

But questions concerning the preconscious tend to become displaced, in the ordinary sense of the word, on to those of the analyst faced with the various forms of dysfunctioning of the preconscious of patients. These questions are in keeping with the history of psychoanalysis and the consideration given to the impact of the functioning of the external object on that of the subject, and on the dynamics of the transference/countertransference in the context of inter- and intrapsychic articulations. Thus, in the case where the articulation between repression and the unconscious gives way to denial, preconscious functioning is undermined, with, in the case of displacement on to the analyst, the attendant danger of leading to a "community of denial", an expression used by Michel Fain and cited by Andrée Bauduin. But before embarking on a discussion of the contemporary relevance of the preconscious, it is necessary to recall the essential place given to the preconscious by Pierre Marty, who went as far as to say that the analyst can "lend" his own preconscious during analysis. It is particularly useful to return to Marty's writings on the subject in that his language sometimes has metaphorical resonances which are reminiscent both of Freud (1950 ([1895d])) in the *Project* and Gerald Edelman (1989) in the *The Remembered Present: A Biological Theory of Consciousness*.

Pierre Marty's work reveals the essential place that he attributes to the dysfunctioning of the preconscious. In what follows, I will refer to three of his contributions. In his book *Mouvements individuels de vie et de mort* (Marty, 1976), he defines the first topography as "centred on a mode of mental functioning that is organised around the necessity of maintaining a constant tension of excitation" (p. 91, note 1, translated for this edition). This is an economic point of view, rarely encountered in such a context with Freudian resonances, except for its reference to a principle of constancy. In *La nuit, le jour*, Braunschweig and Fain (1975) also drew attention to the economic function of the preconscious. The mediating function of the preconscious on the "impact of excitation", Marty continues, occurs through the linking of word-presentations and thing-presentations, "an essential form of mastery" (Marty, 1976, p. 92). The link between the second phase of the anal stage and what Freud noted concerning the preconscious may be seen as analagous to the link between word-presentations and thing-presentations. It was considerations such as these that led Marty to reverse what he called "a classical position in psychoanalysis", where the first topography is considered as one aspect of the second topography. In other words, he advanced the idea that a "suitable functioning of the first topography is necessary to the progressive formation of the second topography . . ." (p. 91). Naturally, as for the first topography, each of the agencies of the second are interdependent, regardless of the question of the qualities of each of the agencies.

Another contribution of Marty's work, present in *L'ordre psychosomatique* (Marty, 1980) is connected with what he calls "sensory-motor accommodation" with quasi-Winnicottian resonances. It concerns what he defines as the "intermediate stage" between a so-called auto-erotic (*anobjectal*) narcissism and a well-differentiated subject/object state. He designates this intermediate stage as an "evolving stage" "at the crossroads of the imaginary and the symbolic". It is a stage "that necessarily precedes the organisation of the second topography" (ibid., pp. 81–82). Marty notes in this connection:

> Preconscious representations, of which we will have evidence later, seem to be formed in which the protagonists are identified (designated, named), but the external objects, oneself, the internal objects, are poorly isolated, have a low level of abstraction, and mixed up in mutual inclusions . . . effective distance is not portrayed . . . in dream life, there are innumerable references to this stage.
>
> (Marty, 1980, p. 82)

Concerning this formation of preconscious representations, we can assume that the fact of "naming" them takes on the nature of "corporealised" proto-language. It remains essential that it is mixed, like the mutual inclusions of which Pierre Marty speaks.

These considerations enter into resonance with Freud's (1891b) work on aphasia, which shows us that what will lead to word-presentations forms part of a "representative complex" with several parameters (those in Fig. 8, p. 77). There is a resonance with Winnicott when he evokes an intermediate area between complete fusion and interpersonal relationships, concerning the layer comprised of maternal substance and infantile substance. The "madness" that Winnicott attributes to himself in such a case refers to the idea that the roots of this intermediate area lie at the placental level, as part of the child and the environment. In such conditions, the acoustic traces of the mother's words with their double valency, erotic and anti-cathecting, will partake in the formation of the *Pcs*. This leads to a generativity of the intermediate area that participates in the formation of the preconscious. Adding greater complexity to this ensemble, we can link it up with the conception of early secondary narcissism developed by Braunschweig and Fain, which includes the narcissistic libidinal cathexes coming from the parents. Finally, it may be added, this intermediate ensemble contains the roots of thirdness.

The third contribution concerns the idea of the "density of the preconscious" that Marty (1990, p. 44) developed in his book *La psychosomatique de l'adulte*. For him, the preconscious is stratified both topographically, its deep layers being "in close contact with the *Ucs.*, the soma, the instincts and the drives", while its higher levels reach the *Cs.*, and also *chronologically* insofar as it "is comprised of successive mental acquisitions particularly during the course of development". Marty adds that "the two systems of stratification interfere with each other constantly and the *Pcs.* is established finally as a reservoir of representations from different epochs which are more or less interrelated and more or less ready to reach the *Cs.*" (p. 39). The result is that the trajectory of a sufficiently differentiated "proto" is that of a representational universe, in which Green was interested.

Marty also tackled the question of the "two major difficulties in the constitution of the *Pcs.* and its functioning" (p. 43). It was in this context that he described the double system of inscription and linkage, synchronic (or transversal) and diachronic (or longitudinal), which extends from the formation to the constitution of representations. This double dynamic system, with its retrogressive movements and its fluidity of associative circulation between transversal and longitudinal linkages, is what suggests the density of the preconscious. The difficulties evoked concerning such a constitution and functioning are, for the author, both fundamental and secondary flaws. As far as the first are concerned, it is a matter of the "quantitative and qualitative insufficiencies of psychic representations as well as the insufficiencies of the affective connotations of these representations", whereas for the second it is a question of the "uncertainty in the phase of remembering more or less vast swathes of unrepressed representations . . . but easily subject to avoidance and suppression" (p. 45). It should be noted that we are not far here from what can lead to associative functioning in the "central phobic position" (Green, 2002c), and which touches upon the unconscious itself. This is indeed the question that Marty's conception of the *Pcs.* raises, namely, that of knowing where to place the cursor between what is still part of the unconscious and what is already preconscious. This debate has existed since Freud, ever since the separation between the descriptive unconscious and the dynamic unconscious. Contrary to what certain statements by André Green might lead us to believe, the issue raised by his contributions is not that of abandoning the first topography, including the preconscious, in the context of contemporary psychoanalysis, but of restoring it, with regard both to what this clinical field confronts us with and to what had led Freud towards embarking on a certain revolution of his ideas concerning the structure of the mind, at least after 1920.

The major point that André Green puts at the centre of his argument is the question of *représentance*. Everything in Freud's work functioned around concepts linked to the sphere of representation – the culminating point being the "Papers on Metapsychology" of 1915 – even if certain prolegomena were present as early as 1890. But *Beyond the Pleasure Principle* (1920g), and even more so, *The Ego and the Id* (1923b), made it necessary to go further than this, aided by the clinical evolution and the psychoanalytic community. Green decrypted, moreover, the elements in Freud's language that translated this evolution. The typical example concerns the concept of instinctual impulse (*Triebregung*). He writes:

> What was defined as the psychical representative of the drive would look very much like the instinctual impulses that the psychical apparatus of 1923 was to present as the raw material of the id, *any allusion to the notion of representation (thing- or object-presentation, still less ideational representative) now disappears.*
>
> (Green, 1999, p. 196)

In fact, although in 1920 or 1923 Freud rarely used the term instinctual impulse, this term remained linked to the sphere of representation. In "The Unconscious" (1915e), Freud writes, for example: "The derivatives of the *Ucs.* instinctual impulses . . . are highly organised" (p. 190). He says the same thing in "Repression" (1915d) of the same year. But it is interesting to point out that we are in the presence of a veritable process in the writing of the text, *The Ego and the Id* (1923b). Thus the first two chapters, titled "Conscious and Unconscious" and "The Ego and the Id", contain extensive considerations on the first topography, but it was in order to lead Freud towards what exceeds it (in particular the unconscious ego, and sensation). For, from the moment he introduced Groddeck's expression, the "id", Freud departed from the reference to the first topography, as was confirmed in the fourth chapter, "The Two Classes of Instincts". This does not seem due to the fact that Freud frequently uses the term instinctual impulse in this text – which moreover is not listed as an entry in the French edition of Freud's work (*Œuvres complètes*) (Bourguignon, Cotet and Laplanche, 1988) – but to the fact that, when he uses it, the citation is eloquent. Thus he writes: "The problem of the quality of instinctual impulses and of its persistence through their various vicissitudes is still very obscure and has hardly been attacked up to the present" (1923b, p. 44). It is important to emphasise that this is the fourth chapter, which deals with the question of the death drive and of the destructive processes that are part of it.

These considerations enable me to make a link with the second major point in the work of André Green after the notion of *représentance*, namely, that of negativity and its different forms. What is important in this ensemble of contributions on negativity is the fact that it is not a matter of an insufficiency, almost in the sense of a deficit, but of what is driven by a force. Moreover, this is what our patients show us when their instinctual impulses are oriented in this direction. Beyond the clinical and psychopathological manifestations of negativity, the important thing at the level of analytic work is what bears witness to the functioning of such negativity. Since Bion's crucial concept of attacks on linking, what André Green advances concerning negativity has to do with the patient's associativity, as well as with all forms of attack on free association, on everything that concerns the potentialities of transference on to speech and transference on to the object. The transference is then above all characterised by the "disobjectalising function", that is to say, a concerted attempt to "whiten" (*blanchir*) representations.[2] Negativisation, with its "colouring of the defences by the drives" (2001b, p. 87), its "negative narcissism", can infiltrate right down to the experience of terror (Freud's *Schreck*), the traces of which are part of the subject. Hence this "negativisation of terror", according to Green (ibid., p. 79), a negativisation of thought processes that is liable to be associated with the traces that are mobilised against all primary thinking, a sort of negativised hallucinatory force entailing an exacerbation of over-secondarisation (p. 79). Free association, which is actively restricted, then becomes a means of avoiding "being invaded by an experience of terror, even negativised" (p. 83). We are then dealing with the undermining of the first topography and consequently of the preconscious.

At the level of the id (*le ça*), we are at best in a state that is situated prior to the distinction affect/representation, and at worst in the unrepresentable. But it is a few lines further on that Green really defines the instinctual impulse: "I would say that the psychical representaive of the drive, synonymous with the instinctual impulse, is what will give birth to affect once the meeting with the object-presentation has occurred" (ibid.). From my point of view this is a way of emphasising, via the "movement" implied by *Regung* that the fate of the instinctual impulse is the linking up of affect and representation, that is to say, a re-objectalisation, the problem being that it does not happen just like "that".

The intermediate notion in its qualificative form appears in *The Interpretation of Dreams* (Freud, 1900a) in the expression "intermediate ideas" (Fr. *représentations intermédiaires*; G. *Mittelvorstellungen*) (p. 596). Everything begins with a thought that emerges in the preconscious and which, because it has not been cathected, is cathected by unconscious wishes, so that the current of thought undergoes transformations, in which the process of condensation plays a part, between "the rational preconscious relations of the dream-thoughts and the attraction exercised by visual memories in the unconscious" (ibid.), although we know that there are not only visual memories in the unconscious. "The outcome of the activity of condensation is the achievement of the intensities required for forcing a way through into the perceptual systems" (ibid.). Thanks to the transference of the intensities, and under the sway of condensation, intermediate ideas are formed. These resemble "compromises", "mixed forms",[3] one of the typical manifestations of which is the slip of the tongue. The ensemble is a model process, referential for whatever departs from it.

Freud resorts to a nominalisation in the article "The Unconscious", as well as for the analytic situation itself: ". . . psychoanalytic treatment is based upon an influencing of the *Ucs.* from the direction of the *Cs.*, and shows that this, though a laborious task, is not impossible" (p. 194). Note that he includes, without confusing them, the *Pcs.* in the *Cs.*, and that earlier he wrote that the *Pcs.* can exert direct influence on the *Ucs.*" Then he continues: "The derivatives of the *Ucs.*, which act as intermediaries between the two systems, open the way towards accomplishing this" (ibid.). Now the movements of the derivatives will occur between the two systems, in other words in the *Pcs*. As for the question of the intermediary, Freud mentions the "*Pcs*. derivatives of the *Ucs*." against which the second censorship is exercised, that which is located between the systems *Pcs*. and the *Cs*. The repressed derivatives of the *Ucs*. which have tried to "circumvent" the censorship at the frontier of the *Pcs*. and to "force themselves" into consciousness can be "repressed afresh" as "derivatives of the Ucs.", but only once they have become "*Pcs*. derivatives of the *Ucs*."[4] And Freud also ascribes an evolving mobile quality to the censorship "so that one might suppose that in the course of individual development the censorship had taken a step forward" (p. 193).

In any case, this evolving mobility that links the two censorships by individualising itself bars all rigidity where they are concerned and thus guarantees movements and fluctuations. It is important to remember that the preconscious "has become" subdivisible between a part "that is capable of becoming conscious without censorship" and another very large part that has "its origin in the *Ucs*." The latter is "submittted to censorship – the second – before it can become conscious" the hyper-cathexis of these derivatives by word-presentations determines their capacity for "becoming conscious" (*Bewußtwerden*). This subdivision has an echo in Pierre Luquet's (1987) work concerning the notions of metaprimary and metaconscious.

In *The Ego and the Id*, Freud (1923b) links analytic work with supplying "*Pcs*. intermediate *links*" (*Pcs. Mittelglieder*), which are word-presentations. *Glied(er)* can also mean member, with its sexual connotation, which is a way of introducing thirdness into the question of the pre-conscious. Freud goes on to discuss the question of sensations and says that "what becomes conscious as pleasure and unpleasure" may be called "a quantitative and qualitative 'something'" (*Ein quantitative-qualitativ Anderes*) (p. 22). This "something" behaves like a repressed "impulse" linked to a compulsion, a sort of prolegomena for the instinctual impulse. However, one page before, in connection with word-presentations, Freud notes that "verbal residues are derived primarily from auditory perceptions, so that the system *Pcs*. has, as it were, a special sensory source" (pp. 20–21). With Freud we find ourselves faced with the same question concerning the formation of the *Pcs*. as we did with Pierre Marty. Although subsequently Freud considered that the "visual components of word-presentations are secondary . . . and may, to begin with, be left on one side" as well as their motor images, he nonetheless names them, thereby making them part of the complexity of the situation. His study on the aphasias (Freud, 1891b) is evidence of this. In *An Outline of Psychoanalysis* (Freud, 1940a[1938]), where he points out that the *Pcs.* belongs exclusively to the ego, he notes that the fact that a process is conditioned by speech allows us to conclude that this process is preconscious in nature, while adding that "it would not be correct, however, to think that connection with mnemic traces of speech is a necessary precondition of the preconscious state" as the latter is "independent of a connection with them" (p. 162). It was this that would lead him to the enigma of the "true nature" of the state of being preconscious (p. 163), throwing light to begin with on the dynamic question of the transformative relationship between free and bound energy.

André Green (1999) draws attention to a remarkable feature concerning the analyses of non-neurotic states: "What is striking about these analyses," he writes, "is the absence of what I call *intermediate formations*, that is, stages between the psychic activity named as instinctual, archaic, primitive, etc., according to preferences, and that of conscious communication" (p. 202 (author's emphasis)). The question of the preconscious is necessarily raised from the angle of negativity. Concerning the functionally inoperative character of intermediate formations in such clinical situations, Green adds that these intermediate formations are defined as "psychic productions organised by primary processes, implying a relative degree of differentiation between affect and representation" (ibid.). The preconscious is thus involved as a potentiality that is attacked and negativised. It is, moreover, well known that in non-neurotic situations, the activity of cathexis is focused on one aim, namely, that of "making every effort to prevent the work of transformation and elaboration, starting from the instinctual impulses or perceptions, taking form in the direction of phantasy thereby helping the unconscious reach a state of preconscious functioning" (p. 219).

The importance of the reference to intermediate formations reappears in relation to the question of *latent thoughts*. Looking at mental functioning in non-neurotic situations, André Green was careful to examine in detail normal neurotic dream functioning and its complexity in order to show more clearly what non-neurotic states are struggling against. He concluded that the general quality of the sequence dream/dream narrative/associations, and its analogons in connection with fantasy activity, must be taken into account in such cases by the analyst. Well after 1920 and 1923, in his *New Introductory Lectures on Psychoanalysis*, Freud (1933a[1932]) expressed his concern and irritation in connection with a certain loss of interest on the part of psychoanalysts for the theory of dreams (p. 8). At the same time his new formulation concerning dreams as an "attempt at the fulfilment of a wish" (p. 29) opened the way to the future relationship between *représentance* and negativity.

For Freud, the question of latent thoughts had an important place in *The Interpretation of Dreams*, which he did not reduce to night life and to their function as the architects of dreams. Indeed, they are comparable for him to waking thoughts. In "A note on the unconscious in psychoanalysis" (1912g) he stresses the fact that "the latent thoughts of the dream differ in no respect from the products of our regular conscious activity" and adds that "they deserve the name of foreconscious thoughts" (p. 265). Thus he writes that, "by entering into connection with the unconscious tendencies during the night, they have become assimilated to the latter, degraded as it were to the condition of unconscious thoughts" (ibid., p. 228).

This "degradation" of dream life is an opportunity for the unconscious, and thus for the infantile sphere of the mind to cathect latent thought. This tendency is present in two types of latent thoughts differentiated by Freud, those that are preconscious, and which may have once been conscious, and those that are unconscious "keeping apart from consciousness in spite of their intensity and activity" (p. 262). We thus find once again the subdivision of the preconscious into two forms, that which is capable of becoming conscious without censorship and that which derives it origin from the unconscious and is subject to censorship. Like the intermediate formations I have been discussing, a preconscious latent thought which has not been cathected, or even "hypercathected", will pass into the unconscious (something Freud mentions even before there is any question of word-presentations), a hypercathexis which thus plays a part in the binding of unbound energy. In analysis, the specificity of latent thoughts resides in the fact that they are only recognised in the aftermath of interpretation. In a similar way, we find the question of latent thoughts in André Green's work, on the subject of the analytic situation and of the pair: the patient's free association/the analyst's free-floating attention. The analyst's task is to be receptive to the latent thoughts to which the patient's words refer. "These latent thoughts," he writes, "must not be confused with the preconscious, even if at certain moments we cannot help comparing them" (Green, 2001a, p. 82).

If we look at what he says a bit more closely, we realise that he does not, however, "linearise" latent thought and the unconscious. He thus looks at the question from the angle of preconscious/conscious relations while adding that, in the context of a relationship between latent thought and the unconscious, the first cannot be reduced to the primary processes by which it is infiltrated, since what is involved is thought-activity and, consequently, a detour, namely, that which differentiates the trajectory of thought identity from that of perceptual identity. He concludes that "the essence of unconscious process" lies in the "relationship between figurability and latent thought" (p. 87).

There are two essential axes to this line of thinking: one which, owing to historicity and as an organisation of progressive differentiations, presents at the same time "qualitative leaps" (the so-called "qualities" of conscious, preconscious and unconscious evoked by Freud in *An Outline on Psychoanalysis* (1940a[1938])), qualitative leaps that are created by the retroactive effect of language, thereby offering a limit to the preconscious space by the exercise of the "second censorship" (*Cs./Pcs*), and by that of the first censorship (*Ucs./Pcs.*). This time, the retroactive process constituting the first censorship, another limit to the preconscious space, can be linked to the hypothesis Freud makes in *An Outline on Psychoanalysis*, after having pointed out that we "know nothing" about the "true nature of the *Pcs*", concerning the "few glimmers of light" that scarcely illuminate the "secret of the nature of the psychical", to use his own terms. These "glimmers of light" hark back to the question of energy and the differentiation between unbound energy and bound energy. Now this differentiation is not only dependent on language, for we must recall what Freud says, again in the *Outline*, when he asserts that "connection with the mnemic traces of speech" is not a necessary precondition of the preconscious state. But, bound energy, as Freud showed, is involved in linking all sorts of elements, from the kinaesthetic to the visual, that are capable of "psychisation" (i.e. of being renered psychic or mentalised).

The unconscious participates in this dynamic through affect, which passes directly from the unconscious to the conscious (Freud says, moreover, with regard to what is kept in the unconscious, that affect "decides" or, at least orients). But these processes of linking can only be organised, from the beginning, in the interpsychic sphere, in the envelope of the parental cathexes and anti-cathexes, something that has been clearly evidenced by the work of Denis Braunschweig and Michel Fain, opening up, as Jean-Luc Donnet has pointed out, the question of identifications in the constitution of the preconscious. Thanks to the pleasure/unpleasure principle, affect is both the motor of the "distortion" of the first censorship (*Ucs./Pcs.*) and of the "filtering" of the second, to use the terms of Michel Neyraut (1997) in *Les raisons de l'irrationnel*. He emphasises that he cannot consider that primary logics, the rational instruments of primary processes, have nothing to do with the preconscious. Concerning primitive logics, which are organised around the Freudian "*Ur*" (primordial), he points out, via Freud's article on "Negation" (1925h), that Freud attributes a language in the first person to what is still only a formless idea. Thus Neyraut writes: ". . . I want to take that (*cela*) into myself and I want to keep that (*cela*) outside of myself. So *ça* (id/it) must either be in me or outside of me" (Neyraut, 1997, p. 179). These are foundational words expressed in the language of the instinctual impulses.

This last point forms a bridge with the second axis, that of the interpsychic. The question of the preconscious can by summarised by the following proposition: the more we are dealing with non-neurotic states, the more the analyst's psychical apparatus is challenged, and the more, as far the preconscious and its protective barrier is concerned, the analyst must remain attentive to the activity of his own preconscious and to its uncertainties in the transference/countertransference dynamics. In effect, his preconscious is particularly threatened in its context of negativity. That is why insisting on the importance of the *Pcs.* does not imply isolation from the other topographical agencies, for it is more a matter of a dialectic between them. In any case, it seems important today to give prominence, in the process of analytic work, to the question of the *Pcs.*, as well as to that of mediation of speech and language, starting from its intermediate elements.

Now the geometrical and dynamic locality of this preconscious mediation is related to the work of symbolisation, to the definition of the primordial function of the *sumbulon*, an object in two halves, which, once reunited by the carriers of each of them, achieve mutual recognition through the constituted object. There is an analogy here with the interpretative dynamic insofar as there is an emergence of this or that element, in the quasi-Bionian sense, in the patient's associativity (and not free association). It is a question of knowing if the analyst's words, in the case of a timely interpretation, will have an interpretative function. For the element of speech that he/she introduces will be constitutive of the analogon, of the sumbulon, in the patient's associativity, as a form of indexation, to use André Green's term. The fact of situating oneself in negative circumstances makes it possible to remain as close as possible to the "level" of the patient's functioning, while at the same time avoiding being intrusive, in a position of waiting and holding, until a symbolising opportunity presents itself to the protective barrier thanks to a redistribution of the diffusion/decondensation of energy.

During my 1987 report to the Congress of French-speaking psychoanalysts (Ody, 1987), I described this type of work of interpreting symbolically not in the sense of interpreting, but in the sense of what constitutes or rests on a symbol. I took up this question again here and there, and by way of illustration, especially concerning the child, in (Ody, 1999b, 2012). Then, I became acquainted with the work of Jean-Claude Rolland,[5] and particularly his book, *Avant d'être celui qui parle* (Rolland, 2006). There he develops the question of analogical interpretation in a sense that is complementary to so-called symbolic interpretation. Thus, he writes: ". . . by comparing two signifiers present in the manifest discourse, the correspondence between which is established by an analogy that is only perceptible to the interlocutor, the interpretation makes a third term appear whose significance had been concealed because it belonged to the latent discourse" (ibid., p. 103). This way of seeing things seemed to me, if I may say so, rather similar to what I was saying about the "abc" of symbolic interpretation, namely, that it "rests on" or "constitutes" a symbol. Thus an element A approximated with an element B produces a psychic event C, which enlarges the field of symbolisation.

In this work, from my point of view, we should not necessarily expect to find on the patient's side, signifiers, constituted forms. We may be dealing with proto-representations, with infra-verbal elements which are part of the associativity. Bion and Winnicott have both given us examples of this in their own way. This takes us back to what Michel Neyraut says about the Freud of "Negation" (1925h), who attributes language in the first person to what is still only a formless idea. In addition, he confirms a rapprochement or complementarity with Jean-Claude Rolland when he writes: "The analogy covers many other domains than that of comparison, and is the very principle of the metaphor . . .", and when he explores the analogical foundations of symbols".[6]

As far as the child is concerned, the symbolic constitution in the interpretative work is more obvious owing to the facility he/she has of gaining access to representability through drawings and games, which we also find in the case of formal regression in the analytic pair, the analyst/adult patient. Concerning the interpretation which is based on a symbol, this no doubt approximates more to the so-called analogical interpretation; in all the cases of interventions of linking that concern what Green referred to as "bifurcations" in processual associativity, the preconscious is involved. It is the ensemble of this work that takes account of the two topographies, concerning two psychical apparatuses interacting with each other interpsychically, which leads in non-neurotic situations to what Green (2001b) describes: "psychoanalytic work, which is laborious, consists in transforming this negativation of thought processes into latent thoughts, the latter finally revealing the subjectivation of which desire is the correlate" (p. 82). Before the process of "becoming conscious" (Bewußtwerden), which is very different from the "symptom", Freud wrote, there is the process of becoming preconscious (Vorbewußtwerden), in processuality.

The second concept, extending Freud's thought, which runs right through this book, is that of Oedipus (Oedipe) as an attractor.[7] The notion of "meta operation", put forward by Donnet (1989), that is, the application of psychoanalysis to the theorisation itself, reverses in certain respects the perspective of a theory built on the basis either of so-called objective experience or of a more directly generative theory, positions that both culminate in theories producing relatively stable objects. At the same time, it may be pointed out that if the specificity of psychoanalysis, compared with any form of scientific enterprise, obliges us to follow the approach suggested by Donnet, there is no absolute heterogeneity between a theorising process operating in psychoanalysis and a process operating in those disciplines considered as more scientific. I am even thinking of those that are furthest removed from the senses, in the full polysemy of the term, as is shown by astrophysicians and microphysicians. Along with psychoanalysis, they share instability, open systems, and constitutive paradoxes. It is nonetheless true that the specificity of psychoanalysis is not to question its theory, its foundations and its history, but rather to operate at a "meta" level in relation to the theorising process that permeates the objects that it creates. Not in a direct manner as the mathematicians, logicians and philosophers of the Vienna Circle did in the interwar period, thereby opening up questions about metalanguage, but in the sense in which the "meta operation", and even "auto-meta" (ibid., p. 192), "denote" the involvement of "unconscious processes".

With regard to this operation which goes as far as to base the theorising process on its navel, "the navel of the theory" (ibid., p. 205), by analogy with what Freud says concerning the dream navel, it seemed worthwhile to re-examine one of the most apparently stable concepts of psychoanalysis, namely, the concept of Oedipus. I say *apparently*, in respect of two examples that are still very representative, even though they are separated by half a century.

In his *Clinical Diary*, Ferenczi (1988[1932]) argues in favour of a "revision of the Oedipus complex" (26 July 1932, pp. 175–176) in connection with the case of a female patient in whom "incestuous fixation" does not appear as a natural product of development but rather is "implanted" in the psyche from the outside. The father's passionate love for his daughter was at the origin of this implantation, leading even to a "fragmentation of the ego", an expression already present in Ferenczi's work. Other publications may be mentioned here as well, such as "The effort to drive the other person crazy" (Searles, 1959), Aulagnier's (1975) notion of assigning identifications, as well as the updating of the Freud-Fliess correspondence, published *in full* and put to a particular use by Masson (1985) in connection with the theory of seduction.

The second example was given by Jean Laplanche (1987) in his *New Foundations in Psychoanalysis*. In this emergence from the solipsism of the endogenous categories of the psyche, also present in Ferenczi, Laplanche considers the generalised theory of seduction as a theoretical foundation stone with reference to the primordial situation between the adult and the child. For Laplanche this relationship is "more firmly rooted in the biological – and above all the instinctual . . . than the Oedipus" (ibid., p. 90) "The sacrosanct universality of the Oedipus," he writes, "can be seen as one of the many solutions to a problem created by the situation in which adults and children relate to one another (and that is universal), and by the entry of the child into the adult universe" (ibid., p. 91).

It can be seen that in both cases the critique is based on the implication of the other, in his entire reality. What about the Oedipus? Thus nominalised, the Oedipus opens out on to two levels.

The first is provisionally solipsistic – a solipsism, moreover, that was necessary in the history of psychoanalytic theory. This first ensemble is a trajectory between two states through which development passes. First through the establishment of the "basic triangulation" as a cathexis arising from what is "not-mother" (Le Guen, 2007, p. 17) or from the cathexis of "the other of the object" (Green, 2002a, p. 200). This first state is linked to notions such as the *depressive position* (Klein, 1935), and *6–8 month anxiety* (Spitz, 1958). And second through the establishment of the Oedipus complex as such, with its four tendencies – wider variations in comparison with the Greek myth – metaphorised by Freud. The transition from the analogy of the Oedipus complex, in both boys and girls, to the asymmetry between the two on account of the particular role played by the castration complex for each of the two sexes as well as the fate of femininity may be linked to this. Between these two poles of the basic triangular situation and the Oedipus complex, the trajectory that unites them in development is affected by a whole series of reorganisations carried out retroactively, including the restructuring by the Oedipus complex of the previous stages (M'Uzan, 1969). The constitution of the post-oedipal superego and the period of latency specific to the human being are the outcomes of this trajectory before they are taken up again in adolescence.

The "completion" of such integration in psychic development is asymptotic and has the value of a theoretical model, and even of a norm, in the non-normative sense of the term (David, 1992). A sufficient completion of this trajectory constitutes the *oedipal organisation of the mind* (Parat, 1967). Let us take a relatively solipsistic clinical example – I say relatively, because it concerns my meeting with a little girl aged five. It is solipsistic insofar as I will not be referring to the external elements surrounding it. It concerns a moment in the trajectory to which I was referring above that crystallises the child's entire mental functioning and is related to the development of the Oedipus complex. Sol (as I shall call her here), who was massively inhibited not so long ago, has made progress in respect of the quality and quantity of this inhibition. She drew a little girl in trousers, holding a notebook, while she herself was wearing a dress. She told me the little girl was her, which, by implicating herself directly, seemed to immobilise the situation somewhat. I suggested an obvious difference: "Is this little girl alone?" Sol replied by drawing a little boy, a production that facilitated a manifestation of the unconscious.

Having drawn the boy's hands, she added large fingers . . . to the notebook of the little girl who was portrayed with a huge hand, in addition to the one that was already holding the note book. Faced with this particular asymmetrical boy/girl situation, I offered her a symbolic interpretation. This type of interpretation has, therefore, a ternary structure. Situated topographically at the level of the preconscious, it is the processual condition leading to the interpretation of the unconscious contents themselves. So I pointed out to Sol that when the little boy appeared alongside the little girl, she immediately found she had a big hand. The immediate and firm reaction of this inhibited child was "No". Negation, as everyone knows, is what opens out on to thought, and it subtly revealed behind the little girl another child, one side of whose body alone was visible, and whose hand ended with the fingers of the notebook, which thus assumed its first function once again.

Once this opening had occurred, things did not stop there. Sol took a few wild and domestic animals out of the box of toys, and then a cowboy, which was the only human figure she took out. She became inhibited again, until I asked her, "What's the cowboy going to do?" "Kill them," she said immediately, thereby throwing light on the meaning of her inhibition at that moment. Then, accompanied by me during a psychodramatic role-play, Sol, identified with the cowboy, starting shooting at each of the animals, beginning with the smallest, before proceeding, after a few inhibited movements, to shoot the most imposing ones. Each one was then methodically devoured by the cowboy, though the excitement did not disorganise Sol, who took her time. When the inhibition appeared again, she was able to understand the fatigue of the cowboy, who then had a nap before resuming his meal when he woke up, a nap that was sometimes interrupted by nightmares in which, through a reversal of the situation, the animals took their vengeance. The coherence – in the sense that there is a certain logic in the processes that were unfolding – organised during the two phases (the drawing and the role-play) made it possible to identify the operative level for the quality of the oedipal triangulation during the trajectory – ranging from the phallic movement of the differences of the sexes to the masculine identification with the cowboy – as an expression of non-disruptive oral instinctuality. This was an achievement in which the maternal image was potentially involved in the oedipal triangle, while it was involved "negatively" through its manifest absence (the female characters all remained in the box of toys), and even through its latent presence in certain devoured animals, not to mention what was going on in the dynamics of the transference.

A second level includes the movements of the endogenous trajectory. This second ensemble is both the "oedipal order" in respect of its cultural and symbolic tendency, which is expressed at the collective level, and what is "refracted" by it at the level of the particular oedipal vicissitudes of the parents' psyche. These may be positive or negative vicissitudes, with reference to the difference not only of the sexes but also of the generations. The oedipal order is consequently marked by a certain "disorder" that is implied by the infinite variation of the expressions of this second ensemble.

I will illustrate these remarks by referring to a consultation with a child and his two parents. The point of view will be different this time insofar as we will not be focusing on the child's mental functioning, but on what provides a structure for it; and, more particularly, on what goes on between the parents in front of the child. The boy in question was eight years old, and equally inhibited; but this inhibition was marked by active phenomena of retention at the level of verbal and graphic expression. The renewed encounters of the psychoanalyst with the child and his parents allowed an exchange to take place between the European psychoanalyst that I am and these African parents, who were modest economic immigrants. I tried to make this exchange more meaningful as I was communicating to them what was happening to their son.

During the consultation to which I am referring, my attempts to communicate made the mother feel uneasy about her son. The father reacted by saying that this boy was the mother's favourite child, in contrast with his elder brother, who apparently posed no problems. The mother defended herself and the father came alive in a way that had not been the case until then. He backed up the point he was making by adding that all the other children complained about this preference. The mother tried to justify herself and, "in passing", called her son by a nickname that I had not heard before. After asking her about it, I discovered that this nickname was that of her father's brother, a paternal uncle who had a certain importance in the mother's history. She seemed shocked when I said to her somewhat psychodramatically that it was now easier to understand that her son had a particular status. After a silence, she regained her composure and returned to describing her son's behaviour. I intervened again playfully: "There you go again, you don't want to listen to me!" Both parents laughed. It was a story of the "Name-of-the-Father" circulated, in short, by the *African Oedipus*

(Ortigues, 1966). What was the consequence of all this for the child? He began raising his finger in class to answer questions. The examples I have given by way of illustration may serve to temper the view that the Oedipal structure is restrictive, prohibiting any *"prescription of one's own dehiscence"*, to take up Donnet's (1989) expression. What has just been said justifies to some extent the positions set out by Deleuze and Guattari (1972) in *Anti-Oedipus*, when they criticise the Freudian point of view of the Oedipus as being a coerced heir of the end of the nineteenth century familialism in which Freud lived.

From this point of view the oedipal order thus crushes the bustling of the unconscious conceived of as a non-oedipal productive desiring-machine. These authors find examples, of course, in the psychoanalytic literature that anticipate the interpretation of the material in the sense of the Oedipus complex, sometimes even to the point of imposing such a meaning in a stereotyped way. And yet the same authors do not contest the "invariant" nature of the oedipal structure (p. 60). Their opposition is based on the match between the productions of the unconscious and this invariant. And that is indeed the question because it is not simply a matter of a match, but of a "gap" between the productions of the unconscious and the Oedipal structure as a whole, and even of the interaction between match and gap.

I will give a last, short example, of an adult session this time. The man in question has been in analysis for several years and had a dream whose level of formal expression was equivalent to that found in children's drawings. The dream seemed to be catalysed by several days of holiday that he had taken outside the usual dates. He immediately said that the dream had occurred between two sessions of analysis on separate days. In the dream he was watching a huge aquatic animal with a lot of teeth that was swallowing two other animals of the same species, one of normal size, the other smaller. Regarding these last two, he commented: "It's like the father and the son." For various reasons that were to do with the material of the analysis, it seemed obvious that the larger animal was the mother. However, not only did he say nothing about it, but he continued telling his dream in a childish tone of voice, extending the dream hallucinatorily in an attempt to master it. Was it for me to say something about it? Had I done so, I would have provided a justification for the critique of Deleuze and Guattari concerning what might appear as a "mere detail". I reminded him that the dream had occurred between two sessions and contrasted, by means of a reversal, the absence of my patient during his holidays and the devouring closeness of the dream. He remained silent for a while, and then told me that he didn't understand what I was trying to say to him because he was obtuse, etc. This went on for a moment until, all of a sudden, he realised that he was complaining in terms that were exactly the same as those in which he complained about . . . his mother. Here, then, is the mother, as he called her. This nomination, which was absent from the dream narrative,[8] occurred within a context of transferential significance. It was in fact he himself who situated this dream between two days on which he usually had sessions. This was reinforced thereafter by my intervention reminding him of this fact. At the same time, I drew a contrast, employing a sort of reversal, between his absence from his sessions and the devouring closeness in the dream suggested by the huge aquatic animal arriving towards "father and son".

The associative sequence is very interesting because first he remained silent, then told me that he didn't understand, that he was "obtuse". Finally, we can say that suddenly "the penny dropped" and it dawned on him that he was complaining as his *mother* did at times, referring to her as such. He did not reach the point, however, during this session, and through this movement of identification with his mother, of becoming aware of his identification with an omnipotent maternal imago, in contradistinction therefore to the complaining mother. On the other hand he understood that in the transference he was ascribing this place to me through the huge aquatic animal in the dream.

A very subtle movement of my patient was all that was needed to justify my remarks, a movement that I would quite simply have prevented from unfolding . . . if I had allowed myself to complete the description of the series of the three aquatic animals. The triangulation involved here shows that the Oedipus complex is not a restrictive structure, but a *welcoming structure*.

In other words, Oedipus (i.e. the Oedipal structure) is an *attractor*, a metaphor that I have borrowed from Ilya Prigogine (Prigogine and Stengers, 1986), though it should be pointed out that borrowing concepts from other disciplines turns them into migrating concepts (Nicolescu, 1996) that undergo transformations. Oedipus is thus an attractor in the sense of an organisation towards complexity, not only in the sense of the Oedipus complex, as it is correctly named, but in the sense of the oedipal ensemble I referred to above, suggesting that neurotic levels are not the only ones involved. It is in this sense, too, that the positive and negative vicissitudes of the Oedipus complex, whether they are present or not in the child in relation to the mental functioning of the parents, will be able to come into play through the encounter of the psycho-analyst with the child or adult. The psychoanalyst presents this wel-coming structure, the attractor, in the form of "waiting". It is thanks to these spaces and these times explored for dehiscences that the cultural dimension and its symbolism, the immediate environment (parents and their substitutes), and the traces of early history can interact with each other. It is this interaction, which is necessary for the subject's mind, that starts to resonate in the encounter with a psychoanalyst, which means that Oedipus is indeed an attractor for the subject. It is again in this sense that the psychoanalyst brings into play evenly-suspended attention rather than free-floating attention. The psychoanalyst's inter-ventions, or his interpretations, his work of binding/unbinding, are based on this type of attention. He finds himself, then, in suspended theory, in *latent theory*, like the latent thoughts that emerge in his con-sciousness by association. This theory is the result of the mutation, the transformation of his own infantile sexual theories which gives rise to the period of latency, recognised as a period in which sexual curiosity is transformed into epistemophilia insofar as it is sufficiently discon-nected from its incestuous roots. What is involved, then, is something different from "the expected Oedipus effect" as envisaged by Karl Pop-per (1976). This author, cited by Assoun (1988) uses this expression to refer to "the effect that a theory, an *expectation* or a prediction exerts on the very event that it predicts or that it describes" (p. 171).

This raises the problem of the influence exerted by the psychoana-lyst consciously or unconsciously, and not only by means of his inter-pretations, on the patient's material, which leads me to think that the expected Oedipus effect does not have a bearing on the dynamic of the Oedipus attractor in the sense that I have envisaged it hitherto. It is true that in the first situation the trajectory can be reduced to the point of imposing meaning in a stereotyped way. In the second, waiting and the tension that it creates between the patient's mind and that of the ana-lyst, the "bearer" of the attractor, makes it possible for unknown and surprising ideas and affects to emerge, a sort of expected anti-effect. The simple reason for this is that the suspended attention is combined with waiting, a combination that leads to "suspended waiting", provid-ing an example of a constitutive and organising paradox. Owing to its gap, Oedipus as an attractor allows all the roads that lead to Rome, I mean to Thebes, to be registered in it as paths of the drives. Oedipus as an attractor is also the necessary condition for their representations and processes. This path known as a destination stands in contrast with the infinitely variable unknown of what leads to it, depending on the specific experiences and unconscious possibilities of each one of us, a path that has to be covered, discovered and rediscovered afresh each time.

Notes

1 This section takes up the article "Modernité du préconscient", initially published in *Libres Cahiers pour la Psychanalyse*, 18: 57–74, Paris: Éditions In Press (Ody, 2008).

2 Translator's note: in the sense of rendering them disaffected, flat, or blank, as in "blank psychosis" (*psychose blanche*).

3 This is also the "mixed blood" (*Mischlingen*) or "mixed race" of "The Unconscious" (1915e, p. 191).

4 "Thus the first of these censorships is exercised against the *Ucs.* itself, and the second against its *Pcs.* derivatives" (1915e, p. 193).

5 I was not aware at the time of this author's text, "Entre remémoration et oubli" (Rolland, 2007), which contains important reflections on the subject of the preconscious.

6 Paper read on 17 December 1997 at the Ecole Propédeutique à la Connaissance de l'Inconscient (ECPI).

7 This section takes up again the article "Œdipe comme attracteur" (Ody, 1989). Translator's note: In French, the nominalization Œdipe refers to a general oedipal structure or configuration.

8 And for good reason: it is all the more understandable in that with the child's tone of voice he employed at this precise moment, it would have been difficult for him to name a fearsome mother.

ADDENDUM

A certain number of clarifications concerning the notion of attractor are given in Chapter 4 of *Entre le temps et l'éternité* (Prigogine and Stengers, 1988). There exist, then, three varieties, three levels of attractor: first, that which corresponds to a fixed-point or occasional attractor, for example, the pendulum which, after a series of oscillations resulting from the impulsion that has been given to it, will find its state of equilibrium in a point; second, that which corresponds to a limit cycle, for example, a chemical clock or a periodical trajectory, etc.; and third, that which corresponds to a complex movement in a multidimensional space. It is called fractal (or strange, or chaotic), like the functioning of the climatic variations on our planet. The attractor is thus characterised by a 3.1 dimension, a system with four independent variables. The interest of this notion is that it concerns open, dissipative and dispersive systems which, consequently, are not isolated or isolable. As far as the fractal attractors, in particular, are concerned, as well as the limit cycles, the systems are open when they are far from their point of equilibrium. This renews the question of determinism, where what is random and what is determined are not mutually exclusive but are subject to productive contradictions. There is a structural instability. It remains true that the application of this notion to the Oedipal structure has its limits despite its interest. Hence the need to highlight its metaphorical value and its position as a migrating concept which is transformed from the moment it is borrowed from another discipline. To return to the example of the climatic variations of our planet, the fractal attractor, albeit very complex, is mathematiseable; however, it would be an illusion to think it can be used for our subject. Moreover, if I. Prigogine cites a possible dimension of the fractal attractor in the case of deep sleep and in the context of electro-encephalographic recordings (here an attractor with two independent variables), he notes that for the waking state no attractor can be identified. Likewise, in the contrary case, that of a pure dynamic system, non-dissipative therefore, as with the theoretical example of perpetual pendular movement, no attractor seems to be definable either.

So I concur with Ilya Prigogine when he points out that in the past our ideas were too simple; they consisted in opposing irregularity and determinism. Today, we see that reality lies somewhere between the two.

REFERENCES

Assoun, P.-L. (1988). *Freud et Wittgenstein*. Paris: Presses Universitaires de France.

Atlan, H. (1972). Du bruit comme principe d'auto-organisation. *Communications*, 18: 21–36.

Aulagnier, P. (2001[1975]). *Violence of Interpretation: From Pictogram to Statement*, trans. A. Sheridan. London, Philadelphia, PA: Brunner Routledge (The New Library of Psychoanalysis).

Baldacci, J.-C. (2005). Dès le début . . . la sublimation? *Revue française de psychanalyse*, 5: 1403–1474.

Balier, C. (2005). La tierceité à l'épreuve de la psycho-criminologie, *Revue française de psychanalyse*, 69(3): 703–715.

Bauduin, A. (1987). Du préconscient. *Revue française de psychanalyse*, 51(2): 449–538.

Bergeret, J. (1993). *La violence fondamentale*. Paris: Dunod.

Bion, W.R. (1967[1959]). Attacks on Linking. Reprinted in: *Second Thoughts*. London: Heinemann.

Botella, C. and Botella, S. (2005[2001]). *The Work of Psychic Figurability: Mental States without Representation*, trans. A. Weller, with M. Zerbib. London: Routledge.

Bourguignon, A., Cotet, P. and Laplanche, J. (eds) (1988). *Sigmund Freud: Œuvres complètes*. Paris: Presses Universitaires de France.

Braunschweig, D. and Fain, M. (1974). Du démon du bien et des infortunes de la vertu. *Nouvelle Revue de psychanalyse*, 10: 161–178.

Braunschweig, D. and Fain, M. (1975). *La nuit, le jour*. Paris: Presses Universitaires de France.

Cahn, R. (2002). *La fin du divan?* Paris: Odile Jacob.

Danon-Boileau, L. and Tamet, J.-Y. (eds) (2016). *Des psychanalystes en séance, Glossaire clinique de psychanalyse contemporaine*. Paris: Gallimard.

David, C. (1992). La vraie normalité se moque de la normalité. In: *La bisexualité psychique*. Paris: Payot, pp. 201–216.

Deleuze, G. and Guattari, F. (1977[1972]). *Anti-Oedipus. Capitalism and Schizophrenia*. London: Penguin.

Diatkine, R. (1969). L'enfant prépsychotique. *Psychiatrie de l'enfant*, 22(2): 413–446.

Diatkine, R. (1982). Propos d'un psychanalyste sur les psychothérapies d'enfant. *Psychiatrie de l'enfant*, 25(1): 389–415.

Diatkine, R. (1988). Destins du transfert. *Revue française de psychanalyse*, 52(4): 803–813.

Diatkine, R. (1989). Interprétations et processus psychanalytique. *Revue française de psychanalyse*, 53(3): 803–811.

Diatkine, R. (1990). Remémoration, prise de conscience. *Revue française de psychanalyse*, 54(4): 911–922.

Diatkine, R., Freud, A. and Segal, H. (1971). La psychanalyse des enfants. *Psychiatrie de l'enfant*, 14(1): 5–81.

Diatkine, R. and Simon, J. (1972). *La psychanalyse précoce*. Paris: Presses Universitaires de France.

Diatkine, R. and Simon, J. (1975). Quelques réflexions sur l'interprétation en psychanalyse des enfants, *Psychiatrie de l'enfant*, 18(1): 89–112.

Diatkine, R. and Van Waeyenberghe, M. (1990). Dysphasies. *Psychiatrie de l'enfant*, 31(1): 37–91.

Donnet, J.-L. (1990[1989]). L'opération méta. In: *La psychanalyse questions pour demain, Monographies, Revue française de psychanalyse*, Paris: Presses Universitaires de France, pp. 191–210.

Eddington, A. (1928). *The Nature of the Physical World*. Cambridge, Cambridge University Press.

Edelman, G. (1989). *The Remembered Present: A Biological Theory of Consciousness*. New York: Basic Books.

Fain, M. (1982). L'interprétation. *Revue française de psychanalyse*, 67(3): 707–716.

Ferenczi, S. and Dupont, J. (eds) (1988[1932]). *The Clinical Diary of Sándor Ferenczi*. Cambridge, MA: Harvard University Press.

Freud, S. (1891b). *On Aphasia*. New York: International University Press, 1953.

Freud, S. (1900a). *The Interpretation of Dreams*. *S.E.*, 4–5. London: Hogarth Press.

Freud, S. (1905d). *Three Essays on the Theory of Sexuality. S.E.*, 7. London: Hogarth Press, pp. 123–243.

Freud, S. (1905e). Fragment of an analysis of a case of hysteria. *S.E.*, 7. London: Hogarth Press, pp. 7–122.

Freud, S. (1909d) Analysis of a phobia in a five-year-old boy, *S.E.*, 10. London: Hogarth Press, pp. 5–149.

Freud, S. (1910c). *Leonardo da Vinci and a Memory of His Childhood. S.E.*, 11. London: Hogarth Press, pp. 57–137.

Freud, S. (1910d). The future prospects of psycho-analytic therapy. *S.E.*, 11. London: Hogarth Press, pp. 141–151.

Freud, S. (1912g). A note on the unconscious in psychoanalysis. *S.E.*, 12. London: Hogarth Press, pp. 260–266.

Freud, S. (1914c). On narcissism: an introduction. *S.E.*, 14. London: Hogarth Press, pp. 73–102.

Freud, S. (1914g). Remembering, repeating, and working-through. *S.E.*, 12. London: Hogarth Press, pp. 145–156.

Freud, S. (1915c). Instincts and their Vicissitudes. *S.E.*, 14. London: Hogarth Press, pp. 117–140.

Freud, S. (1915d). Repression. *S.E.*, 14. London: Hogarth Press, pp. 146–158.

Freud, S. (1915e). The unconscious. *S.E.*, 14. London: Hogarth Press, pp. 166–215.

Freud, S. (1916–1917). *Introductory Lectures on Psycho-Analysis. S.E.*, 15–16. London: Hogarth Press.

Freud, S. (1918b[1914]). From the history of an infantile neurosis. *S.E.*, 17. London: Hogarth Press, pp. 1–122.

Freud, S. (1919e). A child is being beaten. *S.E.*, 17. London: Hogarth Press, pp. 177–224.

Freud, S. (1920g). *Beyond the Pleasure Principle. S.E.*, 18. London: Hogarth Press, pp. 1–66.

Freud, S. (1923b). *The Ego and the Id. S.E.*, 19. London: Hogarth Press, pp. 3–66.

Freud, S. (1924c). *The Economic Problem of Masochism. S.E.*, 19. London: Hogarth Press, pp. 155–170.

Freud, S. (1925h). Negation. *S.E.*, 19. London: Hogarth Press, pp. 233–239.

Freud, S. (1933a[1932]). *New Introductory Lectures on Psychoanalysis S.E.*, 22. London: Hogarth Press, pp. 1–182.

Freud, S. (1937c). Analysis terminable and interminable. *S.E.*, 23. London: Hogarth Press, pp. 209–253.

Freud, S. (1937d). Constructions in analysis, *S.E.*, 23. London: Hogarth Press, pp. 255–269.

Freud, S. (1940a[1938]). *An Outline of Psychoanalysis, S.E.*, 23. London: Hogarth Press, pp. 139–207.

Freud, S. (1950[1895d]). Project for a Scientific Psychology. In: *The Standard Edition (S.E.) of the Complete Psychological Works of Freud*, trans. J. Strachey. London: Hogarth Press (1950–1974), vol. 1, pp. 281–397.

Gammill, J. (1986). Interventions et interprétations exploratoires chez l'enfant. *Journal de la psychanalyse de l'enfant*, 1: 33–48.

Green, A. (1990[1986]). *On Private Madness*. London: Hogarth Press.

Green, A. (2001[1983]). *Life Narcissism, Death Narcissism*. London: Free Association Books.

Green, A. (2001a). Mythes et réalités sur le processus psychanalytique (I). *Revue française de psychosomatique*, 19: 58–88.

Green, A. (2001b). Mythes et réalités sur le processus psychanalytique (II). *Revue française de psychosomatique*, 20: 75–95.

Green, A. (2005[1999]). On discriminating and not discriminating between affect and representation. In: *Psychoanalysis: A Paradigm for Clinical Thinking*, trans. A. Weller. London: Free Association Books.

Green, A. (2005[2002a]). *Key Ideas for a Contemporary Psychoanalysis. Misrecognition and Recognition of the Unconscious*, trans. A. Weller. London: Routledge.

Green, A. (2005[2002b]). On thirdness. In: *Psychoanalysis: A Paradigm for Clinical Thinking*. London: Free Association Books, pp. 233–277.

Green, A. (2005[2002c]). The central phobic position. In: *Psychoanalysis: A Paradigm for Clinical Thinking*, trans. A. Weller. London: Free Association Books.

Green, A. (2006). *Voies nouvelles de la thérapeutique psychanalytique*. Paris: Presses Universitaires de France.

Groddeck, G. (1969). *La maladie, l'art et la symbole*. Paris: Gallimard.

Hollande, C. and Soulé, M. (1970). Pour introduire un colloque sur la compulsion de répétition. *Revue française de psychanalyse*, 34(3): 373–406.

Kaplan-Davids, J. (1999). The family in the child's mind. 25th Colloquium of the Anna Freud Centre, 5–6 November 1999.

Klein, M. (1935). A contribution to the psychogenesis of manic-depressive states. *Int. J. Psycho-Anal.*, 16: 145–174; also in *Contributions to Psycho-Analysis, 1921–45*. London: Hogarth Press, 1948.

Klein, M. (1961). *Narrative of a Child Analysis*. London: The International Psychoanalytical Library, 55.

Klein, M. (1973). *Psychanalyse d'un enfant*. Paris: Tchou.

Lacan, J. (1992[1986]). *The Ethics of Psychoanalysis. The Seminar of Jacques Lacan, Book VII, 1959–1960*. New York: Norton & Co.

Laplanche, J. and Pontalis, J.-B. (1964). Fantasme des origines, origines du fantasme. *Revue les temps modernes*, 215: 1833–1868.

Laplanche, J. (1987). *New Foundations in Psychoanalysis*, trans. D. Macey. Oxford: Blackwell.

Le Guen, Cl. (2007). Comment ça nait, un moi? *Revue française de psychanalyse*, 71(1): 11–26.

Luquet, P. (1987). Langage, pensée et structure psychique (Report to the 47th Conference for French-Speaking Psychoanalysts). *Revue française de psychanalyse*, 52: 267–302.

M'Uzan, M. de (1994). Stratégie et tactique à propos des interprétations freudiennes et kleiniennes. In: *La bouche de l'inconscient*. Paris: Gallimard, pp. 105–114.

M'Uzan, M. de (2013[1969]). The same and the identical. In: *Death and Identity: Being and the Psycho-Sexual Drama*. London: Karnac Books, pp. 3–15.

Marty, P. (1976). *Mouvements individuels de vie et de mort*. Paris: Payot.

Marty, P. (1980). *L'ordre psychosomatique*. Paris: Payot.

Marty, P. (1990). *La psychosomatique de l'adulte*. Paris: Presses Universitaires de France.

Masson J.M. (1985). (ed.) *The Complete Letters of Sigmund Freud to Wilhelm Fliess, 1887–1904*. Cambridge, MA: Belknap Press.

Neyraut, M. (1974). *Le transfert*. Paris: Presses Universitaires de France.

Neyraut, M. (1978). *Les logiques de l'inconscient*. Paris: Hachette.

Neyraut, M. (1988). Les destins du transfert: problèmes méthodologiques. *Revue française de psychanalyse*, 52(4): 815–828.

Neyraut, M. (1997). *Les raisons de l'irrationnel*. Paris: Presses Universitaires de France.

Nicolescu, B. (2008[1996]). *Transdisciplinarity: Theory and Practice*. Cresskill, NJ: Hampton Press.

Ody, M. (1984). Le temps du connaitre/méconnaitre dans l'espace de la consultation familiale, *Les Textes du Centre Alfred Binet*, 4, pp. 101–110.

Ody, M. (1986). A propos du jeu et des pulsions. *Les Textes du Centre Alfred Binet*, 9, pp. 35–43.

Ody, M. (1987). Le langage dans la rencontre entre l'enfant et le psychanalyste. Report to the 47th Congress of French-Speaking Psychoanalysts, *Revue française de psychanalyse*, 52(2): 303–367.

Ody, M. (1989). Œdipe comme attracteur. *Monographies de la Revue française de psychanalyse*. Paris: Press Universitaires de France, pp. 211–219.

Ody, M. (1994a). Limites du 'tout analyser' chez l'enfant, et fin de la cure. *Revue française de psychanalyse*, 4: 1107–1115.

Ody, M. (1994b). L'adulte dans l'enfant et 'l'insight'. *Revue française de psychanalyse*, 3: 681–689.

Ody, M. (1997). L'angoisse chez l'enfant et chez l'adolescent. *Revue française de psychanalyse*, 2: 53–66.

Ody, M. (1998). Quelques réflexions et illustrations à propos du trajet des sublimations. *Revue française de psychanalyse*, 4: 1265–1278.

Ody, M. (1999a). A propos de la notion freudienne de représentation-limite. *Revue française de psychanalyse*, 63(5): 1633–1636.

Ody, M. (1999b). À propos des interprétations en psychanalyse des enfants. In: Monograph of the *Revue française de psychanalyse (Interprétation: un processus mutative)*. Paris Presses Universitaires de France, pp. 137–158.

Ody, M. (2001) Interventions, interprétations dans le travail psychanalytique avec l'enfant. *Revue Psychanalyse et Enfance du Centre Alfred Binet*, 30: 39–51.

Ody, M. (2003a). La névrose de l'enfant existe-t-elle? *Revue française de psychanalyse*, 4: 1333–1350.

Ody, M. (2003b). Troubles de la représentance chez un enfant de parent homosexuel. *Revue française de psychanalyse*, 1: 219–228.

Ody, M. (2004). Régression, repli. Lecture presented within the framework of the "Thursday Lectures of the Paris Psychoanalytic Society", 13 October 2004 (www.spp.asso.fr).

Ody, M. (2008). Modernité du préconscient. *Libres Cahiers pour la Psychanalyse*, 18: 57–74, Paris: Éditions In Press.

Ody, M. (2011). La psychanalyse, la réflexivité, et l'enfant. SPP Deauville Colloquium ("La psychanalyse et la réflexivité"), 8–9 October 2011. *Revue française de psychanalyse*, 76(3): 649–664.

Ody, M., Donnet, J.-L., Botella, S. and Smadja, C. (2011a). Oral intervention on the relationship of associativity and free association in the child at the 3rd St Malo Colloquium, 17–18 September 2011 ("L'opposition entre l'association libre (le procédé) et l'associativité (a partir de la dérive de la règle)". Unpublished.

Ody, M. (2012). Interprétations symboliques, symbolisantes. *L'interprétation, Monographies et débats de psychanalyse*. Paris: Presses Universitaires de France, pp. 34–42.

Ortigues, M. and Ortigues, E. (1966). *Œdipe africain*. Paris: L'Harmattan, 2000.

Parat, C. (1967). L'organisation oedipienne du stade génital. *Revue française de psychanalyse*, 5–6: 743–911.

Pasche, F. (1965). *À partir de Freud*, Paris: Payot.

Popper, K. (1976). *Unended Quest: An Intellectual Autobiography*. London: Routledge.

Prigogine, I. and Stengers, I. (1979). *La nouvelle alliance*. Paris: Gallimard ("Folios essais").

Prigogine, I. and Stengers, I. (1988). *Entre le temps et l'éternité*. Paris: Fayard.

Ribas, D. and Lechartier-Atlan, C. (eds) (2010). *Avancées freudiennes, Textes 1954–2009, Revue française de psychanalyse*. Paris: Presses Universitaires de France, pp. 189–198.

Rolland, J-C. (1997). Le rhythme et la raison. *Revue française de psychanalyse*, 61(5): 1589–1635.

Rolland, J.-C. (2006). *Avant d'être celui qui parle*. Paris: Gallimard.

Rolland, J.-C. (2007). Entre remémoration et oubli. *Psychanalyse en Europe, Bulletin*, 61: 49–57.

Rosolato, G. (1978). *La relation d'inconnu*. Paris: Gallimard.

Sandler, J., Kennedy, H. and Tyson, R.L. (1980). *The Technique of Child Psychonalysis: Discussions with Anna Freud*. Cambridge, MA: Harvard University Press.

Searles, H. (1959). The effort to drive the other person crazy: An element in the aetiology and psychotherapy of schizophrenics. In: the *British Journal of Medical Psychology*, 32: 1–18. Also in *Collected Papers on Schizophrenia and Related Subjects*. London: Hogarth Press, 1965.

Segal, H. (1981). *Délire et créativité*. Paris: Des Femmes.

Segal, H. (1986) *Delusion and Artistic Creativity and Other Psychoanalytic Essays*. London: Free Association Books.

Simon, J. (1991). De la stratégie des interventions en analyse d'enfant. *Psychiatrie de l'enfant*, 34(2): 469–478.

Spitz, R.A. (1965[1958]). *The First Year of Life. A Psychoanalytic Study of Normal and Deviant Development in Object Relations*. New York: International Universities Press.

Strachey, J. (1934). The nature of the therapeutic action of psychoanalysis. *International Journal of Psychoanalysis*, 15: 127–159.

Sulloway, F. (1979). *Freud, Biologist of the Mind: Beyond the Psychoanalytic Legend*. Syracuse, NY: Burnett Books.

Varela, F. (1989). Connaitre les sciences cognitives. Paris: Seuil.

Viderman, S. (1970). *La construction de l'espace psychanalytique*. Paris: Denoël.

Villa, F. and Danon-Boileau, L. (eds) (2008). Quand la clinique nous impose la dialogue. *Monograph of the Alfred Binet Centre*, Paris: Éditions In Press.

Widlöcher, D. (1970). *Freud et le problème du changement*. Paris: Presses Universitaires de France.

Widlöcher, D. (1980). Genèse et changement. Report to the 40th Congress of French-speaking psychoanalysts. *Revue française de psychanalyse*, 4: 889–976.

Winnicott, D.W. (1958[1947]). Hate in the countertransference. In: *Through Paediatrics to Psychoanalysis: Collected Papers*. London: Tavistock Publications, pp. 194–203.

Winnicott, D.W. (1958[1954]). Metapsychological and clinical aspects of regression within the psychoanalytical set-up. In: *Through Paediatrics to Psychoanalysis, Collected Papers*. London: Tavistock Publications, pp. 278–294.

Winnicott, D.W. (1989[1965]). Notes on Withdrawal and Regression. In: *Psycho-Analytic Explorations*, ed. D.W. Winnicott, C. Winnicott, R. Shepherd and M. Davis. Cambridge, MA: Harvard University Press, pp. 149–151.

Winnicott, D.W. (1971). *Playing and Reality*. London: Tavistock Publications.

Winnicott, D.W. (1987). *The Spontaneous Gesture: Selected Letters of D.W. Winnicott*, ed. R. Rodman. London: Karnac Books.

INDEX

Note: numbers preceded by *n* are chapter endnote numbers.

For Product Safety Concerns and Information please contact our EU
representative GPSR@taylorandfrancis.com
Taylor & Francis Verlag GmbH, Kaufingerstraße 24, 80331 München, Germany

www.ingramcontent.com/pod-product-compliance
Lightning Source LLC
Chambersburg PA
CBHW070403270326
41926CB00014B/2682